Quilting to Go ™

Edited by Jeanne Stauffer & Sandra L. Hatch

HOUSE of
WHITE
BIRCHES

PUBLISHERS
SINCE 1947

Quilting to Go

Editors: Jeanne Stauffer & Sandra L. Hatch
Associate Editor: Dianne Schmidt
Book Design: Jessi Butler
Copy Editors: Michelle Beck, Sue Harvey, Mary Martin, Nicki Lehman

Photography: Tammy Christian, Christena Green, Kelly Heydinger
Photo Stylist: Tammy Nussbaum
Photography Assistant: Linda Quinlan

Publishing Services Manager: Brenda Gallmeyer
Graphic Artist: Edith Teegarden
Production Assistant: Janet Bowers
Technical Artist: Connie Rand
Traffic Coordinator: Sandra Beres

Chief Executive Officer: John Robinson
Publishing Director: David McKee
Book Marketing Director: Craig Scott
Editorial Director: Vivian Rothe
Publishing Services Director: Brenda R. Wendling

Printed in the United States of America
First Printing: 2003
Library of Congress Number: 2002107208
ISBN: 1-59217-005-6

Every effort has been made to ensure the accuracy and completeness of the instructions in this book. However, we cannot be responsible for human error or for the results when using materials other than those specified in the instructions, or for variations in individual work.

Welcome!

We had a great time planning this book for you and know you will enjoy stitching these designs to give as gifts or to use yourself.

We selected the general focus for this book by responding to a comment that we have read over and over in the letters we receive from quilters across the United States and Canada. They tell us about how much they love to quilt and what their favorite projects are. Then they tell us about their biggest problem: finding time to quilt.

So we decided to help! We asked designers for projects that could be made by busy quilters on the go. Instead of reading out-of-date magazines while you wait to see the doctor, you can quilt. Whether you are taking a break at a ski resort, sitting at the airport, waiting for your child to finish practice, stalled in traffic or taking a short break at the office, you will have more time to quilt if you have the right projects.

Many of the projects in this book are quilted in sections or blocks so they are easily transportable, even the full-size bed quilts. We also included small projects that can be made quickly. And we've included a few bags that you can make; they're just right for taking your quilting with you throughout the day.

Not all the projects are easy because we know some of you want a challenge, but they are all projects you can quilt on the go. So what are you waiting for? There are over 40 designs from which to choose. Gather your needle and thread, and begin!

Happy stitching,

Jeanne Stauffer

Sandra L. Hatch

Contents

Dimensional Classics

Points & Curves

Fancy Threads

One Block at a Time

Dimensional Classics

Many 3-D techniques are completed
by hand, making them perfect for those
moments when you are waiting at
the doctor's or dentist's office

Summer Door Banner

By Connie Kauffman

Visiting family and friends is a summertime activity.
Welcome all your visitors to your home with this floral door banner.

Project Note

The instructions are given for hand appliqué for the fence and letters. You may choose to use machine methods if you don't want to quilt as you go. Increase fusible transfer web to 1 yard and refer to the General Instructions for machine appliqué.

Project Specifications

Skill Level: Intermediate
Banner Size: 12" x 21"

Materials

+ Scraps blue and purple fabrics for fringed flowers
+ 1/8 yard green mottled for leaves
+ 1/8 yard dark print for letters
+ 1/8 yard each light and dark pink prints for yo-yo flowers
+ 3/8 yard white-on-white print for fence
+ 3/8 yard blue mottled for sky
+ Batting 16" x 25"
+ Backing 16" x 25"
+ All-purpose thread to match fabrics
+ Light blue hand-quilting thread
+ Brown and green 6-strand embroidery floss
+ 1 package yellow rickrack
+ 12 (3/8") brown variegated buttons
+ 1/2 yard fusible transfer web
+ Basic sewing tools and supplies, rotary cutter, mat and ruler, marking pencil and pinking shears

Instructions

Preparing Background

Step 1. Cut a 12 1/2" x 21 1/2" rectangle blue mottled for sky background.

Step 2. Fold and crease rectangle to mark the center. Fold both bottom corners at the center mark and crease to make an angle as shown in Figure 1; cut along crease lines to make angled corners, again referring to Figure 1.

Figure 1
Fold both bottom corners at the center mark and crease to make an angle; cut along crease lines to make angled corners.

Step 3. Prepare templates for fence pieces using patterns given; cut as directed on each piece, adding a 1/4" seam allowance all around when cutting for hand appliqué.

Step 4. Prepare fence pieces for hand-appliqué, referring to the General Instructions, leaving the bottom edges unturned.

Step 5. Arrange the fence pieces on the background, matching bottom edges; pin or baste in place to hold.

Step 6. Hand-appliqué the fence pieces in place using matching all-purpose thread to complete background preparation.

Making Yo-Yo Flowers

Step 1. Prepare templates for yo-yo pieces using patterns given; cut as directed on each piece.

Step 2. To make a yo-yo flower, fold and finger-press a 1/8" hem around each circle edge. Hand-sew gathering stitches all around with a doubled strand of knotted thread; pull thread to gather tightly as shown in Figure 2. Use fingers to move the small opening to the center to make a yo-yo flower. Repeat for all yo-yo flowers.

Figure 2
Make yo-yo flowers as shown.

Making Fringed Flowers

Step 1. Prepare templates for fringed flowers using the A, B and C patterns given. Cut as directed on each piece using pinking shears to give a zigzag edge.

Step 2. Layer A, B and C pieces with right sides up working from large on bottom to small on top to complete one fringed flower; pin to hold. Repeat to make 12 fringed flowers.

Making Rickrack Flowers

Step 1. To make one rickrack flower, cut a 6" length of yellow rickrack. Knot a piece of all-purpose thread to match the rickrack and hand-stitch a line of long stitches through the center length of the rickrack as shown in Figure 3.

Figure 3
Hand-stitch a line of long stitches through the center length of the rickrack.

Step 2. Gather the rickrack on the thread and draw up to make a circle as shown in Figure 4; overlap beginning and end, and stitch layers together at overlapped ends to make a flower as shown in Figure 5. Repeat for 17 rickrack flowers.

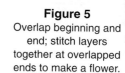

Figure 4
Gather the rickrack on the thread and draw up to make a circle.

Figure 5
Overlap beginning and end; stitch layers together at overlapped ends to make a flower.

Making Leaves

Step 1. Bond fusible transfer web to the wrong side of the green mottled fabric.

Step 2. Prepare templates for leaf pieces using patterns given; trace shapes onto the fused side of the green mottled as directed for number to cut. Cut out shapes on marked lines. Remove paper backing.

Stitching Stems

Step 1. Mark stem placement lightly with marking pencil referring to the Placement Diagram or photo of finished project for positioning.

Step 2. Using 2 strands brown or green embroidery floss, chain-stitch stem lines referring to Figure 6.

Figure 6
Make a chain stitch using 2 strands of embroidery floss.

Finishing

Step 1. Prepare templates for letters for message using patterns given. **Note:** *Use the inside line as the finished edge of the letters for this project.* Cut out letters, adding a seam allowance all around for hand appliqué.

Step 2. Arrange message on the longest fence piece and hand-appliqué in place, turning under seam allowance as you stitch.

Step 3. Position the leaves on the background referring to the Placement Diagram and photo of finished project for positioning. Fuse in place when satisfied with placement. **Note:** *See special hint for making dimensional leaves.*

Step 4. Arrange the fringed flowers on the background referring to the Placement Diagram or photo of project for positioning. Stitch in place using a 3/8" variegated brown button in the center and leaving pinked edges free as shown in Figure 7.

Figure 7
Stitch fringed flower in place with button in the center, leaving pinked edges free.

Step 5. Arrange clusters of yo-yo flowers as shown in Figure 8 for large and small flowers. Hand-stitch in place around edges, taking stitches on the inside edges as shown in Figure 9.

Figure 8
Arrange the yo-yo flowers in clusters as shown.

Figure 9
Tack each yo-yo in place from underneath.

Step 6. Arrange the rickrack flowers on the large leaves referring to the Placement Diagram or project photo for positioning. Hand-stitch in place.

Step 7. Place the completed top right side up on a flat surface; place the backing right sides together with quilt top and smooth. Place the batting on the backing/top layers; smooth and pin. Turn over and trim backing and batting even with the completed top.

Step 8. Stitch around edges, leaving a 6" opening on one side; clip corners. Turn right side out through opening; press opening seam under. Hand-stitch opening closed.

Step 9. Hand-quilt around the fence pieces and message letters and as desired in background using light blue hand-quilting thread.

Step 10. Cut a 3 1/2" x 11 1/2" strip any leftover fabric. Fold under each short end of the strip 1/4" and press; press under 1/4" again and stitch to hem ends.

Step 11. Fold the strip with right sides together along length; stitch along length to make a tube. Turn the tube right side out; press with seam centered to complete a hanging sleeve.

Step 12. Hand-stitch the hanging sleeve to the top backside of the banner, being careful that stitches do not show on the right side. ✦

Making Dimensional Leaves

To give the large leaves a dimensional look, iron/fuse the base of the leaf near a flower; arch the leaf and iron/fuse the tip or center and leave the remainder of the leaf loose as shown in Figure 10. This adds interest to a quilted project that won't receive wear and tear, or require frequent washing.

Figure 10
Fuse the tip or center of leaf in place.

Summer Door Banner
Placement Diagram
12" x 21"

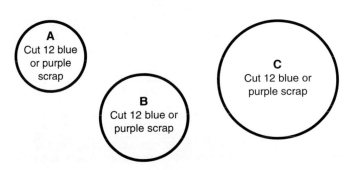

A
Cut 12 blue or purple scrap

B
Cut 12 blue or purple scrap

C
Cut 12 blue or purple scrap

Large Leaf
Cut 20 green mottled

Large Yo-Yo
Cut 8 dark pink & 6 light pink prints

Small Yo-Yo
Cut 4 each light & dark pink prints

Narrow Leaf
Cut 2 green mottled (reverse 1)

Fence 2
Cut 1 white-on-white print

Add 10" between lines to make complete pattern.

Letters
Cut 1 each L, C and O and 2 E's and M/W's dark print

Make templates using the inner lines, adding a 1/4" seam allowance all around when cutting. Outer lines are used for letters in the Winter Door Banner on page 110 and for the Autumn Door Banner on page 167.

Small Leaf
Cut 8 green mottled

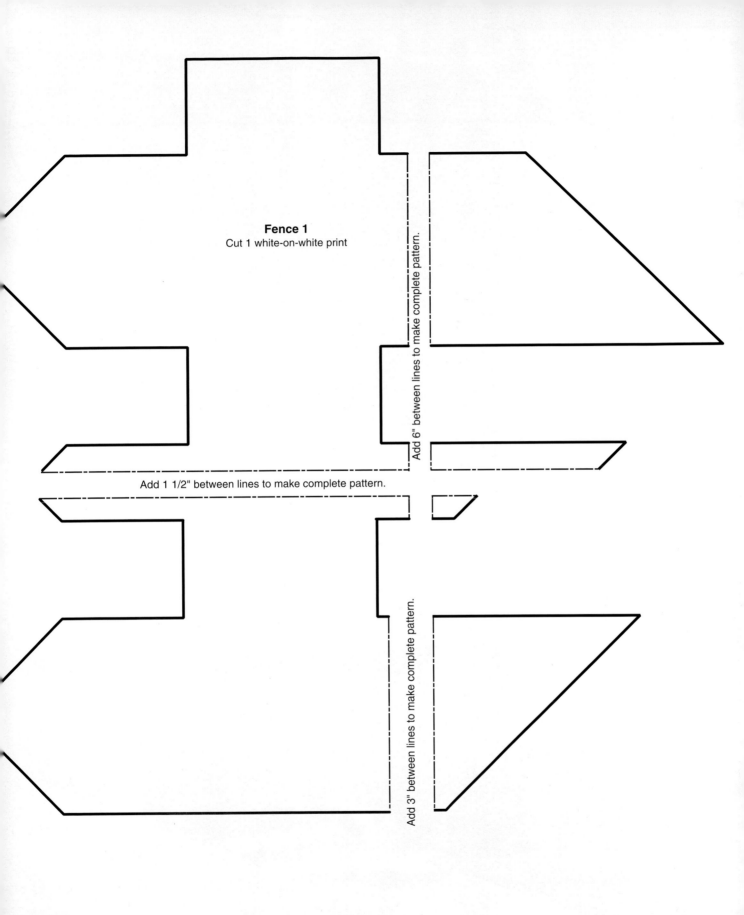

Fence 1
Cut 1 white-on-white print

Add 6" between lines to make complete pattern.

Add 1 1/2" between lines to make complete pattern.

Add 3" between lines to make complete pattern.

Star-Spangled Yo-Yos

By Julie Weaver

Scraps of red, white and blue were used to make the yo-yo's which form the star design in this patriotic table cover.

Project Notes

If you don't like the shading created by the use of scraps, you may purchase fabric yardage as listed to make a more formal looking project.

You will need a large, flat surface on which to lay out all the yo-yos to form the pattern. The yo-yos are joined one to another in rows, and it would be very easy to mix up the rows if the pieces were constantly picked up and moved. It would help to pin yo-yos together in pairs for one row, stitch the pair, lay it back down and pin to join the pairs.

Project Specifications

Skill Level: Beginner

Quilt Size: Approximately 38" x 38"

Materials

- ◆ 1 3/4 yards blue fabric or assorted scraps to equal this amount
- ◆ 2 1/4 yards white/cream fabric or assorted scraps to equal this amount
- ◆ 2 3/4 yards red fabric or assorted scraps to equal this amount
- ◆ Hand-quilting thread to match fabrics
- ◆ Basic sewing tools and supplies

Instructions

Step 1. Prepare template for circle using pattern given; cut as directed on piece.

Figure 1
Run a gathering stitch on the turned-under edges of the circle.

Step 2. Turn under edges of each circle 1/8"; finger-press to hold.

Step 3. To make one yo-yo, knot a length of quilting thread to match fabric and run a gathering stitch on the turned-under edges of the circle as shown in Figure 1.

Step 4. Pull thread tight to form a yo-yo as shown in Figure 2. Tie a knot and clip threads. Finger-press flat to complete the yo-yo. Repeat for 184 blue, 248 white/cream and 352 red yo-yos.

Figure 2
Pull thread tight to form a yo-yo.

Step 5. Arrange the yo-yos in rows referring to the Placement Diagram for positioning.

Step 6. With right sides together, join two yo-yos using small whipstitches at the outer edges as shown in Figure 3, stitching an area of at least 1/4" on yo-yo sides, again referring to Figure 3.

Figure 3
Join 2 yo-yos using small whipstitches at the outer edges, stitching an area of at least 1/4" on yo-yo sides.

Step 7. Continue joining yo-yos to create rows; join rows to complete the entire top. ✦

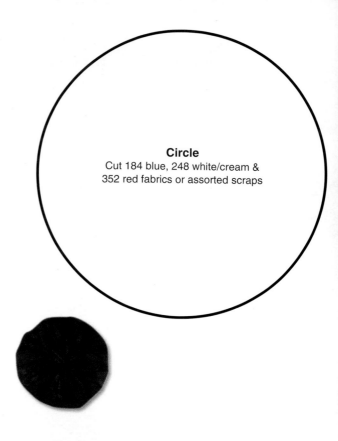

Circle
Cut 184 blue, 248 white/cream & 352 red fabrics or assorted scraps

Star-Spangled Yo-Yos
Placement Diagram
Approximately 38" x 38"

Blossom Basket Medallion

By Pearl Louise Krush

*Create the center panel of this medallion quilt on the go
and combine with machine stitching to put it all together.*

Project Specifications

Skill Level: Intermediate

Quilt Size: Approximately 77 3/4" x 103 1/4" (without prairie points)

Block Size: 9" x 9"

Number of Blocks: 20

Materials

+ Scraps light and dark green prints for leaves
+ 1 fat quarter peach print for ruched flowers
+ 1/8 yard rose print for flower centers
+ 1/4 yard yellow print for petal flowers
+ 1/4 yard lavender print for grapes
+ 1/4 yard each 9 different print fabrics for Nine-Patch blocks
+ 2/3 yard basket print for basket
+ 1 yard dark green print for borders
+ 1 3/4 yards yellow tone-on-tone for borders
+ 1 3/4 yards cream-on-cream print for background and triangles
+ 5 3/4 yards large floral print for plain blocks and backing
+ 3 1/4 yards green-and-white check for prairie points
+ 5 3/4 yards large floral print for plain blocks and backing
+ 6 3/4 yards small floral print for backing
+ 9 yards 45"-wide batting
+ All-purpose thread to match fabrics
+ 12 skeins light green 6-strand embroidery floss
+ Basic sewing tools and supplies, rotary cutter, mat and ruler, marking pencil and large safety pin

Making Center Panel

Step 1. Cut one 23 1/2" x 23 1/2" square cream-on-cream print for center panel; fold and crease to mark center. Cut a backing and batting square 30" x 30".

Step 2. Prepare templates for basket, yo-yo circles and leaves using patterns given; cut as directed on each piece for hand appliqué, adding a seam allowance all around when cutting.

Step 3. Turn under the edges of the basket all around; pin in place matching center line of basket to creased lines on the background, 6 1/2" from diagonal point as shown in Figure 1; hand-stitch in place using matching all-purpose thread.

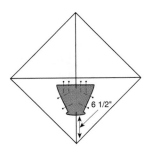

Figure 1
Pin basket in place matching center line
of basket to creased lines on the
background, 6 1/2" from diagonal point.

Step 4. Mark the background square in a 1" cross-hatch design referring to Figure 2.

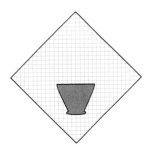

Figure 2
Mark the background square in
a 1" crosshatch design.

Figure 3
Sew the shorter strips to 2
opposite sides and the longer
strips to the remaining sides.

Step 5. Cut two strips each 2 1/2" x 23 1/2" and 2 1/2" x 27 1/2" dark green print. Sew the shorter strips to two opposite sides and the longer strips to the remaining sides as shown in Figure 3; press seams toward strips.

Step 6. Sandwich batting between the marked and bordered top, and the prepared backing piece; pin or baste layers together to hold. Quilt on the marked lines using 2 strands light green embroidery floss.

Step 7. When quilting is complete, trim backing and batting edges even with the top.

Step 8. Cut three 2 1/2" by fabric width strips basket print. Fold the raw edges of each strip to the center and press as shown in Figure 4; fold again and press, again referring to Figure 4.

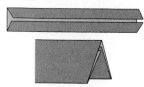

Figure 4
Fold the raw edges of each strip to
the center; fold again and press.

Step 9. Pin one end of each strip together using a large safety pin. Braid the three strips together into a tight braid for basket handle; pin the remaining ends when finished to hold.

Step 10. Pin one end of the braided basket handle to one top edge of the appliquéd basket; shape the handle so the top center is 12" from the center of the basket and pin in place. Trim excess at the other side of the basket. Hand-stitch the inner and outer edges of the braided handle in place. **Note:** *Don't worry about ends; they will be covered with flowers.*

Step 11. To prepare yo-yos, carefully fold the outer edge of each circle in about 1/8"; sew a large gathering stitch around the folded area using all-purpose thread to match fabric and referring to Figure 5.

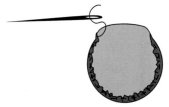

Figure 5
Fold the outer edge of each
circle in about 1/8"; sew a
large gathering stitch
around the folded area.

Step 12. Pull the thread to gather the circle and tie to complete one yo-yo as shown in Figure 6. Repeat for 19 lavender print and nine rose print yo-yos.

Figure 6
Pull the thread to
gather the circle and tie
to complete 1 yo-yo.

Step 13. Cut three 2 1/2" by fabric width strips yellow print; subcut into 2 1/2" squares. You will need 45 squares for flower petals.

Step 14. To make petal flowers, fold five 2 1/2" x 2 1/2" yellow print squares in half diagonally with wrong sides together. Using a knotted double strand of matching all-purpose thread, sew large gathering stitches on the raw edges of one folded square as shown in Figure 7. Continue with the remaining squares on the same thread to connect; connect the first and last triangle and pull to gather to make a petal flower as shown in Figure 8. Repeat for nine petal flowers.

 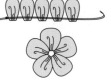

Figure 7
Sew large gathering
stitches on the raw edges
of 1 folded square.

Figure 8
Connect the first and
last triangle and pull
to gather to make a
petal flower.

Step 15. Sew a rose yo-yo to the center of each petal flower using matching all-purpose thread.

Step 16. Cut seven 3" x 18" strips peach print. Fold one raw edge of each strip to the center; fold again as shown in Figure 9.

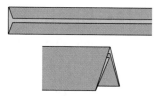

Figure 9
Fold 1 raw edge of each strip
to the center; fold again.

Step 17. Using a knotted, doubled strand of matching all-purpose thread, sew large zigzag stitches the entire length of the strip as shown in Figure 10. Pull the gathering stitches as tight as possible to form a circle of the gathered strip. Tack each round of the circle in place to make a ruched flower; repeat for seven ruched flowers.

Figure 10
Using a knotted, doubled strand of
matching all-purpose thread, sew large
zigzag stitches the entire length of the strip.

Step 18. Arrange leaves on the basket with the petal flowers, ruched flowers, and lavender yo-yos in grape clusters, referring to Figure 11 for positioning suggestions. Hand-stitch all pieces in place using matching all-purpose thread to finish the center panel; set aside.

Figure 11
Arrange leaves on the basket with the petal
flowers, ruched flowers and lavender yo-yos.

Making the Nine-Patch Blocks

Step 1. Cut two 3 1/2" by fabric width strips from each of the nine different prints.

Step 2. Join three different print strips along length with right sides together to make a strip set; repeat for six strip sets. Press seams in one direction. Subcut each strip set into 3 1/2" segments.

Step 3. Join three segments to complete one Nine-Patch block as shown in Figure 12; repeat for 20 blocks.

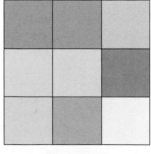

Figure 12
Join 3 segments to
complete 1 Nine-
Patch block.

Nine-Patch
9" x 9" Block

Completing Quilted Rows

Step 1. Cut eight strips 9 1/2" by fabric width large

floral print; subcut strips into 9 1/2" square segments for A. You will need 30 A squares.

Step 2. Cut five 14" x 14" squares cream-on-cream print; cut each square in half on both diagonals to make B triangles; you will need 20 B triangles.

Step 3. Cut two 7 1/4" x 7 1/4" squares cream-on-cream print; cut each square in half on one diagonal to make four C triangles.

Step 4. Sew B to opposite sides of A; add C to make a corner row as shown in Figure 13. Repeat for two corner rows; press seams away from A.

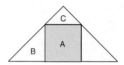

Figure 13
Sew B to opposite sides of A;
add C to make a corner row.

Step 5. Join one Nine-Patch block with two A and two B pieces to make Row 1X as shown in Figure 14; repeat for Row 1Y. Press seams toward A.

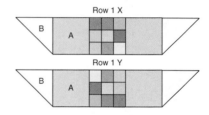

Figure 14
Join 1 Nine-Patch block with 2 A and
2 B pieces to make Rows 1X and 1Y.

Step 6. Join two Nine-Patch blocks with three A and two B pieces to make Row 2X as shown in Figure 15; repeat for Row 2Y. Press seams toward A.

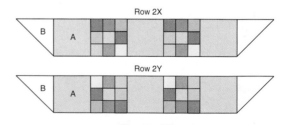

Figure 15
Join 2 Nine-Patch blocks with 3 A and
2 B pieces to make Rows 2X and 2Y.

Step 7. Join three Nine-Patch blocks with four A and two B pieces to make Row 3X as shown in Figure 16; repeat for Row 3Y. Press seams toward A.

Step 8. Join two Nine-Patch blocks with two A squares and one C triangle to make Row 4X as shown in Figure 17; repeat for Row 4Y. Press seams toward A.

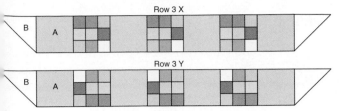

Figure 16

Join 3 Nine-Patch blocks with 4 A and 2 B pieces to make Rows 3X and 3Y.

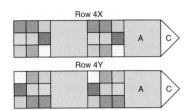

Figure 17
Join 2 Nine-Patch blocks with 2
A squares and 1 C triangle to
make Rows 4X and 4Y.

Step 9. Join one Nine-Patch block with two A squares and one B triangle to make Row 5X as shown in Figure 18; repeat for Row 5Y. Press seams toward A.

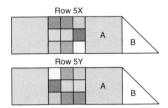

Figure 18
Join 1 Nine-Patch block with
2 A squares and 1 B triangle
to make Rows 5X and 5Y.

Step 10. Join one Nine-Patch block with one A square and one B triangle to make Row 6X as shown in Figure 19; repeat for Row 6Y. Press seams toward A.

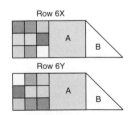

Figure 19
Join 1 Nine-Patch block with
1 A square and 1 B triangle
to make Rows 6X and 6Y.

Step 11. Cut 16 strips each 11" by fabric width small floral print and batting. Join strips on short ends as necessary to make strips at least 2" larger all around for Rows 1–6. Cut two strips each 16" by fabric width small floral print and batting. Trim to make strips at

least 2" larger all around than corner rows.

Step 12. Sandwich a batting strip between a small floral print strip and a pieced row; pin or baste layers together to hold. Mark a 1" crosshatch design on each B triangle and a large X on the A squares and Nine-Patch blocks. Quilt on the marked lines as for center panel; when quilting is complete, remove pins or basting. Trim excess backing and batting even with top.

Joining Quilted Rows

Step 1. Cut 15 strips 1 1/2" by fabric width small floral print for connecting strips. Measure edges of rows and create connecting strips long enough to cover the edge of each row by joining strips with right sides together on the short ends.

Step 2. Fold each connecting strip along length with wrong sides together; press.

Step 3. To connect rows, begin with Rows 5X and 6X; pin the rows right sides together, matching seams. Align the raw edge of a connecting strip with the raw edges of the rows as shown in Figure 20; sew through all layers.

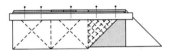

Figure 20
Pin the rows right sides together, matching seams. Align the raw edge of a connecting strip with the raw edges of the rows.

Step 4. Trim seam allowance to 1/8"; fold the folded edge of the connecting strip to cover the seam and

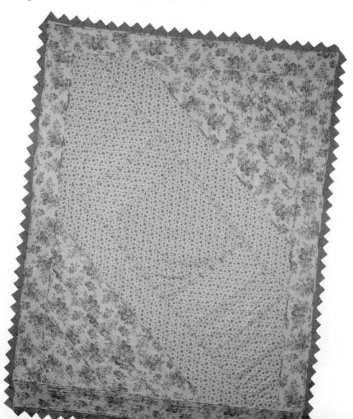

hand-stitch in place. Repeat with Row 4X on the opposite side of Row 5X to make an X side panel as shown in Figure 21; repeat for a Y side panel.

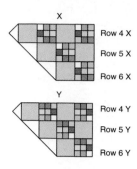

Figure 21
Join rows to make X and Y side panels.

Step 5. Make X and Y corner panels in the same manner referring to Figure 22 for positioning of rows.

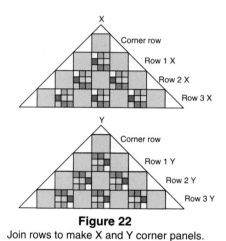

Figure 22
Join rows to make X and Y corner panels.

Step 6. Join the side panels to the center panel in the same manner and add the corner panels to complete the quilt center as shown in Figure 23.

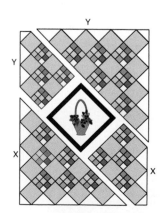

Figure 23
Join the side and corner panels with the center panel to complete the quilt center.

Adding Borders

Step 1. Cut and piece two strips each 2" x 64 1/4" and 2" x 89 3/4" dark green print. Cut and piece two strips each 6" x 64 1/4" and 6" x 89 3/4" yellow tone-on-tone.

Step 2. Sew a dark green print strip to a same-length yellow tone-on-tone strip; press seams toward the dark green print strip. Repeat for all strips.

Step 3. Cut four 6" x 6" squares yellow tone-on-tone for D. Cut four each 2" x 6" (E) and 2" x 7 1/2" (F) rectangles dark green print.

Step 4. Sew E to D and add F to make a corner unit; repeat for two corner units and two corner units reversed as shown in Figure 24.

Figure 24
Sew E to D and add F to make a corner unit; repeat to make a reverse corner unit.

Step 5. Sew a corner unit to the ends of each shorter pieced border strip as shown in Figure 25; press seams away from corner units.

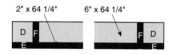

Figure 25
Sew a corner unit to the ends of each shorter pieced border strip.

Step 6. Cut nine strips each 10" by fabric width large floral print and batting.

Step 7. Piece backing and batting strips to make strips at least 2" larger than the border strips all around. Sandwich the batting strips between the border strips and backing pieces; pin or baste to hold. Mark four large V shapes along the top and bottom yellow strips and six large V shapes along the side yellow strips. Quilt on the marked lines and as desired as for the center panel. When quilting is complete, remove pins or basting; trim excess batting and backing even with top.

Step 8. Cut nine 1 1/2" by fabric width strips large floral print; prepare connecting strips as instructed in Joining Quilted Rows. Sew quilted border strips with right sides together to the quilted top, adding longer strips to opposite long sides and shorter strips to the top and bottom, and adding connecting strips to the back seams as instructed in Joining Quilted Rows.

Adding Prairie Points

Step 1. Cut eight 12" by fabric width strips and two 12" x 22" strips green-and-white check.

Step 2. Join two fabric width strips and one 12" x 22" section with right sides together on 12" ends to make a long strip; repeat for two strips. Join two fabric width strips on 12" ends to make a long strip; repeat for two strips.

Step 3. Fold the stitched strips in half with wrong sides together along length; press. Unfold and mark a line every 6" on both sides of the creased center line on the wrong side of each strip, alternating the marked lines as shown in Figure 26.

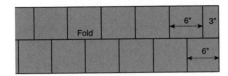

Figure 26
Mark the strips on the wrong side of the fabric every 6" to the pressed fold, alternating the marked lines.

Step 4. Cut on the marked lines to the creased line on each strip; trim off the 3" tabs on the strip ends. Fold each cut section diagonally into a triangle and press; fold again as shown in Figure 27 and press. Fold the pressed triangle strip in half along length to form a line of prairie points and press as shown in Figure 28.

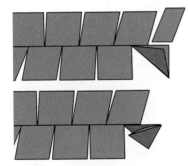

Figure 27
Cut on the marked lines to the fold area on each strip. Trim off the 3" tabs. Fold each cut section into a triangle and press; fold again.

Fold

Figure 28
Fold the pressed triangle strip to form a line of triangles and press.

Step 5. Cut nine 1 1/2" by fabric width strips large floral print; prepare connecting strips as instructed in Joining Quilted Rows.

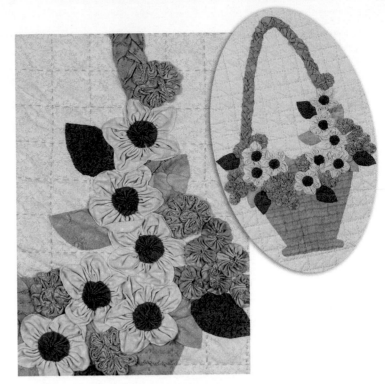

Step 6. Lay the folded edge of a shorter prairie-point strip right sides together with the top edge of the quilt, aligning the end of the prairie-point strip with one end of quilt edge. Trim any excess from the opposite end of the prairie-point strip, leaving a 1/4" seam allowance. Turn seam allowance in and hand-stitch in place. Lay a connecting strip about 1/8" from the bottom folded edge of the strip and quilt. Sew through all layers; hand-stitch the folded edge of the connecting strip to the back of the quilt. Repeat with bottom and side prairie-point strips and connecting strips to complete the quilt. ✦

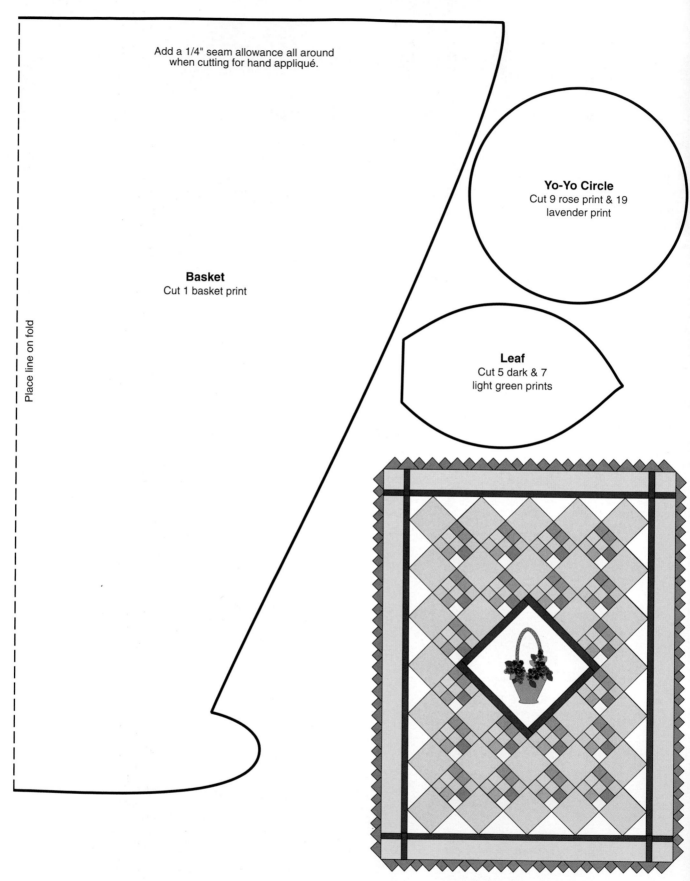

Add a 1/4" seam allowance all around
when cutting for hand appliqué.

Place line on fold

Basket
Cut 1 basket print

Yo-Yo Circle
Cut 9 rose print & 19
lavender print

Leaf
Cut 5 dark & 7
light green prints

Blossom Basket Medallion
Placement Diagram
Approximately 77 3/4" x 103 1/4"
(without prairie points)

Garden View Wall Quilt

By Susan Parr

When nature's blossoms are taking a rest, bring the flowers inside in this fabric garden.

Project Specifications

Skill Level: Intermediate
Wall Quilt Size: 20" x 28"

Materials

- Scraps bright pink tone-on-tone and gold/green print for cone flowers
- 1/4 yard green leaf print for leaves
- 1/2 yard green print for stems
- 1 1/4 yards brown tone-on-tone for borders
- 2 rectangles 17 1/2" x 25 1/2" blue mottled for background
- Batting 20 1/2" x 28 1/2"
- All-purpose thread to match fabrics
- White hand-quilting thread
- Black, green and bright pink 6-strand embroidery floss
- 4 yards 100-percent acrylic blue/purple variegated chenille yarn for fuzzy flowers
- Fabric tube turner
- 1 roll 1/4" fusible web tape
- Basic sewing tools and supplies, rotary cutter, mat and ruler, and marking pencil

Instructions

Step 1. Mark lines on one 17 1/2" x 25 1/2" background piece using the marking pencil referring to Figure 1.

Step 2. Cut three strips each 1" x 19" and 1" x 27" brown tone-on-tone. Fold each strip right sides together

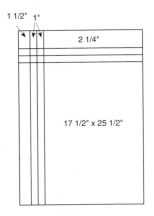

Figure 1
Mark lines on a 17 1/2" x 25 1/2" background piece.

along length; stitch, using a 1/8" seam allowance, to make a narrow tube. Use the fabric tube turner to turn tubes right side out; press with seam centered in the back. Bond fusible web tape to the seam side of each strip; remove paper.

Step 3. Center the strips on the marked lines on the background, weaving the overlapping area in the top corner as shown in Figure 2. Fuse strips in place; hand-stitch in place using invisible stitches with all-purpose thread to match the strips. Trim strips even with background piece.

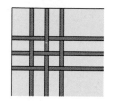

Figure 2
Weave the overlapping
area in the top center.

Step 4. Prepare templates for leaf and flower shapes using patterns given; cut as directed on each piece.

Step 5. To make the 3-D leaves, place two same-size leaves right sides together; stitch all around. Cut the backside of the leaf in a Y shape as shown in Figure 3; turn right side out through opening. Push out points and smooth curves; press. When shape is smooth, cut a small piece of fusible web tape, remove paper backing, insert inside cut opening and press to hold layers together. Repeat for all leaves.

Figure 3
Cut the backside of
the leaf in a Y shape.

Step 6. Cut 1"-wide bias strips from the green print to equal 4 yards for stems. Prepare stem pieces referring to Step 2 in the following lengths: (2) 4 1/2"; (3) 7"; (2) 11"; (1) 13"; (2) 14"; (1) 16"; and (1) 18".

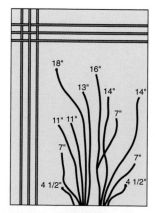

Figure 4
Arrange stem pieces
on background.

Step 7. Tie a small knot in the end of three of the stem pieces to create leaf buds referring to the Placement Diagram of positioning suggestions. Arrange the stem pieces on the open area of the fused background piece referring to Figure 4 for positioning. **Note:** *Your stems may curve more or less than those shown on the completed sample.*

Step 8. Fuse and hand-stitch stems in place using invisible stitches, leaving knotted bud ends loose, using all-purpose thread to match the stem fabric.

Step 9. Cut two strips each 3 1/2" x 20 1/2" and 3 1/2" x 28 1/2" brown tone-on-tone for borders. Sew a shorter strip to the bottom edge and longer strip to the long right edge of the fused background piece, mitering the corner seam as shown in Figure 5; press seams toward strips with mitered seam pressed open. Repeat with the second background piece, sewing the longer strip on the left edge to make a reverse piece for backing, again referring to Figure 5. Set aside backing piece.

Figure 5
Miter corner seams. Make
front and back reverse.

Step 10. Arrange the stitched leaves on the stems referring to the Placement Diagram for positioning suggestions; stem-stitch down the center of each leaf using 2 strands green embroidery floss as shown in Figure 6, continuing stitching to create small stems to attach to fabric stems, again referring to Figure 6.

Figure 6
Stem-stitch down the center of
each leaf using 2 strands
green embroidery floss.

Step 11. Add stem-stitched tendrils as desired on the fabric stems referring to the Placement Diagram for positioning suggestions.

Step 12. Prepare flower shapes for hand appliqué referring to the General Instructions. Pin flower shapes in place referring to the Placement Diagram for positioning suggestions.

Step 13. Using a buttonhole stitch and 2 strands bright pink embroidery floss, stitch around each flower shape. Stem-stitch on the flower lines to create petals. Buttonhole-stitch around flower centers using 2 strands black embroidery floss.

Step 14. Cut a 36" length of chenille yarn. Beginning at one end, make three loops approximately 1" long as shown in Figure 7; do not cut yarn. Using matching thread, join

the loops in the center, again referring to Figure 7.

Step 15. Position the loops at the end of one appliquéd stem as shown in Figure 8 and referring to the Placement Diagram for positioning suggestions. Hand-stitch loops in place along center on the same appliquéd stem.

Figure 7
Make 3 loops 1"
long; join in center.

Figure 8
Position stitched
loops at the end of
a stem; secure.

Step 16. Continue looping chenille yarn, making loops a little larger, tacking each loop in the center before making another loop as shown in Figure 9. Continue this process until the resulting looped flower is 2"–2 1/2" long. Make another three-loop piece as in Step 14; stitch in place at the top end of flower. Cut yarn and tuck end under loops. Backstitch down the flower center to secure all loops. Repeat for four fuzzy flowers.

Figure 9
Continue to make
loops, tacking each
loop in the center.

Step 17. Place the batting on a flat surface; place the appliquéd top on the batting. Place the prepared backing piece right sides together with the layered batting and front matching brown tone-on-tone borders; pin to hold. Stitch all around, leaving an 8" opening on the bottom edge for turning.

Step 18. Clip corners; trim batting close to seam. Turn right side out through opening; pull out corners and press seams flat. Hand-stitch opening closed.

Step 19. Hand-quilt close to narrow brown tone-on-tone strips, in the ditch of border seams, around flowers and as desired using white hand-quilting thread to finish. ✦

Garden View Wall Quilt
Placement Diagram
20" x 28"

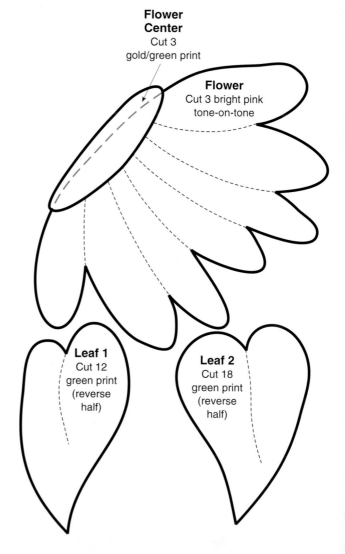

**Flower
Center**
Cut 3
gold/green print

Flower
Cut 3 bright pink
tone-on-tone

Leaf 1
Cut 12
green print
(reverse
half)

Leaf 2
Cut 18
green print
(reverse
half)

Cathedral Windows Sewing Projects

By Donna Friebertshauser

Turn a purchased canvas tote into an elegant bag with Cathedral Window patchwork.

Project Specifications

Skill Level: Intermediate

Tote Patchwork Size: Approximately 12" x 12"

Needle Case Size: Approximately 3" x 6"

Pincushion Size: Approximately 3" x 3"

Thimble Holder Size: Approximately 2 1/4" x 3"

Materials

+ Purchased canvas tote with at least a 14"-square front
+ 1/4 yard each 8 assorted bright prints for windows
+ 1 3/4 yards tan solid
+ All-purpose thread to match tan solid
+ No. 7 embroidery or fine crewel needle
+ 32 (1/2") white pearl buttons
+ 2 (2 1/2" x 11") pieces plastic canvas for bag base
+ 18" (3/8") cotton cord for padded handles
+ Basic sewing tools and supplies, rotary cutter, mat and ruler, template material, and water-erasable marker or pencil

Cathedral Windows Tote Bag

Instructions

Step 1. Wash, dry and press all fabrics.

Step 2. Cut 18 squares tan solid 9" x 9".

Step 3. Fold each square with right sides together; sew both end seams as shown in Figure 1 to make a fabric canoe.

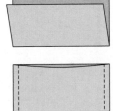

Figure 1
Fold each square with right sides together; sew both end seams.

Step 4. Open the fabric canoe and place the two seam allowances with right sides together as shown in Figure 2, matching seams.

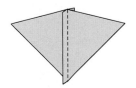 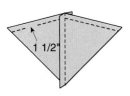

Figure 2
Open the fabric canoe and place the 2 seam allowances with right sides together.

Figure 3
Sew along the open edge, leaving 1 1/2" unsewn in the center of 1 side.

Step 5. Press one seam allowance to the right and one to the left; sew along the open edge, leaving 1 1/2" unsewn in the center of one side as shown in Figure 3. Trim fabric from corners.

Step 6. Turn the piece right side out through the opening; press carefully to avoid stretching on bias-edge sides.

Step 7. To make Cathedral Window A shapes, fold the four points of nine of the squares to the center of the square with the seams on the inside as shown in Figure 4.

Step 8. Blind-stitch the points together as shown in Figure 5.

Step 9. Place the smooth side of two squares together and blind-stitch edges together as shown in Figure 6. **Note:** *There is no seam allowance; pieces butt against each other.* Stitch a third square to the unit to complete a row as shown in Figure 7. Repeat for three rows. Join the rows as for the squares to complete the base unit.

Figure 4
Fold the 4 points of 9 of the squares to the center of the square with the seams on the inside.

Figure 5
Blind-stitch the points together.

Figure 6
Place the smooth side of 2 squares together and blind-stitch edges together.

Figure 7
Stitch a third square to the unit to complete a row.

28 *Quilting to Go*

Step 10. Measure the window area formed where two squares are joined together as shown in Figure 8. This space should be approximately 2 1/2" x 2 1/2". Cut nine different bright print squares this size for Z, referring to the photo for color suggestions. Place a Z square in a window to cover the blind-stitched seam as shown in Figure 9; do not turn under a seam allowance.

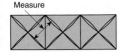

Figure 8
Measure the window area formed where 2 squares are joined together.

Figure 9
Place a Z square in a window to cover the seam.

Step 11. Lift the center of one of the folded flaps and roll over the edge of the Z square approximately 1/4"; pin until ready to sew. Gradually taper the rolled edge to the corners of the Z square as shown in Figure 10. Repeat to cover the remaining edges of the Z square. Blind-stitch the rolled edges in place. Repeat with all Z squares. **Note**: *The flaps will completely cover the raw edges of the window fabrics.* Roll the remaining flaps over the tan solid background areas; taper edges and blind-stitch in place.

Figure 10
Turn the remaining portions of the flap back and taper to nothing at the corners.

Step 12. Center and hand-stitch the completed unit to one side of the canvas tote.

Cathedral Windows Tote Bag Side A
Placement Diagram
At least 14" x 14"

Step 13. To make Cathedral Window B shapes, repeat Steps 7–9 to make a base unit except do not blind-stitch the folded points together, pin in place as shown in Figure 11.

 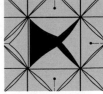

Figure 11
Pin folded points in place.

Figure 12
Insert a bright print square under the folded points.

Step 14. Cut nine 4" x 4" squares assorted bright prints referring to the photo for color suggestions. Remove pin holding folded points on one square. Insert a bright print square under the folded points as shown in Figure 12: blind-stitch points together. Repeat for all squares.

Step 15. Lift the center of one of the folded flaps and roll the flap down, tapering the rolled edge to the corners to expose the bright print square as shown in Figure 13; pin in place. Repeat with all folded flaps on all squares. Blind-stitch the rolled edges in place.

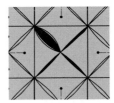

Figure 13
Roll the flap to expose the bright print square, tapering the rolled edge to the corners.

Cathedral Windows Tote Bag Side B
Placement Diagram
At least 14" x 14"

Step 16. Center and hand-stitch the completed unit to the remaining side of the canvas tote.

Step 17. Sew a 1/2" white pearl button at the intersections of the Cathedral Window units referring to the Placement Diagrams for positioning.

Step 18. Reinforce the bottom of the tote bag by whipstitching two 2 1/2" x 11" pieces of plastic canvas together and inserting in the bottom of the bag.

Step 19. To reinforce handles, place a 9" length of 3/8" cotton cord along the center of each handle. Wrap the handle around the cord and whipstitch the butted handle edges together.

Cathedral Windows Needle Case

Additional Materials

+ Felt, thermal fleece or other fabric for needle pages
+ 1/2 yard 1/4"-wide polyester/satin ribbon to blend with fabrics
+ 2 (5" x 5") squares tan solid
+ 2 (3" x 3") squares bright prints for windows
+ 2 (3 1/4" x 3 1/4") squares coordinating fabric for lining

Instructions

Step 1. Complete two Cathedral Window B blocks referring to Steps 2–7, and 14 and 15 for tote, except use the 5" x 5" tan solid squares and the 3" x 3" bright print squares.

Step 2. Sew a 1/2" pearl button in the center of each block.

Step 3. Place the smooth sides of the squares together; whipstitch one edge.

Step 4. Cut the 1/4"-wide polyester/satin ribbon length in half to make two 9" lengths. Tie a knot in one end of each length.

Step 5. Fold under all edges of each 3 1/4" x 3 1/4" square coordinating lining fabric 1/4" and press.

Step 6. Center a lining square on the inside of each of the joined squares as shown in Figure 14. Place the unknotted end of each ribbon between the lining squares and the joined squares as shown in Figure 15. Hand-stitch lining squares in place, securing ribbon ends.

Figure 14
Center a lining square on the inside of each of the joined squares.

Figure 15
Place the unknotted end of each ribbon between the lining squares and the joined squares.

Step 7. Cut two 2 3/4" x 5 1/2" rectangles felt, thermal fleece or other fabric for needle pages. Fold the pages in half; insert inside cover and stitch down the center to secure as shown in Figure 16.

Figure 16
Stitch down the center of the needle pages.

Hint

To differentiate between needle sizes, the needle pages may be labeled with embroidered letters to indicate size. Use 2 strands any color embroidery floss and a straight stitch, and label pages with needle sizes such as Quilting, Tapestry, Milliner, Crewel, etc.

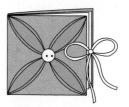

Cathedral Windows Needle Case
Placement Diagram
Approximately 3" x 6"

Cathedral Windows Pincushion

Additional Materials

- 2 (5" x 5") squares tan solid
- 2 (3" x 3") squares bright prints
- Fiberfill or other stuffing material

Instructions

Step 1. Prepare two Cathedral Windows B blocks referring to Steps 2–7 and 14 and 15 for tote, except use the 5" x 5" tan solid squares and the 3" x 3" bright print squares.

Step 2. Sew a 1/2" white pearl button in the center of each block.

Step 3. Place the two blocks with smooth sides together. Whipstitch the edges together all around, leaving one side open.

Step 4. Stuff firmly using fiberfill or other stuffing material. Hand-stitch opening closed when desired fullness is achieved to finish.

Cathedral Windows Pincushion
Placement Diagram
Approximately 3" x 3"

Cathedral Windows Thimble Holder

Additional Materials

- 3 (4" x 7") rectangles assorted bright prints
- Lightweight cardboard
- Black permanent pen
- Plastic—cottage cheese, coffee, etc. lids

Instructions

Step 1. Trace the C pattern given onto lightweight cardboard to make template.

Step 2. Trace the pattern on the plastic using black permanent pen; cut out pieces and set aside.

Step 3. Place two C pieces with right sides together; stitch all around, leaving a 1 1/2" opening on one side. Trim points; turn right side out; press. Repeat for three C units.

Step 4. Insert a piece of plastic inside the opening of each C unit; fold in the seam allowance and hand-stitch the openings closed.

Step 5. Sew a 1/2" white pearl button in the center of two C units for side units. The remaining unit is the bottom.

Step 6. Blind-stitch one side unit to one side of bottom unit as shown in Figure 17, stitching along seam allowance with close stitches. Sew the remaining side unit to the remaining side of the bottom unit as shown in Figure 18.

Figure 17
Blind-stitch 1 side unit
to 1 side of bottom unit.

Figure 18
Sew the remaining side
unit to the remaining side
of the bottom unit.

Step 7. Gently squeeze the ends of the stitched holder to open and insert a thimble, beeswax, needle threader or other tiny sewing aids. ✦

Cathedral Windows Thimble Holder
Placement Diagram
Approximately 2 1/4" x 3"

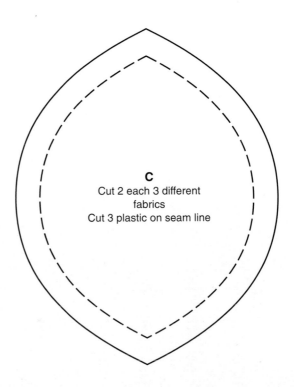

C
Cut 2 each 3 different
fabrics
Cut 3 plastic on seam line

Tumbling Blocks Raggy Quilt

By Barbara Clayton

Combine machine stitching and on-the-go techniques to complete this frayed-edge baby quilt.

Project Specifications

Skill Level: Beginner

Quilt Size: 44 7/8" x 51"

Block Size: 6 1/8" x 7"

Number of Blocks: 59

Materials

- 3 1/4 yards pink print flannel
- 3 1/4 yards blue print flannel
- 3 1/4 yards white with blue dots flannel
- Low-loft batting 45" x 65"
- White all-purpose thread
- White hand-quilting thread
- Basic sewing tools and supplies, rotary cutter, mat and ruler, marking pencil, template material and freezer paper

Instructions

Step 1. Prepare templates using pattern pieces given; cut as directed on each piece using a rotary cutter.

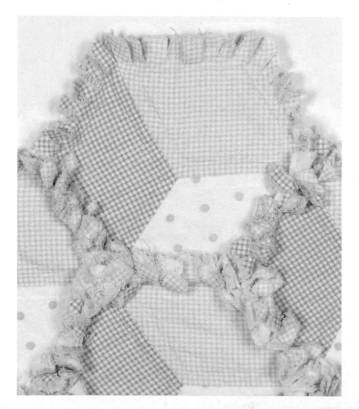

Step 2. Press the waxy side of the freezer paper to the wrong side of the flannel A pieces using a dry iron, positioning the shape 1/4" from two sides and 1" from the opposite sides as shown in Figure 1.

Figure 1
Position the freezer-paper
shape 1/4" from 2 sides
and 1" from the opposite
sides of the fabric A.

Step 3. Baste the seam allowances to the wrong side, through the paper as shown in Figure 2. When folding over points, fold one side first, then fold the other side over the first fold at midpoint as shown in Figure 3.

Figure 2
Baste the seam
allowances to the
wrong side, through
the paper.

Figure 3
Fold 1 side first,
then fold the other
side over the first
fold at midpoint.

Step 4. Place a basted white with blue dots piece right sides together with a blue print piece with sharp point pointing down as shown in Figure 4, keeping edges even.

Figure 4
Place a basted white with blue dots
piece right sides together with a blue
print piece with sharp point pointing
down, keeping edges even.

Step 5. Whipstitch the two basted pieces together, stitching from the end point of the paper to the folded point at the top of the side as shown in Figure 5. Insert a pink print diamond between the two stitched pieces to form three sides of a cube referring to Figure 6.

Figure 5
Whipstitch the 2 basted
pieces together, stitching
from the end point of the
paper to the folded point at
the top of the side.

Figure 6
Insert a pink diamond between
the 2 stitched pieces to form
three sides of a cube.

Step 6. Whipstitch the pink print diamond to the top of the blue piece, starting at the paper points; continue to the top of the white and blue dots piece, ending at the paper point, referring to Figure 7, leaving the seam unsewn in the 1" seam allowance area for fraying, to complete one Tumbling Block.

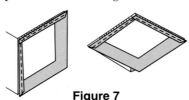

Figure 7
Whipstitch to the top of the blue piece,
starting at the paper points; continue to the
top of the white and blue dots piece, ending
at the paper point, leaving the seam
unsewn in the 1" seam allowance area for
fraying, to complete 1 Tumbling Block.

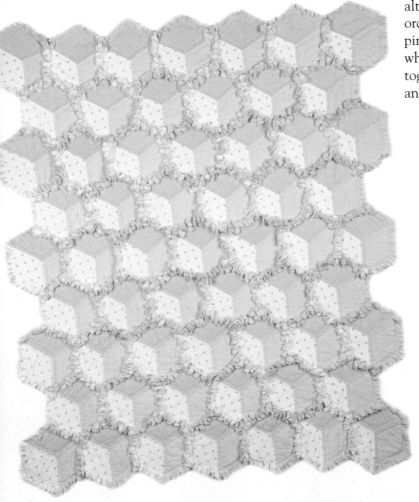

Step 7. Repeat to complete 59 blocks; remove the basting stitches and paper.

Step 8. Lay the backing hexagons on a table wrong side up. Center the smaller batting hexagon on the backing hexagon. Place a finished Tumbling Block on top of the batting, lining up the sides with the backing hexagon.

Step 9. Place a pin in the middle of each side. Machine-stitch around the six sides of the hexagon, along the 1" seam line as shown in Figure 8.

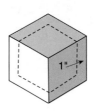

Figure 8
Machine-stitch around the
6 sides of the hexagon,
along the 1" seam line.

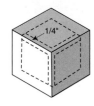

Figure 9
Hand-quilt each diamond
1/4" from the interior
pieced edge.

Step 10. Hand-quilt each diamond 1/4" from the interior pieced edge as shown in Figure 9, using white hand-quilting thread.

Step 11. Join the blocks in five rows with seven blocks and four rows with six blocks as shown in Figure 10, alternating the backs of each block in the following order: all rows of seven blocks—pink, white, blue, pink, white, blue, pink; all rows of six—blue, pink, white, blue, pink, white. Place blocks with backings together and join on side seams only; 1" seam allowances will be on the top of the quilt.

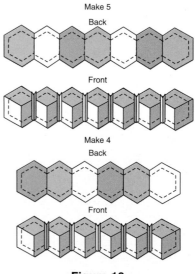

Make 5
Back

Front

Make 4
Back

Front

Figure 10
Join the blocks in 5 rows with 7
blocks and 4 rows with 6 blocks,
placing colors as shown.

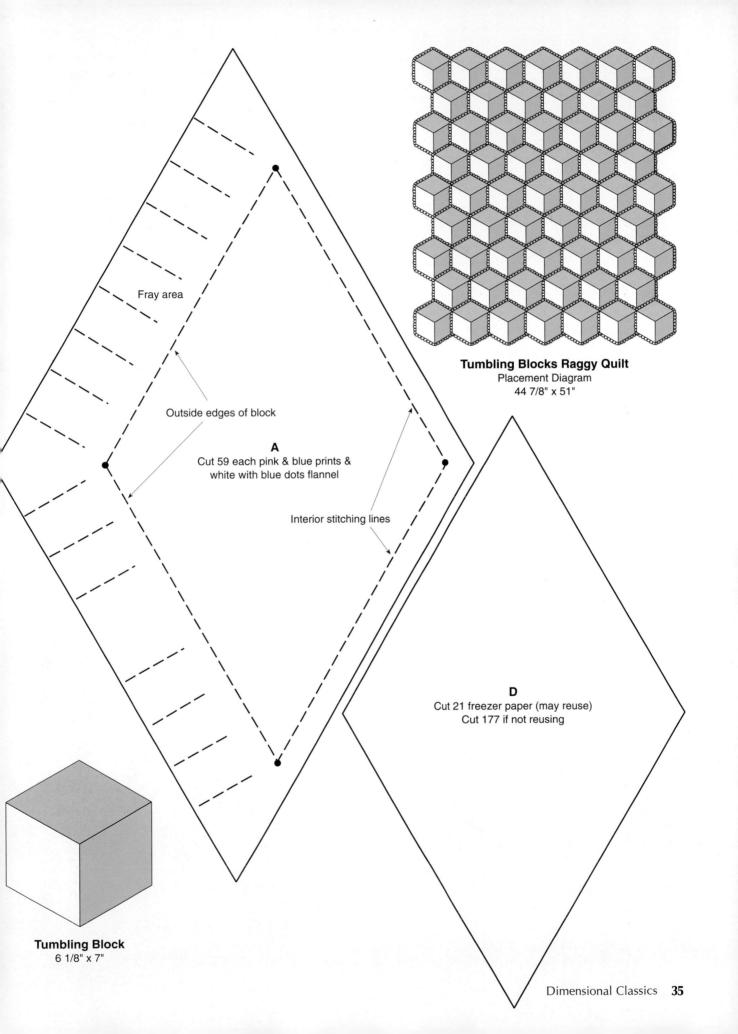

Fray area

Outside edges of block

A
Cut 59 each pink & blue prints &
white with blue dots flannel

Interior stitching lines

Tumbling Blocks Raggy Quilt
Placement Diagram
44 7/8" x 51"

D
Cut 21 freezer paper (may reuse)
Cut 177 if not reusing

Tumbling Block
6 1/8" x 7"

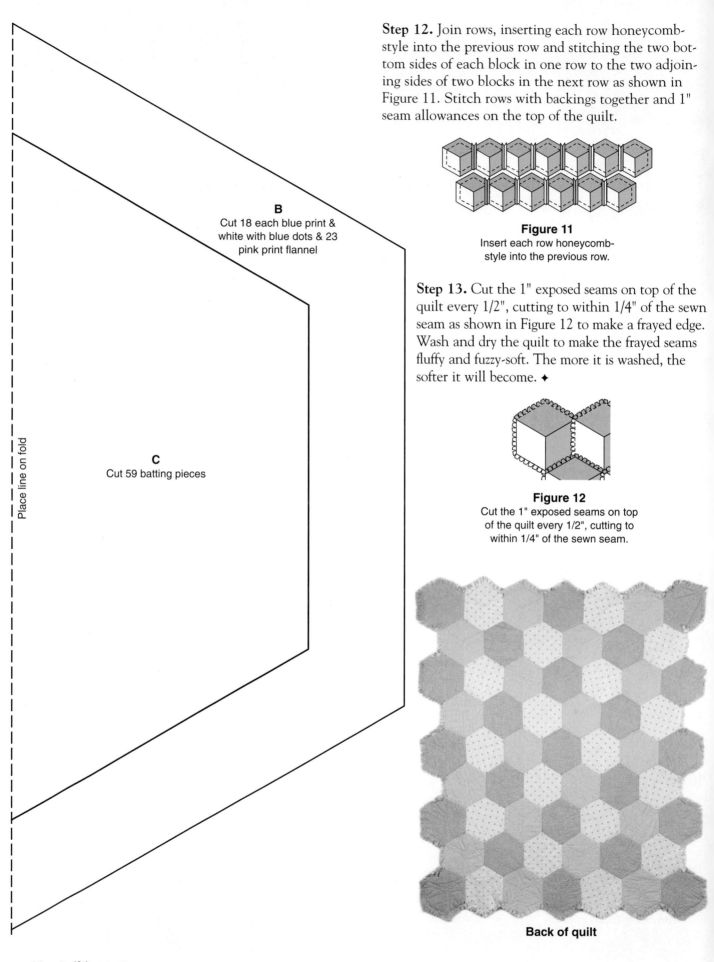

B
Cut 18 each blue print &
white with blue dots & 23
pink print flannel

Place line on fold

C
Cut 59 batting pieces

Step 12. Join rows, inserting each row honeycomb-style into the previous row and stitching the two bottom sides of each block in one row to the two adjoining sides of two blocks in the next row as shown in Figure 11. Stitch rows with backings together and 1" seam allowances on the top of the quilt.

Figure 11
Insert each row honeycomb-style into the previous row.

Step 13. Cut the 1" exposed seams on top of the quilt every 1/2", cutting to within 1/4" of the sewn seam as shown in Figure 12 to make a frayed edge. Wash and dry the quilt to make the frayed seams fluffy and fuzzy-soft. The more it is washed, the softer it will become. ✦

Figure 12
Cut the 1" exposed seams on top of the quilt every 1/2", cutting to within 1/4" of the sewn seam.

Back of quilt

Irish Chain Biscuit Quilt

By Chris Malone

Create the traditional Irish Chain design using blocks made with biscuit units.

Project Specifications

Skill Level: Beginner
Quilt Size: 80 1/2" x 91"
Unit Size: 3 1/2" x 3 1/2"
Block Size: 10 1/2" x 10 1/2"
Number of Blocks: 56

Materials

+ 2 yards green print
+ 3 yards pink print
+ 7 yards total assorted white, cream and light tan prints, and tone-on-tones
+ 7 yards muslin
+ Backing 85" x 95"
+ 3–4 pounds polyester fiberfill
+ Ecru all-purpose thread
+ Ecru crochet cotton for ties
+ 75 (1") safety pins
+ Basic sewing tools and supplies, rotary cutter, mat and ruler, and marking pencil

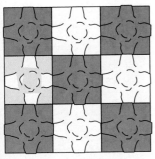

Pink Nine-Patch
10 1/2" x 10 1/2" Block

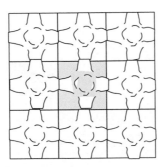

White Nine-Patch
10 1/2" x 10 1/2" Block

Instructions

Step 1. Prewash all fabrics; press.

Step 2. Cut 12 strips green print, 18 strips pink print and a total of 46 strips assorted white, cream and light tan prints or tone-on-tones (referred to as white in subsequent steps) 5" by fabric width for A. Subcut strips into 5" square segments to make 94 green print, 140 pink print and 364 assorted white, cream and light tan prints, or tone-on-tones A squares.

Step 3. Cut 60 strips muslin 4" by fabric width; subcut strips into 4" square segments for B. You will need 598 B squares.

Step 4. To make one biscuit unit, place an A square on a B square with wrong sides together. Match corners and pin, creating a bunch between corners as shown in Figure 1.

Step 5. Make a double pleat on the center of three sides of A to ease in excess fabric as shown in Figure 2.

Figure 1
Match corners of squares and pin, creating a bunch between corners.

Figure 2
Make a double pleat in the center of 3 sides of A to ease in excess fabric; pin pleats.

Step 6. Pin and then stitch pleats in place by hand or machine using a 3/16" seam as shown in Figure 3; remove pins.

Figure 3
Stitch pleat in place by
hand or machine using
a 3/16" seam.

Step 7. Insert a small amount of stuffing through
opening in remaining side; pleat, pin and stitch as in
Steps 5 and 6 to complete one biscuit unit as shown
in Figure 4. Repeat for 598 biscuit units using a similar
amount of fiberfill in each one. **Note:** *If using a sewing
machine for basting, it is more time efficient to stitch and
stuff multiple units at a time.*

Figure 4
Insert a small amount of stuffing
through opening in remaining
side; pleat, pin and stitch to
complete 1 biscuit unit.

Step 8. Join two pink biscuit units with one white
biscuit unit to make a row as shown in Figure 5;
repeat for 56 pink/white/pink rows. Join two white
biscuit units with one pink biscuit unit to make a row
as shown in Figure 6; repeat for 28 white/pink/white
units. Press seams in one direction.

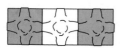   

Figure 5
Join 2 pink biscuit units with 1
white biscuit unit to make a row.

Figure 6
Join 2 white biscuit units with 1
pink biscuit unit to make a row.

Step 9. Sew a white/pink/white row between two
pink/white/pink rows to complete one Pink Nine-
Patch block as shown in Figure 7; repeat for 28 blocks.
Press seams in one direction.

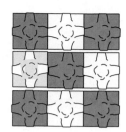

Figure 7
Sew a white/pink/white row between 2 pink/white/pink rows to complete 1 Pink Nine-Patch block.

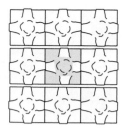

Figure 8
Join 3 rows to complete 1 White Nine-Patch block.

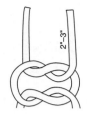

Figure 10
Make a square knot, leaving a 2"–3" tail.

Figure 11
Tie square knots at seam intersections.

Step 10. Join the remaining white biscuit units in rows of three. Join three rows to complete one White Nine-Patch block as shown in Figure 8; repeat for 28 blocks. Press seams in one direction.

Step 11. Join four Pink Nine-Patch blocks with three White Nine-Patch blocks to make a row as shown in Figure 9; repeat for four rows. Press seams open or in one direction.

Make 4

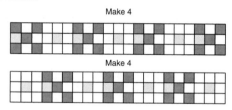

Make 4

Figure 9
Join blocks to make rows as shown.

Step 12. Join four White Nine-Patch blocks with three Pink Nine-Patch blocks to make a row, again referring to Figure 9; repeat for four rows.

Step 13. Join the rows referring to the Placement Diagram for positioning; press seams open or in one direction.

Step 14. Join 21 green print biscuit units to make a row; repeat for two rows. Press seams open or in one direction. Sew a row to the top and bottom of the pieced center.

Step 15. Join 26 green print biscuit units to make a row; repeat for two rows. Press seams open or in one direction. Sew a row to opposite long sides of the pieced center.

Step 16. Place the backing fabric right side down on a flat surface; lay the completed top right side up over backing, leaving an equal amount of backing showing all around edges. Secure top to backing with 1" safety pins placed evenly across the top.

Step 17. Using ecru crochet cotton, take a stitch at each intersection between squares; backstitch over stitch and tie a square knot, leaving a 2" tail as shown in Figures 10 and 11.

Step 18. When tying is complete, remove 1" safety pins.

Step 19. Trim backing 3/4" larger than quilt top all around referring to Figure 12.

Figure 12
Trim backing 3/4" larger than quilt top.

Figure 13
Hand- or machine-stitch backing/binding edge in place on the quilt's top side.

Step 20. Fold edge of backing to the wrong side 1/4" and fold over again to cover edge of blocks to make a 3/8" self-binding edge. Hand- or machine-stitch backing/binding edge in place on the quilt's top side as shown in Figure 13 to finish. ✦

Irish Chain Biscuit Quilt
Placement Diagram
80 1/2" x 91"

My Garden Basket

By Julie Weaver

Ruched and yo-yo flowers fill this appliquéd basket bordered with a black-and-white checkerboard.

Project Specifications

Skill Level: Intermediate

Quilt Size: 23" x 27"

Materials

- Scraps 2 different green and 2 different blue tone-on-tones
- 9" x 16" rectangle brown print
- 1 fat quarter each 2 different gold tone-on-tones
- 1/3 yard black print No. 2
- 1/3 yard red tone-on-tone
- 1/2 yard black print No. 1
- 3/4 yard white-on-white print
- Backing 27" x 31"
- Batting 27" x 31"
- Neutral color all-purpose thread
- Green rayon embroidery floss
- White and tan hand-quilting thread
- 5 (3/4") wooden buttons
- Basic sewing tools and supplies

Instructions

Completing Basic Quilt Top

Step 1. Cut a 13 1/2" x 17 1/2" rectangle white-on-white print for center background. Fold and crease to mark the center.

Step 2. Cut six 1 1/2" by fabric width strips black print No. 2; subcut two of these strips into two 15 1/2" (A) and two 17 1/2" (B) lengths. Set aside remaining strips for outer borders.

Step 3. Sew the B strips to opposite long sides and the A strips to the top and bottom of the center background rectangle; press seams toward strips.

Step 4. Cut six strips 1 1/2" by fabric width each white-on-white print and black print No. 1. Sew a white-on-white print strip between two black print No. 1 strips with right sides together along length to make a strip set; press seams toward dark strips. Repeat to make two X strip sets.

Step 5. Sew a black print No. 1 strip between two white-on-white print strips with right sides together along length to make a strip set; press seams toward dark strip. Repeat to make two Y strip sets.

Step 6. Subcut strip sets into 1 1/2" segments to make X and Y units as shown in Figure 1. You will need 40 of each unit.

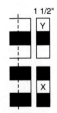

Figure 1
Subcut strip sets into
1 1/2" segments to
make X and Y units.

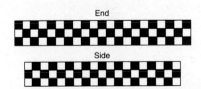

Figure 2
Join X and Y segments to make border strips.

Step 7. Join nine X and 10 Y segments to make a side border strip as shown in Figure 2; press seams in one direction. Repeat for two side strips.

Step 8. Sew a strip to opposite sides of the bordered center background; press seams away from the pieced strip.

Step 9. Join 11 X segments and 10 Y segments to make an end border strip, again referring to Figure 2; press seams in one direction. Repeat for two end strips. Sew a strip to the top and bottom of the bordered center; press seams toward strips.

Step 10. From the black print No. 2 strips set aside in Step 2, cut two strips each 23 1/2" (C) and 25 1/2" (D). Sew the D strips to opposite sides and C strips to the top and bottom; press seams toward strips.

Step 11. Prepare templates for appliqué shapes using patterns given; cut as directed on each piece and prepare for hand appliqué referring to the General Instructions.

Step 12. Center the basket and handle pieces on the background with top of handle and bottom of basket 1 5/8" from the outside center edges as shown in Figure 3; hand-stitch in place referring to the General Instructions.

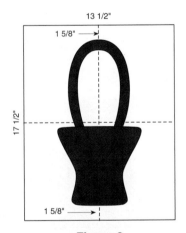

Figure 3
Center the basket and handle pieces on the background with top of handle and bottom of basket 1 5/8" from the outside center edges.

Step 13. Prepare the pieced and appliquéd top for quilting referring to the General Instructions. Quilt as desired by hand or machine. *Note: The sample was hand-quilted in an echo design around the basket and handle in the center background, in the ditch of seams between border strips and with an X through the center of each white-on-white print border square using white hand-quilting thread. The basket and handle were hand-quilted in a 3/4" diagonal crosshatch pattern using tan hand-quilting thread.*

Step 14. Prepare 3 1/4 yards straight-grain binding

from black print No. 1. Bind edges of quilt referring to the General Instructions.

Making Red Ruched Flowers

Step 1. Cut two 2" x 22" and three 1 1/2" x 22" bias strips from red tone-on-tone.

Step 2. Fold under 1/4" on one of the long raw edges on each of the bias strips; press. Press each strip in half with wrong sides together so raw edges meet. Mark dots, beginning 1/2" in from the side every 1" along the top fold referring to Figure 4. Mark dots along the bottom 1/4" fold every 1", beginning from the side, again referring to Figure 4.

Figure 4
Mark dots, beginning 1/2" in from the side every 1" along the top fold. Mark dots along the bottom 1/4" fold every 1", beginning from the side.

Step 3. Using matching all-purpose thread and beginning at the first dot, take a running stitch to connect the dots to make a zigzag pattern along the strip as shown in Figure 5.

Figure 5
Connect the dots to make a zigzag pattern along the strip.

Step 4. Gather the strip to an approximate 12" length, measuring from beginning dot to ending dot; tie off.

Step 5. Begin at one end and start forming a small circle, keeping the center-folded edge on the outside. Continue building outward, tacking as you go, until the ruched strip forms a circular flower as shown in Figure 6. Tack edges and ungathered tails to the back to make a 2 1/2" flower. Trim tails, if necessary. Repeat for two 2 1/2" ruched flowers.

Figure 6
Begin at 1 end and start forming a small circle, keeping the folded edge on the outside. Continue building outward, tacking as you go, until the ruched strip forms a circular flower.

Step 6. Repeat Steps 2–5 with the 1 1/2"-wide bias strips to make three 2" ruched flowers.

Making Gold Ruched Flowers

Step 1. Cut five 2 1/2" x 11" bias strips from gold tone-on-tones.

Step 2. Prepare each strip as in Step 2 for Making Red Ruched Flowers except mark dots every 1 1/2" beginning 3/4" in from the side along the top fold as shown in Figure 7. Mark dots along the bottom 1/4" fold every 1 1/2", again referring to Figure 7, beginning from the side.

Figure 7
Mark dots every 1 1/2" beginning 3/4" in from the side along the top fold. Mark dots along the bottom 1/4" fold every 1 1/2".

Step 3. Connect the dots in a zigzag pattern with a running stitch. Gather the strip to an approximate 5" length, measuring from beginning dot to ending dot to make six petals; tie off.

Step 4. Join petals into a circle, tucking ungathered tails to the back; arrange petals and tack in place to make an approximate 2 1/2" flower. Trim tails, if

necessary. Sew a wooden button to the center; repeat for five gold ruched flowers.

Making Yo-Yo Flowers

Step 1. Prepare template for circle; cut as directed on the piece.

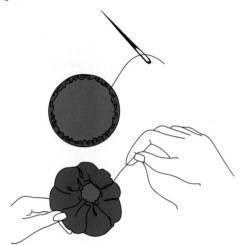

Figure 8
Make yo-yo flowers as shown.

Step 2. To make one yo-yo flower, turn under 1/8" along outer edge of one circle and finger-press. Hand-stitch a basting stitch on the right side using a knotted thread as

My Garden Basket
Placement Diagram
23" x 27"

shown in Figure 8. Pull thread to gather and knot tightly; press yo-yo flat to complete one yo-yo flower, again referring to Figure 8. Repeat for nine yo-yo flowers.

Completing the Quilt

Step 1. Arrange the leaf shapes on the quilted center background referring to the Placement Diagram for positioning; hand-stitch in place as for basket and handle.

Step 2. Using 3 strands of green rayon embroidery floss and an outline stitch, stitch detail lines on leaf shapes,

being careful to stitch through only to the batting layer.

Step 3. Arrange the yo-yo and ruched flowers on the center background referring to the Placement Diagram for positioning; stitch in place, tacking edges through to batting layer only.

Step 4. Stitch vine lines using an outline stitch and 3 strands of green rayon embroidery floss tacking edges through to batting layer only and referring to the Placement Diagram for design suggestions. ✦

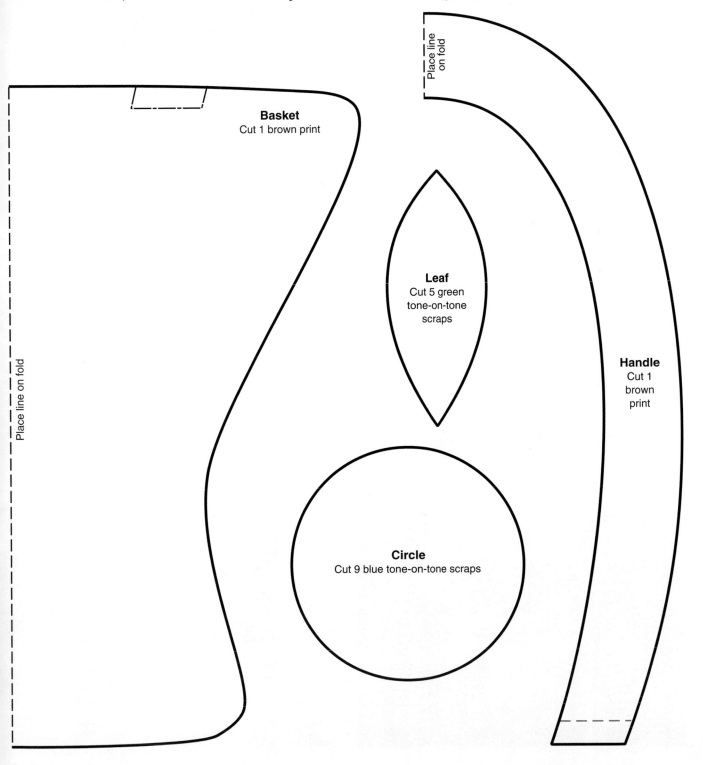

Popping Prairie Points

By Christine Carlson

Open the centers of the prairie-point boxes to find a surprise ribbon.

Project Specifications

Skill Level: Beginner
Quilt Size: 13" x 15 3/8" (includes binding)
Block Size: 1 3/4" x 1 3/4"
Number of Blocks: 12

Materials

+ 12 (4 1/2") squares assorted coordinating fabrics for A
+ 12 (2 1/4" squares) assorted coordinating fabrics for B
+ 8" x 11" rectangle teal print for D and E
+ 10" x 12" rectangle gold print for F and G
+ 10" x 15" rectangle purple print for H and J
+ 1 fat eighth burgundy print for C
+ Batting 17" x 20"
+ Backing 17" x 20"
+ 2 yards 1"-wide self-made or purchased straight-grain or bias binding
+ All-purpose thread to match fabrics
+ Hand-quilting thread to match fabrics
+ 10 assorted 1/2" buttons
+ 4 matching 5/8" buttons
+ Assorted 1/8"-wide silk ribbons

+ Spray sizing
+ Basic sewing tools and supplies, rotary cutter, mat and ruler, marking pencil and large-eye, sharp-tip needle

Popping Prairie Points
1 3/4" x 1 3/4" Block

Instructions

Step 1. Cut 48 squares 1 3/4" x 1 3/4" from burgundy print for C.

Step 2. Fold each A square into quarters as shown in Figure 1; cut into four equal 2 1/4" x 2 1/4" A squares.

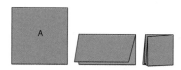

Figure 1
Fold as shown.

Step 3. Fold each A square on one diagonal to make a triangle as shown in Figure 2. Fold the corners over to the center to make a folded square as shown in Figure 3; use spray sizing to press folds flat.

 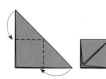

Figure 2
Fold each A square
on 1 diagonal to
make a triangle.

Figure 3
Fold the corners over
to the center to make
a folded square.

Step 4. Place four matching folded A squares on a matching B square with the folded edges of A in the center as shown in Figure 4; pin and baste in place.

Step 5. Draw a diagonal line on the wrong side of each C square.

Figure 4
Place 4 matching
folded A squares on a
matching B square
with the folded edges
of A in the center.

Figure 5
Place a C square on
1 corner of an A-B
unit; stitch on the
marked line.

Figure 6
Trim excess seam
allowance to 1/4"
through all layers.

Figure 7
Press C to the right side
and trim off triangle tails.

Step 6. Place a C square on one corner of an A-B unit as shown in Figure 5; stitch on the marked line, again referring to Figure 5.

Step 7. Trim excess seam allowance to 1/4" through all layers as shown in Figure 6; press C to the right side as shown in Figure 7.

Step 8. Repeat with a matching C square on the opposite corner of the A-B unit; trim and press as shown in Figure 8.

Step 9. Repeat with a matching C on the remaining corners of the A-B unit to complete

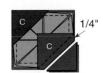

Figure 8
Repeat with a matching C
square on the opposite
corner of the A-B unit.

one Popping Prairie Points block as shown in Figure 9. Repeat for 12 blocks.

Figure 9
Repeat with a
matching C on the
remaining corners of
the A-B unit to
complete 1 Popping
Prairie Points block.

Step 10. Cut eight 1 1/8" x 2 1/4" (D) and three 1 1/8" x 7" (E) sashing pieces from the 8" x 11" rectangle teal print.

Step 11. Join three blocks with D to make a row as shown in Figure 10; press seams toward D. Repeat for four rows.

Figure 10
Join 3 blocks with D to make a row.

Step 12. Join the rows with E; press seams toward E referring to the Placement Diagram.

Step 13. Cut two 2" x 9 3/8" (F) and two 2" x 10" (G) strips from the 10" x 12" gold print rectangle.

Step 14. Sew F to opposite long sides of the pieced center and G to the top and bottom; press seams toward strips.

Step 15. Cut two 2" x 12 3/8" (H) and two 2" x 13" (J) strips from the 10" x 15" purple print rectangle.

Step 16. Sew H to opposite long sides of the pieced center and J to the top and bottom; press seams toward strips.

Step 17. Prepare quilt top for quilting and quilt referring to the General Instructions. **Note:** *The sample was hand-quilted with a diagonal line on each C triangle, through the center of the sashing strips, in the ditch of seams between blocks and in a double channel line on the gold print strips using hand-quilting thread to match fabrics.*

Step 18. When quilting is complete, trim batting and backing edges even with quilted top.

Step 19. Bind edges with self-made 1"-wide bias or straight-grain binding referring to the General Instructions.

Step 20. Cut 12 pairs of 1/8"-wide silk ribbon 5" long. Stitch two matching ribbon pieces through the center of each block inside the pocket area and tie ends in a square knot as shown in Figure 11. Trim ends to 1" lengths.

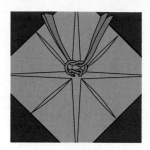

Figure 11
Stitch 2 matching ribbon pieces
through the center of each
block inside the pocket area
and tie ends in a square knot.

Step 21. Sew a 1/2" button at the intersections of the D-E sashing strips and in the center of the F and G strips. Sew a 5/8" button in the corners of each G strip referring to the photo and Placement Diagram for positioning. ✦

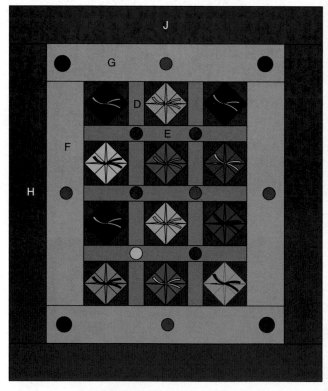

Popping Prairie Points
Placement Diagram
13" x 15 3/8"
(includes binding)

Points & Curves

Stitch points and curves by hand for your next quilt project while you are waiting for your child to finish practicing.

Spring Door Banner

By Connie Kauffman

Spring brings us welcome showers, sunshine and pretty flowers.

Project Specifications

Skill Level: Beginner
Quilt Size: 12" x 21 1/2"

Materials

+ Scraps light and medium gray, green and brown mottleds
+ 6" x 6" square dark yellow mottled
+ 1/8 yard light yellow mottled
+ 1/8 yard pink tone-on-tone
+ 1/4 yard each light and medium blue mottleds
+ 1/4 yard each light and medium green tone-on-tones
+ Backing 16" x 25"
+ Batting 16" x 25"
+ Neutral color all-purpose thread
+ Hand-quilting thread to match fabrics
+ 3/8" pearl button
+ Basic sewing tools and supplies, rotary cutter, mat and ruler, pinking shears, and marking pencil

Instructions

Step 1. Cut sunbeams from light yellow mottled in the following sizes: 1 1/4" x 2 1/2" (A), 1 1/4" x 4" (B), 1 1/4" x 8" (C) and 1 1/4" x 6 1/2" (D). Turn under long edges of each piece 1/4"; press.

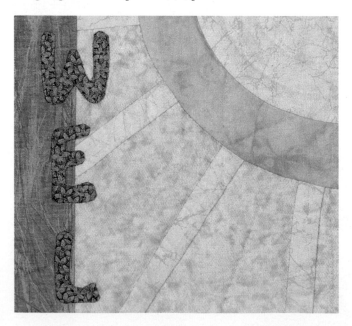

Step 2. Cut one rectangle each 6 1/2" x 11 1/2" light and medium blue mottleds. Arrange the sunbeam pieces on the light blue mottled rectangle referring to Figure 1 for positioning; hand-appliqué in place. Sew the rectangles together on the 11 1/2" side, stitching the sunbeam ends into the seam. Press seam toward darker fabric.

Figure 1
Arrange the sunbeam
pieces on the light blue
mottled rectangle.

Step 3. Cut one rectangle each 6 1/2" x 11" light and medium green tone-on-tones; sew the rectangles together on the 11" side. Press seam toward lighter fabric.

Step 4. Join the two stitched units as shown in Figure 2; press seam toward green fabrics.

Figure 2
Join the 2
stitched units.

Step 5. Lay the stitched unit on a flat surface with blue fabrics on top; fold up the corners of the green fabrics to the center seam and crease to mark as shown in Figure 3. Cut along creased lines to make the bottom angled corners, again referring to Figure 3.

Figure 3
Fold up the corners of the green
fabrics to the center seam and
crease to mark as shown. Cut
along creased lines to make the
bottom angled corners.

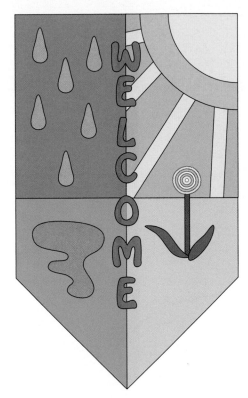

Spring Door Banner
Placement Diagram
12" x 21 1/2"

Step 6. Prepare templates for appliqué shapes using patterns given; cut as directed on each piece, adding a 1/8"–1/4" seam allowance all around when cutting for hand appliqué. Cut a 3/4" x 4 1/4" piece brown mottled for stem.

Step 7. Arrange the pieces on the stitched background referring to Figure 4 and the Placement Diagram for positioning. When satisfied with the positioning, hand-appliqué shapes in place, turning under edges as you stitch, using all-purpose thread to match fabrics.

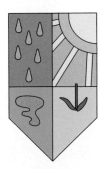

Figure 4
Arrange the pieces on
the stitched
background.

Step 8. Trace the smaller, inside Welcome letters given on page 10 with the *Summer Door Banner* on the pink tone-on-tone. Arrange the letter message along

the center seam on the background pieces and hand-appliqué in place as in Step 7.

Step 9. Lay the batting on a flat surface; place the backing on the batting with right side up. Place the stitched top right sides together with the backing piece; pin layers together to hold.

Step 10. Machine-stitch around edges of the stitched top using a 1/4" seam allowance, leaving a 3" opening on one side. Trim excess backing and batting even with the stitched top as shown in Figure 5; trim corner points.

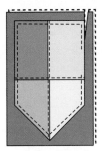

Figure 5
Trim excess backing
and batting even with
the stitched top.

Step 11. Turn the stitched unit right side out through the opening; press to make seam edges flat. Hand-stitch the opening closed.

Step 12. Using pinking shears, cut five different-size circles from yellow mottled and gray scraps. Clip into circles almost to the center as shown in Figure 6.

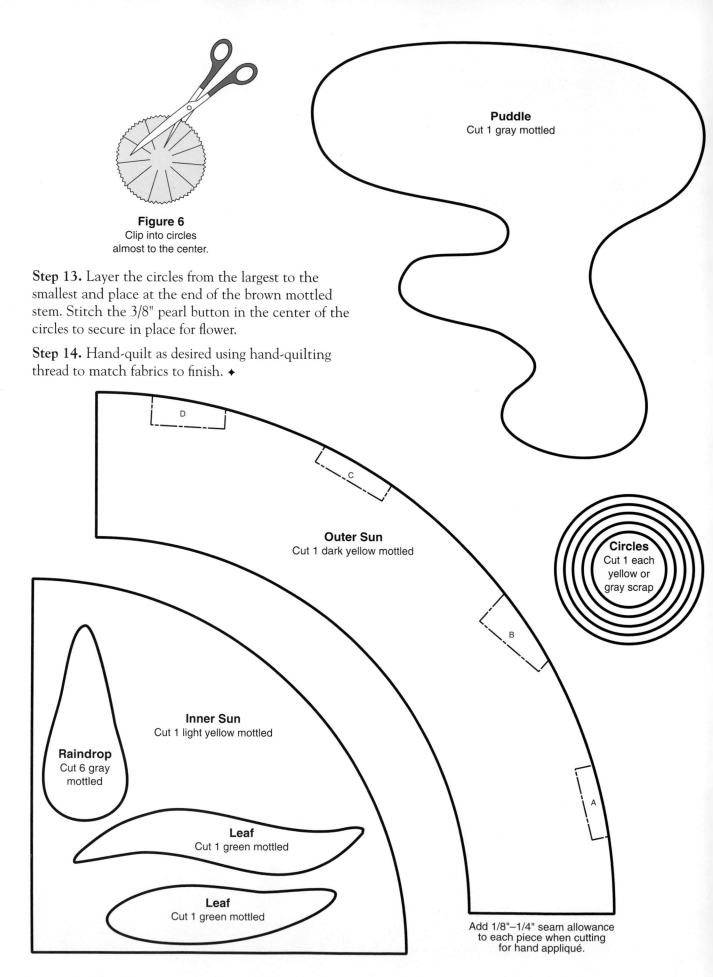

Figure 6
Clip into circles
almost to the center.

Step 13. Layer the circles from the largest to the smallest and place at the end of the brown mottled stem. Stitch the 3/8" pearl button in the center of the circles to secure in place for flower.

Step 14. Hand-quilt as desired using hand-quilting thread to match fabrics to finish. ✦

Puddle
Cut 1 gray mottled

D

C

Outer Sun
Cut 1 dark yellow mottled

Circles
Cut 1 each
yellow or
gray scrap

B

Inner Sun
Cut 1 light yellow mottled

Raindrop
Cut 6 gray
mottled

A

Leaf
Cut 1 green mottled

Leaf
Cut 1 green mottled

Add 1/8"–1/4" seam allowance
to each piece when cutting
for hand appliqué.

Fall Flourish

By Connie Kauffman

Choose six fabrics in autumn colors and an autumn print
to create a splash of color to rival Mother Nature's fall display.

Project Specifications

Skill Level: Intermediate
Quilt Size: 22" x 32"

Materials

+ 1/8 yard rust-and-gold print
+ 1/8 yard each copper, olive green and rust mottleds
+ 1/4 yard each dark green and gold mottleds
+ 3/8 yard black solid
+ 1/2 yard tan splatter print
+ 1/2 yard autumn print
+ Backing 26" x 36"
+ Batting 26" x 36"
+ All-purpose thread to match fabrics
+ Gold metallic thread
+ Basic sewing tools and supplies, and freezer paper

Instructions

Step 1. Cut 60 squares tan splatter print 2 1/2" x 2 1/2" for A.

Step 2. Cut 12 squares each black solid and gold mottled 2 1/2" x 2 1/2" for A.

Step 3. Cut 12 squares each autumn print, dark green, copper, olive green and rust mottleds and rust-and-gold print 2 1/2" x 2 1/2" for B.

Step 4. Place the pattern for B under a piece of freezer paper with the shiny side down. Drawing on the top of the freezer paper, trace 72 B shapes; cut out each shape on the traced line.

Step 5. Place one freezer paper B with the shiny side down on the right side of each fabric B square cut in Step 3, aligning corners of the freezer paper B with the fabric B as shown in Figure 1.

Figure 1
Place 1 freezer paper B
with the paper side
against the wrong side of
a fabric B square, aligning
corners of the freezer
paper B with the fabric B.

Step 6. Cut each pattern along the curve, leaving a 1/4" seam allowance beyond the edge of the freezer paper as shown in Figure 2; do not cut along the edge of the freezer paper.

Figure 2
Cut each pattern along the
curve, leaving a 1/4" seam
allowance beyond the edge
of the freezer paper.

Step 7. To press seam allowance over on the curved edge of B, remove the freezer-paper B and place the fabric B right side down on the ironing board. Place the freezer paper with the shiny side up on the fabric square, aligning straight edges. Turn the curved edge of the fabric B over onto the freezer-paper B and press as shown in Figure 3, being careful not to place the iron onto the freezer paper area.

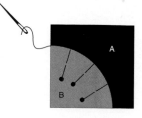

Figure 3
Turn the curved edge of the fabric B
over onto the freezer-paper B and
press, being careful not to place the
iron onto the freezer paper area.

Step 8. Place the pressed autumn print B pieces on top of the black solid A squares, matching corners; pin in place. Hand-stitch the curved edges as shown in Figure 4 using matching all-purpose thread; remove freezer paper shapes.

Figure 4
Place the pressed autumn
print B pieces on top of the
black solid A squares,
matching corners; pin in place.
Hand-stitch the curved edges.

Step 9. Place the pressed rust-and-gold print B pieces on the gold mottled A squares; repeat Step 8.

Step 10. Place the remaining B pieces on the tan splatter print A squares; repeat Step 8. **Note:** *When all B pieces have been appliquéd to the A squares, the A layer beneath B may be trimmed away to reduce bulk as shown in Figure 5.*

Figure 5
Trim away the A layer
beneath the B piece to
reduce bulk as shown.

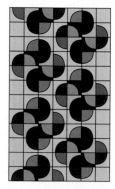

Figure 6
The A-B units create an
overlapping design as shown.

Step 11. Arrange the A-B units in rows with the remaining tan splatter A squares referring to the

Placement Diagram for positioning. **Note:** *The A-B units create an overlapping design, which is shown in Figure 6.*

Step 12. Join the units in rows; press seams in alternating rows in opposite directions. Join the rows to complete the pieced center; press seams in one direction.

Step 13. Cut two strips each 1" x 15 1/2" and 1" x 24 1/2" gold mottled. Sew the longer strips to opposite sides and shorter strips to the top and bottom of the pieced center; press seams toward strips.

Step 14. Cut two strips each 1 1/2" x 17 1/2" and 1 1/2" x 25 1/2" dark green mottled. Sew the longer strips to opposite sides and shorter strips to the top and bottom of the pieced center; press seams toward strips.

Step 15. Cut two strips each 3" x 22 1/2" and 3" x 27 1/2" autumn print. Sew the longer strips to opposite sides and shorter strips to the top and bottom of the pieced center; press seams toward strips. Use the corner pattern given to round the corners of the autumn print border.

Step 16. Prepare quilt top for quilting and hand-quilt as desired referring to the General Instructions. **Note:** *The quilt shown was hand-quilted in the ditch of the appliquéd A-B seam, in the ditch of all border seams and in a scallop pattern in the outer border using gold metallic thread.*

Step 17. Prepare 3 3/8 yards self-made straight-grain binding from black solid and apply to the quilted top to finish referring to the General Instructions. ✦

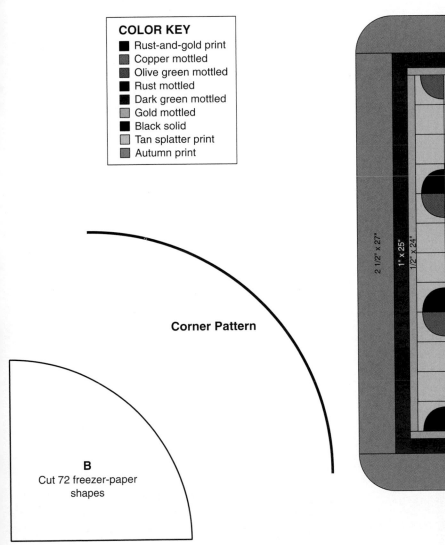

COLOR KEY
- ■ Rust-and-gold print
- ■ Copper mottled
- ■ Olive green mottled
- ■ Rust mottled
- ■ Dark green mottled
- ■ Gold mottled
- ■ Black solid
- ■ Tan splatter print
- ■ Autumn print

Corner Pattern

B
Cut 72 freezer-paper shapes

2 1/2" x 22"

1" x 17"

1/2" x 15"

2 1/2" x 27"

1" x 25"

1/2" x 24"

Fall Flourish
Placement Diagram
22" x 32"

Magic Carpet Quilt

By Christine A. Schultz

An octagonal pieced center creates a unique compass-design block made with a paisley border print.

Project Notes

Select a paisley border print and place the A template on the design; trace and cut out referring to Photo 1.

Photo 1

Roughly trace the motif onto the template, using the cut piece as a guide as shown in Photo 2.

Photo 2

Using the traced motif as a guide, place the template on the fabric on the same design on the print to create identical A pieces referring to Photo 3. When joining the A pieces, a kaleidoscopic effect appears in the center of the pieced octagon as shown in the close-up of the center of one block.

Photo 3

When using fabric for special cutting of the A patches and use of other border motifs in the border print in this manner, yardage will be significantly increased. To estimate yardage needed most accurately, cut template A from clear template material and trace the designed motif in the chosen position on the template. Lay the template over desired fabric motifs, in position, and determine how much fabric is needed for eight A pieces. Multiply this amount by six (the number of blocks in this top). If spaces between the A pieces are large enough for F, this yardage should suffice. If not, add 1/4 yard for F patches. Cut border strips from the length of the fabric before cutting smaller patches to avoid piecing long strips.

Magic Carpet
15 1/2" x 15 1/2" Block

Project Specifications

Skill Level: Advanced

Quilt Size: 45" x 63"

Block Size: 15 1/2" x 15 1/2"

Number of Blocks: 6

Materials

+ 3/4 yard each light and dark brown prints
+ 1 yard dark blue print
+ 1 1/2 yards beige tone-on-tone
+ 2 yards blue/brown paisley print
+ Backing 49" x 67"
+ Batting 49" x 67"
+ All-purpose thread to match fabrics
+ Neutral color all-purpose thread
+ Cream hand-quilting thread
+ Basic sewing tools and supplies, and clear template material

Instructions

Step 1. Cut two identical strips each along the length of a stripe portion of the blue/brown paisley print 3 1/2" x 45 1/2" and 3 1/2" x 63 1/2". Set aside for outside borders.

Step 2. Prepare see-through templates using pattern pieces given; cut as directed on each piece.

Step 3. To piece one block, join two A pieces, stopping stitching at the end of the marked seam allowance to make pivot point as shown in Figure 1; repeat for four A units. Join two A units, again stopping at the marked seam allowance; repeat. Join the two halves to complete the center A unit. Press seams in one direction and center seam in a swirling pattern as shown in Figure 2.

Figure 1
Join A pieces, stopping stitching at the marked seam allowance; join the units as shown to complete the center A unit.

Figure 2
Press seams in 1 direction and center seam in a swirling pattern.

Step 4. Sew C and CR to B as shown in Figure 3; repeat for eight B-C units; press seams away from B.

Figure 3
Sew C and CR to B.

Figure 4
Sew D to opposite sides of 4 B-C units.

Step 5. Sew D to opposite sides of four B-C units as shown in Figure 4; press seams away from D.

Step 6. Sew a B-C unit to the A unit as shown in Figure 5. Set a B-C-D unit onto the pieced unit as shown in Figure 6. Continue to add a B-C unit and then a B-C-D unit around the center A unit until all B-C and B-C-D units have been added. Press seams away from the A unit.

Figure 5
Sew a B-C unit to the A unit.

Figure 6
Set a B-C-D unit onto the pieced unit.

Step 7. Set E and ER pieces in between the B and D points as shown in Figure 7; press seams toward E and ER.

Figure 7
Set E pieces in between the B and D points.

Step 8. Sew F around the outside referring to Figure 8 to complete one block; repeat for six blocks. Press seams toward F.

Figure 8
Sew F around the outside to complete 1 block.

Figure 9
Join 3 blocks to make a row.

Step 9. Join three blocks to make a row as shown in Figure 9; press seams in one direction. Repeat for two rows.

Step 10. Join the rows with H squares and G and L triangles as shown in Figure 10; press seams away from rows.

Step 11. Cut and piece two 1 1/2" x 47" strips beige tone-on-tone. Sew a strip to opposite long sides of the pieced center; press seams toward strips.

Figure 10
Join the rows with
H squares and G
and L triangles.

Step 12. Cut two 2 3/4" x 33 1/2" strips beige tone-on-tone. Sew a strip to the top and bottom of the pieced center; press seams toward strips.

Step 13. Set aside two each light and dark brown prints and four dark blue print I squares for corner units. Sew a J triangle to opposite sides of each remaining I square as shown in Figure 11; press seams toward J pieces.

Figure 11
Sew a J triangle to
opposite sides of I.

Figure 12
Sew 1 J and 2 K
pieces to the I pieces.

Step 14. Sew one J and two K pieces to the I squares set aside in Step 13 to make corner units as shown in Figure 12; press seams away from I.

Step 15. Join nine I-J units to make a strip as shown in Figure 13; repeat for two strips. Press seams in one direction. Sew a light brown print corner unit to one end of each strip and a dark brown print corner unit to the remaining end, again referring to Figure 13. Sew a strip to the top and bottom of the pieced center; press seams away from pieced strips.

Figure 13
Join 9 I-J units to make a strip; add a corner unit to each end.

Step 16. Join 17 I-J units to make a strip as shown in Figure 14; repeat for two strips. Sew a corner unit to each end of each strip, again referring to Figure 14; press seams

in one direction. Sew a strip to opposite long sides of the pieced center; press seams away from pieced strips.

Figure 14
Join 17 I-J units to make a strip; add a corner unit to each end.

Step 17. Using the border strips cut in Step 1, sew the shorter strips to the top and bottom and longer strips to opposite sides of the pieced center, mitering corners referring to the General Instructions.

Step 18. Prepare quilt top for quilting and hand-quilt as desired referring to the General Instructions. *Note: The quilt shown was hand-quilted 1/4" from seams of A, B, D and J pieces, in the ditch of border seams and F pieces and in the pattern given in the G and H pieces using cream hand-quilting thread.*

Step 19. Prepare 6 1/2 yards straight-grain binding using dark blue print. Apply binding to the quilted top to finish referring to the General Instructions. ✦

Magic Carpet Quilt
Placement Diagram
45" x 63"

A
Cut 48 identical
blue/brown paisley print

B
Cut 48 beige tone-on-tone

C
Cut 96 dark
blue print
(reverse half
for CR)

D
Cut 48 light brown print

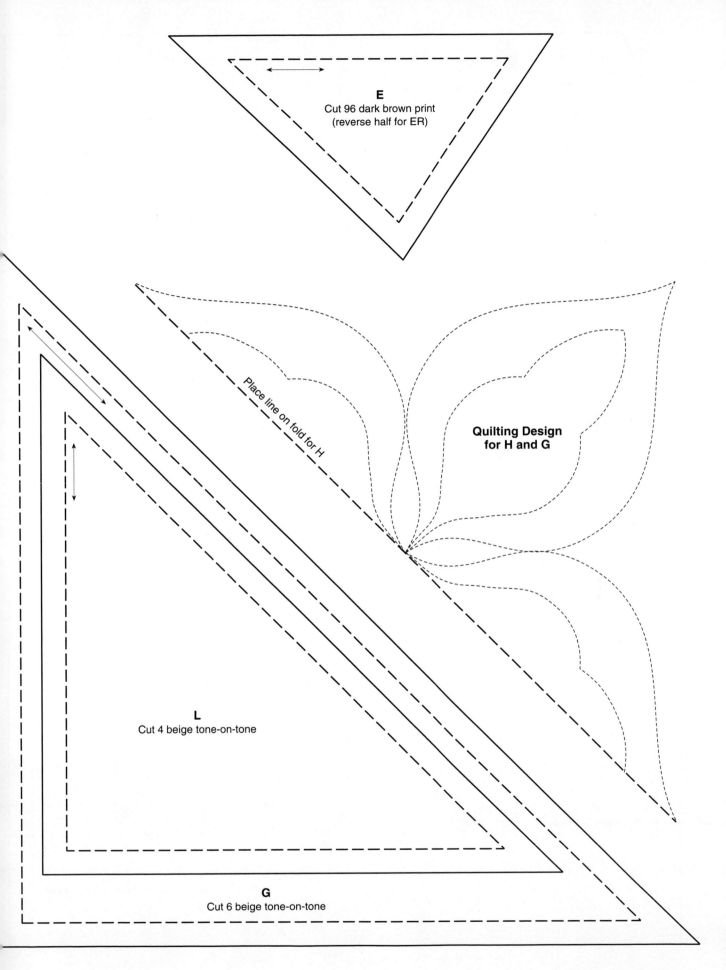

E
Cut 96 dark brown print
(reverse half for ER)

Place line on fold for H

**Quilting Design
for H and G**

L
Cut 4 beige tone-on-tone

G
Cut 6 beige tone-on-tone

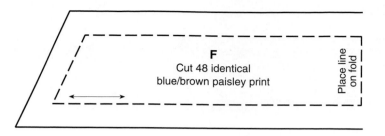

F
Cut 48 identical
blue/brown paisley print

Place line on fold

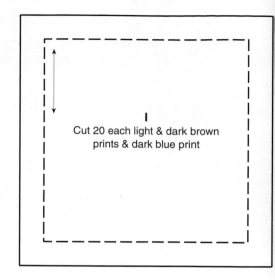

I
Cut 20 each light & dark brown
prints & dark blue print

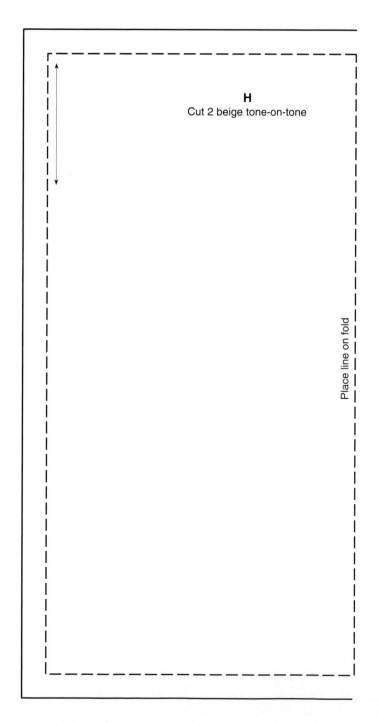

H
Cut 2 beige tone-on-tone

Place line on fold

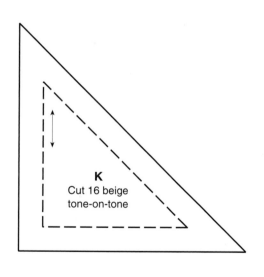

K
Cut 16 beige
tone-on-tone

J
Cut 112 beige tone-on-tone

Merry-Go-Round Medallion

By Holly Daniels

Cutting identical A pieces creates a circular pattern in the center of the Compass block.

Project Notes

Identical A pieces were cut from the same section of the paisley print to create a kaleidoscope design in the center of the Compass block. The corner G pieces were also cut from the same section of the paisley print to make identical corners.

Project Specifications

Skill Level: Advanced

Quilt Size: 32" x 32"

Block Size: 16" x 16"

Number of Blocks: 1

Materials

+ 1/4 yard large floral
+ 1/2 yard green tone-on-tone
+ 1 yard rose paisley print
+ 1 yard cream solid
+ Backing 36" x 36"
+ Batting 36" x 36"
+ Neutral color all-purpose thread
+ Cream hand-quilting thread
+ Basic sewing tools and supplies

Compass
16" x 16" Block

Instructions

Step 1. Prepare templates using patterns given; cut as directed on each piece.

Step 2. To piece the block, join two A pieces; repeat for four pairs. Join two pairs; repeat. Join the halves to complete the center as shown in Figure 1; press seams in one direction.

Figure 1
Join 2 A pieces;
repeat for 4 pairs.
Join 2 pairs; repeat.
Join the halves to
complete the center.

Figure 2
Sew B to F.

Step 3. Sew B to F as shown in Figure 2; press seam toward B. Repeat for all F pieces.

Step 4. Sew D to each long side of C and add E as shown in Figure 3; repeat for all C pieces. Press seams away from C.

Figure 3
Sew D to each long
side of C and add E.

Figure 4
Sew a C-D-E unit
to a B-F unit.

Step 5. Sew a C-D-E unit to a B-F unit as shown in Figure 4; repeat for all B-F units. Press seams toward the B-F units.

Step 6. Join the pieced units to form a circle as shown in Figure 5; press seams away from the B-F units.

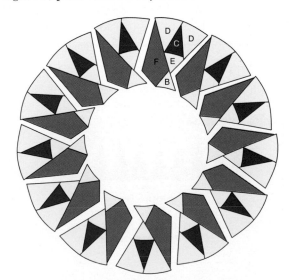

Figure 5
Join the pieced units to form a circle.

Step 7. Turn under edges of the pieced A unit 1/4"; press. Center and appliqué the A unit onto the pieced circle unit.

Step 8. Center and sew G to the pieced unit to complete the Compass block; press seams toward G.

Step 9. Cut two strips each 1 1/4" x 16 1/2" and 1 1/4" x 18" cream solid. Sew the shorter strips to opposite sides and longer strips to the top and bottom of the pieced center; press seams toward strips.

Step 10. Cut two strips each 1" x 18" and 1" x 19" green tone-on-tone. Sew the shorter strips to opposite sides and longer strips to the top and bottom of the pieced center; press seams toward strips.

Step 11. Cut two strips each 1 1/4" x 19" and 1 1/4" x 20 1/2" cream solid. Sew the shorter strips to opposite sides and longer strips to the top and bottom of the pieced center; press seams toward strips.

Step 12. Join 10 rose paisley print H pieces with nine cream solid H pieces and I and IR to make a side strip as shown in Figure 6; press seams in one direction. Repeat for four strips.

Figure 6
Join 10 H rose paisley print H
pieces with 9 cream solid H pieces
and I and IR to make a side strip.

Step 13. Sew an H-I strip to opposite sides of the pieced center; press seams away from the H-I strips. Sew J to each end of the remaining two H-I strips referring to Figure 7. Sew to the top and bottom of the pieced center; press seams away from the H-I strips.

Figure 7
Sew J to each end of an H-I strip.

Step 14. Cut two strips each 1 1/2" x 28 1/2" and 1 1/2" x 30 1/2" cream solid. Sew the shorter strips to opposite sides and longer strips to the top and bottom of the pieced center; press seams toward strips.

Step 15. Cut two strips each 1 1/2" x 30 1/2" and 1 1/2" x 32 1/2" green tone-on-tone. Sew the shorter strips to opposite sides and longer strips to the top and bottom of the pieced center; press seams toward strips.

Step 16. Prepare quilt top for quilting and hand-quilt as desired referring to the General Instructions. **Note:** *The quilt shown was hand-quilted 1/4" from seams in all B, C and H pieces using cream hand-quilting thread.*

Step 17. Prepare 4 yards self-made straight-grain binding from rose paisley print and apply to the quilted top to finish referring to the General Instructions. ✦

Merry-Go-Round Medallion
Placement Diagram
32" x 32"

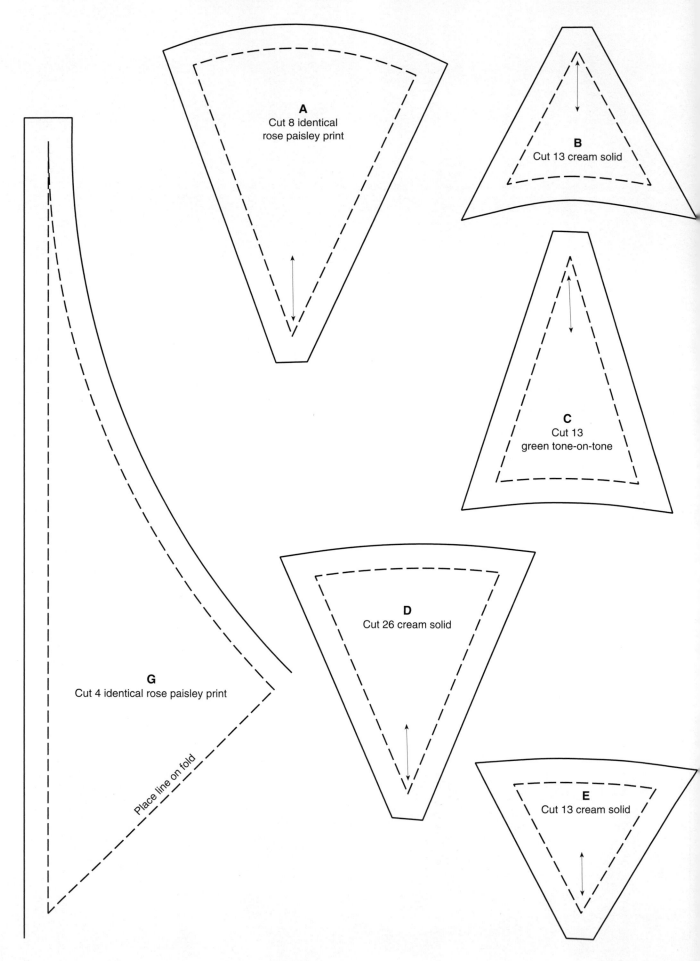

A
Cut 8 identical
rose paisley print

B
Cut 13 cream solid

C
Cut 13
green tone-on-tone

D
Cut 26 cream solid

E
Cut 13 cream solid

G
Cut 4 identical rose paisley print

Place line on fold

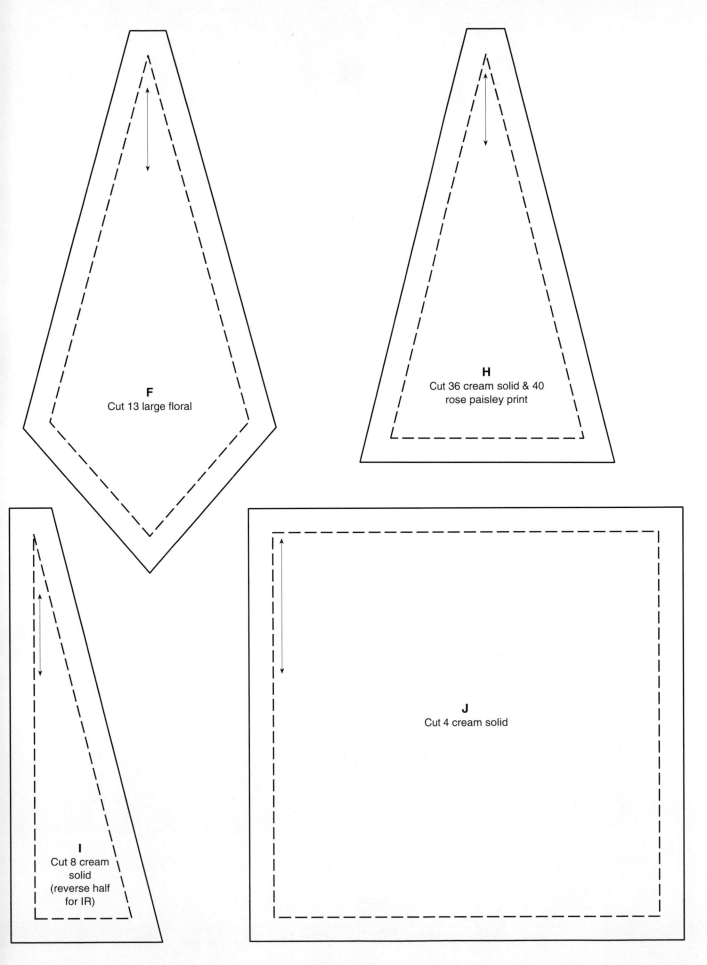

F
Cut 13 large floral

H
Cut 36 cream solid & 40
rose paisley print

I
Cut 8 cream
solid
(reverse half
for IR)

J
Cut 4 cream solid

Compass Garment Bag

By Marian Shenk

Three Compass blocks set on point make the perfect center panel for a quilted garment bag.

Project Specifications

Skill Level: Intermediate

Garment Bag Size: 22" x 36"

Block Size: 8 1/2" x 8 1/2"

Number of Blocks: 3

Materials

+ Scrap taupe solid
+ 1 fat quarter each teal, burgundy, green and rose tone-on-tones
+ 1 yard cream-on-cream print
+ 1 1/2 yards lining fabric
+ 1 1/4 yards tan/rose floral
+ 1 1/4 yards lightweight batting
+ Neutral color all-purpose thread
+ Cream hand-quilting thread
+ 2 yards 3/4"-wide cream lace trim
+ 3 cream floral appliqués
+ 1 package cream wide bias tape
+ Purchased wooden or plastic coat hanger
+ Basic sewing tools and supplies

Compass
8 1/2" x 8 1/2" Block

Instructions

Step 1. Prepare templates using pattern pieces given; cut as directed on each piece.

Step 2. To piece one block, join one each color B and three C pieces as shown in Figure 1; press seams in one direction.

Figure 1
Join 4 B and
3 C pieces.

Step 3. Sew A and AR to the B ends of the B-C unit; press seams toward A and AR.

Step 4. Center the A-B-C unit on D with right sides together; pin ends and ease remainder of D to fit the pieced unit as shown in Figure 2; stitch. Clip curved seam; press seam away from D.

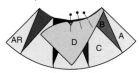

Figure 2
Center the A-B-C unit on D with right
sides together; pin ends and ease
remainder of D to fit the pieced unit.

Step 5. Add E to the pieced unit as in Step 4 to complete one block as shown in Figure 3; press seam away from E. Repeat for three blocks.

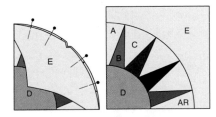

Figure 3
Add E to the pieced unit
to complete 1 block.

Step 6. Cut three 13 1/4" lengths 3/4"-wide cream lace. Hand- or machine-stitch one piece of lace along the seam between the A-B-C unit and E on each pieced block. Cut three 6 1/2" lengths and hand-stitch along D seam.

Step 7. Hand- or machine-stitch a cream floral appliqué motif on the D piece in each block referring to the photo of the finished project for positioning.

Step 8. Cut one 13 1/4" x 13 1/4" square cream-on-cream print for F; cut the square in half on both diagonals to make four F triangles.

Step 9. Cut two 6 7/8" x 6 7/8" squares cream-on-cream print for G; cut each square in half on one diagonal to make four G triangles.

Step 10. Arrange the pieced blocks with F and G in diagonal rows as shown in Figure 4; join the units in rows. Press seams toward F and G. Join the rows to complete the pieced center.

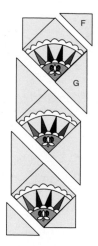

Figure 4
Arrange the pieced
blocks with F and G
in diagonal rows.

Step 11. Cut two 5 1/2" x 36 1/2" strips tan/rose floral. Sew a strip to opposite long sides of the pieced center; press seams toward strips.

Step 12. Lay the pieced top on a flat surface. Mark the top center. Measure down 5" from each top corner and mark as shown in Figure 5. Using a coat hanger as a guide for the curve, mark a gently curving line from the top center to the marked spot again referring to Figure 5; repeat on both top edges. Trim along marked line.

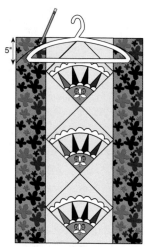

Figure 5
Measure down 5" from each
top corner and mark. Using a
coat hanger as a guide for the
curve, mark a gently curving
line from the top center to the
marked spot.

Step 13. Mark chosen quilting design on the pieced top referring to the General Instructions.

Step 14. Cut one backing from tan/rose floral, two batting and two lining pieces to match the pieced front.

Step 15. Pin a batting piece to the wrong side of the pieced front and one to the backing piece; baste to hold.

Step 16. Place the layered backing and pieced front pieces right sides together; stitch along both long edges and across the curved top edge, leaving a 1" opening at the center top and leaving bottom edge open. Secure seam on both sides of top opening. Press seam open; turn right side out.

Step 17. Place the lining pieces right sides together; stitch as in Step 16; press. Do not turn right side out.

Step 18. Insert lining inside the stitched outside bag piece, matching side seams and center openings. Hand-stitch the layers together at the top opening to secure.

Step 19. Quilt the pieced front on marked lines and as desired using cream hand-quilting thread. ***Note:*** *The sample shown was hand-quilted in the ditch of seam in the pieced blocks, in a curving arch design in the shape of the E arch in E and in a curved design on the F triangles using cream hand-quilting thread.*

Step 20. When quilting is complete, sew the cream bias tape to the bottom edge through all layers, overlapping beginning and end. Turn bias tape to the inside of the bag and hand-stitch in place.

Step 21. Insert the wooden or plastic hanger through top center opening to use. ✦

Compass Garment Bag
Placement Diagram
22" x 36"

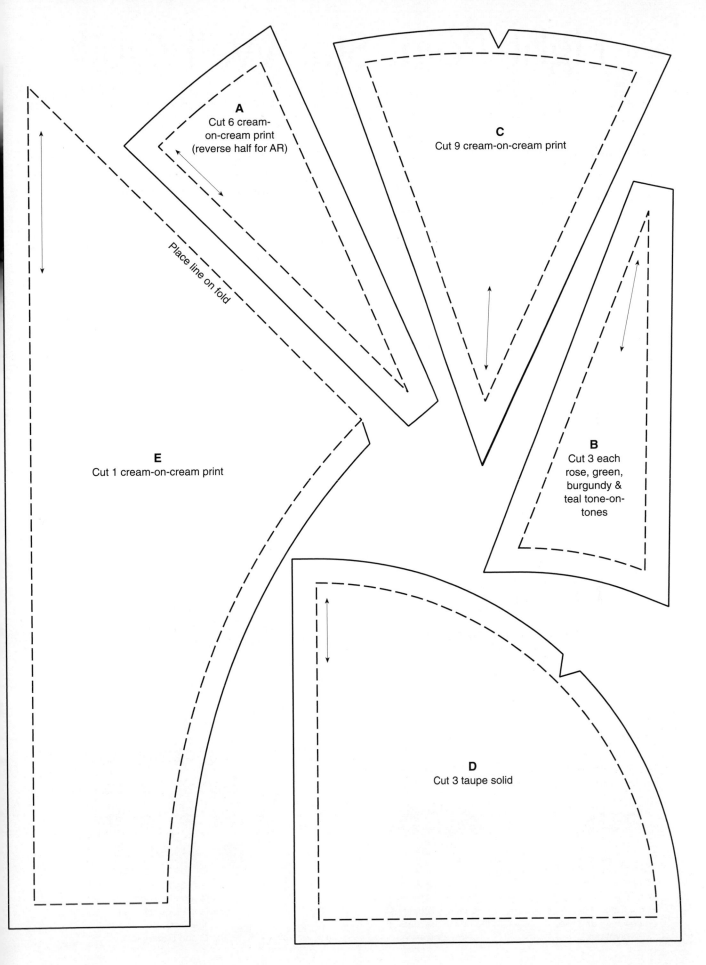

A
Cut 6 cream-on-cream print (reverse half for AR)

C
Cut 9 cream-on-cream print

Place line on fold

E
Cut 1 cream-on-cream print

B
Cut 3 each rose, green, burgundy & teal tone-on-tones

D
Cut 3 taupe solid

Eight-Point Star Wall Quilt

By Christine A. Schultz

A simple Eight-Point Star block makes a nice little wall quilt.

Project Specifications

Skill Level: Intermediate

Quilt Size: 34 1/2" x 41 5/8"

Block Size: 5" x 5"

Number of Blocks: 20

Materials

+ 9" x 9" squares 20 different blue-and-white prints
+ 1/6 yard navy-and-white stripe
+ 1/6 yard blue-and-white print
+ 1 yard muslin
+ 1 yard yellow print
+ Backing 39" x 46"
+ Batting 39" x 46"
+ 4 1/2 yards self-made or purchased navy binding
+ Neutral color all-purpose thread
+ Cream hand-quilting thread
+ Basic sewing tools and supplies

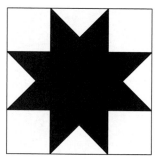

Eight-Point Star
5" x 5" Block

Instructions

Step 1. Prepare templates using pattern pieces given; cut as directed on each piece.

Figure 1
Join 2 same-fabric A pieces, stopping stitching at the end of the marked seam allowance to make pivot point.

Figure 2
Join the 2 A units, stopping stitching at the end of the marked seam allowance.

Step 2. To piece one block, join two same-fabric A pieces, stopping stitching at the end of the marked seam allowance to make pivot point as shown in Figure 1; repeat for four A units. Join two A units, again stopping at the marked seam allowance; repeat. Join the two units, stopping stitching at the end of the marked seam allowance as shown in Figure 2.

Step 3. Connect center points to close up the small hole that sometimes appears when points are joined with pivot points, joining one pivot point to the next all around the center. Press the center seam in a swirling pattern as shown in Figure 3.

Figure 3
Press center seam points in a swirling design.

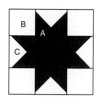

Figure 4
Set-in B squares and C triangles to complete 1 block.

Step 4. Set in a B square at each corner and add a C triangle on each side to complete one block as shown in Figure 4; repeat for 20 blocks.

Step 5. Cut 12 squares yellow print 5 1/2" x 5 1/2" for D. Arrange the pieced blocks in diagonal rows with the D squares and the G and F triangles as shown in Figure 5; join in rows. Press seams toward D. Join the rows to complete the pieced center; press seams in one direction.

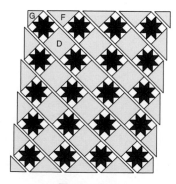

Figure 5
Arrange the pieced blocks in diagonal rows with the D squares and the G and F triangles.

Step 9. Sew a partial star unit to one end and a partial star reversed unit to the other end of each strip cut in Step 7 as shown in Figure 7. Press seams toward strips.

Step 10. Sew the longer strips to opposite sides and shorter strips to the top and bottom of the pieced center; press seams toward strips.

Step 11. Set B squares in at each corner as shown in Figure 8 to complete the pieced top.

Figure 8
Set B squares in
at each corner.

Step 12. Prepare quilt top for quilting and hand-quilt as desired referring to the General Instructions. ***Note:*** *The quilt shown was hand-quilted 1/4" from seams of A pieces, in a 3/4" grid in the background and D pieces, and in the cable design given in the outside borders using cream hand-quilting thread.*

Step 13. Apply binding to the quilted top to finish referring to the General Instructions. ✦

Step 6. Cut two strips each 1" x 30" and 1" x 36 1/8" blue-and-white print. Sew the longer strips to opposite long sides and shorter strips to the top and bottom of the pieced center; press seams toward strips.

Step 7. Cut and piece two muslin strips each 3" x 25" and 3" x 32 1/8"; set aside.

Step 8. Join three navy-and-white stripe A pieces as in Step 2; repeat for two A units. Join with one each B, C and E pieces as shown in Figure 6 to make partial stars for corners. Repeat for four partial stars and four partial stars reversed.

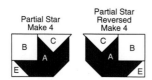

Figure 6
Join an A unit with 1 each B,
C and E pieces to make
partial stars for corners.

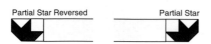

Figure 7
Sew a partial star unit to 1 end and a partial
star reversed to the other end of each strip.

Eight-Point Star Wall Quilt
Placement Diagram
34 1/2" x 41 5/8"

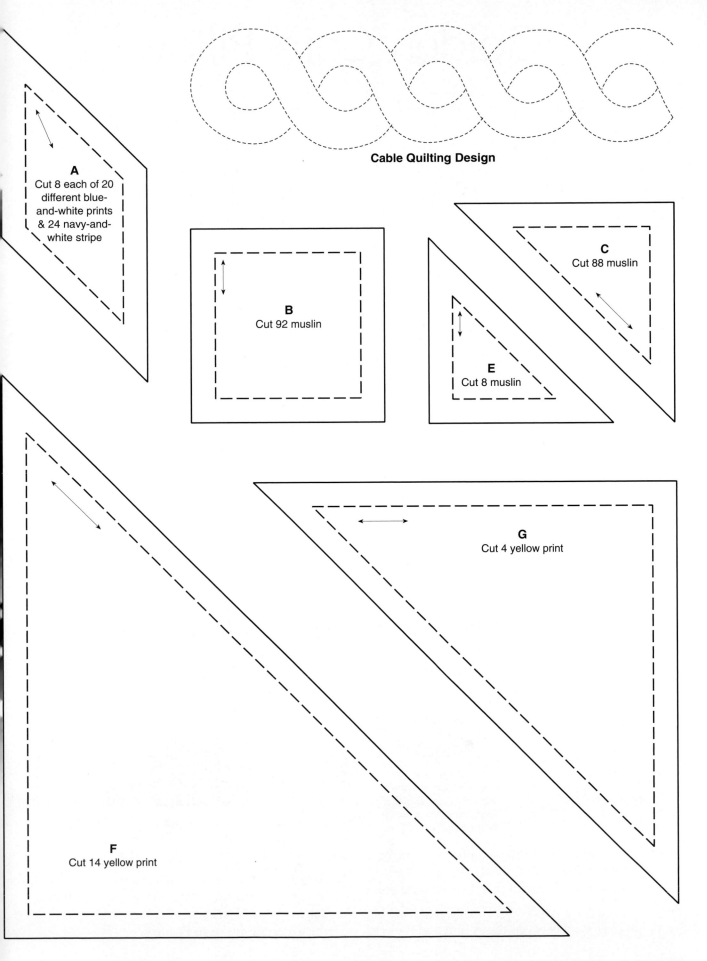

Cable Quilting Design

A
Cut 8 each of 20 different blue-and-white prints & 24 navy-and-white stripe

B
Cut 92 muslin

C
Cut 88 muslin

E
Cut 8 muslin

G
Cut 4 yellow print

F
Cut 14 yellow print

Golden Cord Pillow

By Marian Shenk

Make an elegant pillow by adding a touch of gold lamé, cord and tassels to a simple block.

Project Specifications

Skill Level: Intermediate

Pillow Size: Approximately 14" x 14"

Materials

- Scraps 2 different burgundy and teal tone-on-tones for A
- Scraps burgundy print for A
- 4" x 4" square teal tone-on-tone for B
- 7" x 22" rectangle each burgundy and teal tone-on-tones for C and D units
- 1 fat quarter cream tone-on-tone
- Backing 16" x 16"
- Batting 16" x 16"
- All-purpose thread to match fabrics
- Cream hand-quilting thread
- 2 yards gold cord piping
- 4 gold tassels
- 3/4 yard 1/2"-wide gold lamé bias trim
- 14" x 14" pillow form
- Basic sewing tools and supplies

Instructions

Step 1. Prepare templates using pattern pieces given; cut as directed on each piece.

Step 2. Join the A pieces, alternating colors referring to Figure 1; press seams in one direction.

Figure 1
Join the A pieces,
alternating colors.

Figure 2
Pin the B piece to the A
unit, matching centers; pin
ends and ease A onto B
between center and end.

Step 3. Pin the B piece to the A unit, matching centers as shown in Figure 2; pin ends and ease A onto B between center and end. Stitch; clip seams and press.

Step 4. Cut a 6 1/2" piece of 1/2"-wide gold lamé bias trim; pin over seam between the A unit and B piece.

Hand-stitch in place on both sides of the trim.

Step 5. Cut two strips each 2 1/8" x 22" cream and teal tone-on-tones. Join one strip of each color with right sides together along length to make a strip set; press seams toward darker fabric. Repeat for two strip sets.

Step 6. Subcut strip set into 2 1/8" D segments as shown in Figure 3.

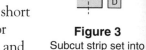

Figure 3
Subcut strip set into
2 1/8" D segments.

Step 7. Join five segments on short ends to make a strip; repeat for two strips with four segments, and two strips with three segments.

Step 8. Join the pieced strips as shown in Figure 4 to make a staggered pieced unit.

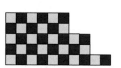

Figure 4
Join the pieced strips
to make a staggered
pieced unit.

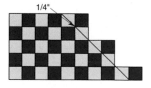

Figure 5
Draw a diagonal line from
corner to corner 1/4" from
the seam on the cream
tone-on-tone squares on
the staggered end.

Step 9. Draw a diagonal line from corner to corner 1/4" from the seam on the cream tone-on-tone squares on the staggered end as shown in Figure 5 to make an angled piece; set aside.

Step 10. Join the C triangles to make rows as shown in Figure 6; press seams toward darker C pieces.

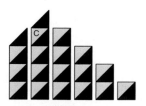

Figure 6
Join the C triangles
to make rows.

Step 11. Join the rows to make a pieced unit as shown in Figure 7. Starting at the top left corner, draw a diagonal line from the corner though all rows; cut off the excess as shown in Figure 8.

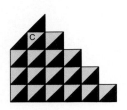

Figure 7
Join the rows to
make a pieced unit.

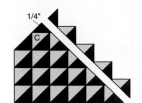

Figure 8
Starting at the top left corner,
draw a diagonal line from the
corner through all rows; cut
off the excess.

Step 12. Stitch the two pieced units along the angled seam and press the seam toward the pieced C unit.

Step 13. Lay the pieced fan shape at the lower block intersections as shown in Figure 9. Measure and move the pieced fan shape until the fan shape aligns with the outer edges of the pieced unit. **Note:** *The pinned unit should measure approximately 15" x 15".*

Figure 9
Lay the pieced fan
shape at the lower block
intersections.

Step 14. Baste the curved edge of the fan shape onto the pieced unit.

Step 15. Cut a 17" length of 1/2"-wide gold lamé bias trim; pin over the raw edges of the basted sections. Hand-stitch in place; trim ends even with fan shape.

Step 16. Trim excess pieced section from behind the section to reduce bulk.

Step 17. Pin the batting square to the wrong side of the pieced top; pin or baste to hold.

Step 18. Hand-quilt in the ditch of seams and at the edges of the bias trim using cream hand-quilting thread.

Step 19. When quilting is complete, trim batting even with quilted top.

Step 20. Trim gold cord piping seam edge to 1/4".

Pin and stitch the gold cord piping to the edge of the pillow top using a zipper foot, and clipping into seam edge of piping at corners as shown in Figure 10.

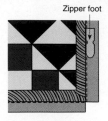

Figure 10
Pin and stitch the gold cord
piping to the edge of the
pillow top using a zipper
foot, and clipping into seam
edge of piping at corners.

Step 21. Place the backing piece right sides together with the quilted-and-corded top; stitch all around, leaving an 8" opening on one side. Clip corners, turn right side out.

Step 22. Insert pillow form; hand-stitch opening closed.

Step 23. Hand-stitch a gold tassel to each corner to finish. ✦

Golden Cord Pillow
Placement Diagram
Approximately 14" x 14"

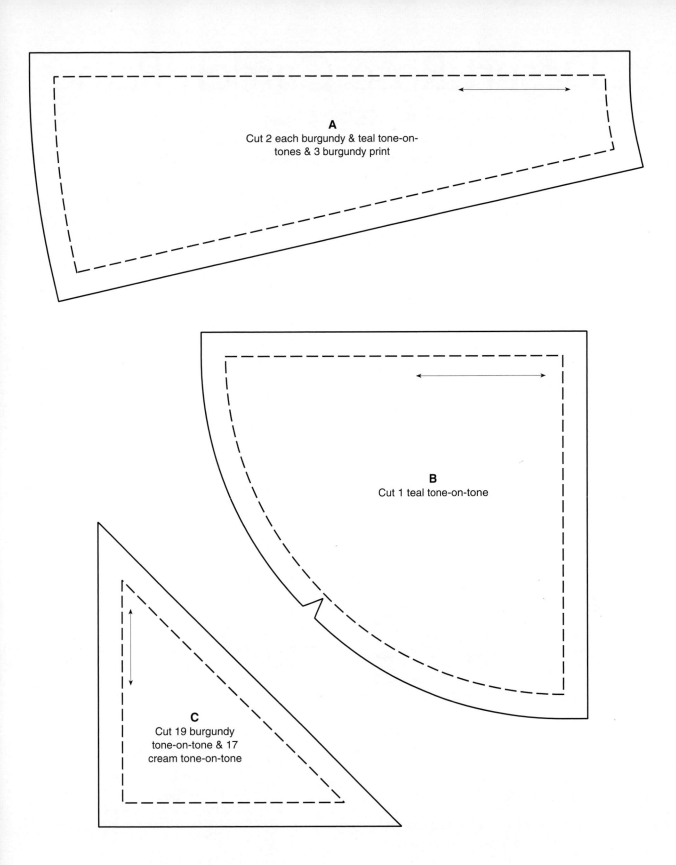

A
Cut 2 each burgundy & teal tone-on-tones & 3 burgundy print

B
Cut 1 teal tone-on-tone

C
Cut 19 burgundy tone-on-tone & 17 cream tone-on-tone

Desert Rose Garden Path

By Susan Parr

A pieced flower block with sharp points combines with a curved
Drunkard's Path-type block to make this pretty wall quilt.

Project Specifications

Skill Level: Intermediate
Quilt Size: 45" x 45"
Block Size: 12" x 12"
Number of Blocks: 9

Materials

- 1/4 yard rose tone-on-tone
- 3/8 yard light green print
- 1/2 yard burgundy tone-on-tone
- 1 1/2 yards dark green tone-on-tone
- 1 1/2 yards tan mottled
- Backing 49" x 49"
- Batting 49" x 49"
- All-purpose thread to match fabrics
- Cream hand-quilting thread
- Basic sewing tools and supplies, and freezer paper

Cactus Rose
12" x 12" Block

Drunkard's Path
12" x 12" Block

Instructions

Making Cactus Rose Blocks

Step 1. Prepare templates for A–D using patterns given; cut as directed on each piece. Make freezer paper templates for the E and F pieces, cutting as directed on each piece.

Step 2. Press the freezer-paper templates to the wrong side of the green print. Cut out shapes, adding a 1/4" seam allowance all around when cutting.

Step 3. Turn under seam allowance on each E and F

piece along edge of freezer-paper shapes; press. **Note:** *Do not turn under seam allowance on the ends of the E pieces. They will be sewn into the block seams.*

Step 4. Place E in the center of C referring to the placement line on C. Hand-stitch in place. Repeat with the F leaf shape.

Step 5. To piece one block, sew a burgundy tone-on-tone D to a rose tone-on-tone D; repeat for two units.

Step 6. Join the D units as shown in Figure 1; set in A squares and a B triangle as shown in Figure 2.

Figure 1
Join the D units.

Figure 2
Set in A squares
and a B triangle.

Step 7. Sew two green print D pieces to C as shown in Figure 3.

Figure 3
Sew 2 green print
D pieces to C.

Step 8. Sew the C-D unit to the A-B-D unit and set in B to complete one Cactus Rose block as shown in Figure 4; repeat for five blocks. Press and trim seam points.

Figure 4
Sew the C-D unit to the A-B-D
unit and set in B to complete 1
Cactus Rose block.

Making Drunkard's Path Blocks

Step 1. Prepare G and H templates using patterns given; cut as directed on each piece.

Step 2. To piece one block, pin H to G, matching centers. Pin ends, easing in fullness between and pin as necessary as shown in Figure 5. Stitch, removing

pins as you sew. Clip seam as shown in Figure 6; press seam toward H. Repeat for 64 G-H units.

Figure 5
Pin H to G, matching centers.
Pin ends, easing in fullness
between, and pin as necessary.

Figure 6
Clip seam.

Step 3. Arrange 16 G-H units in four rows of four units each, referring to Figure 7 for positioning. Join the units in rows; press seams in one direction. Join the rows to complete the blocks; press seams in one direction. Repeat for four blocks.

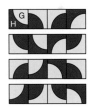

Figure 7
Arrange 16 G-H units in
4 rows of 4 units each.

Completing the Quilt

Step 1. Join two Cactus Rose blocks with one Drunkard's Path block to make a row as shown in Figure 8; repeat for two rows. Press seams toward Drunkard's Path blocks.

Step 2. Join two Drunkard's Path blocks with one Cactus Rose block to make a row, again referring to Figure 8; press seams toward Drunkard's Path blocks.

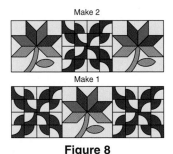

Make 2

Make 1

Figure 8
Join blocks to make rows as shown.

Step 3. Join the rows referring to the Placement Diagram for positioning; press seams in one direction.

Step 4. Cut two strips each 1 1/2" x 36 1/2" and 1 1/2" x 38 1/2" burgundy tone-on-tone. Sew the shorter strips to opposite sides and longer strips to the top and bottom of the pieced center; press seams toward strips.

Step 5. Cut and piece two strips each 4" x 38 1/2" and 4" x 45 1/2" dark green tone-on-tone. Sew the shorter

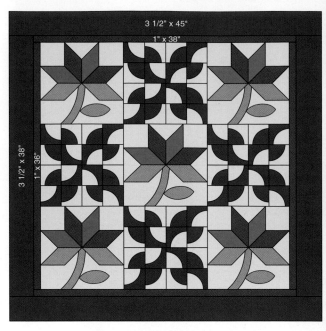

Desert Rose Garden Path
Placement Diagram
45" x 45"

strips to opposite sides and longer strips to the top and bottom of the pieced center; press seams toward strips.

Step 6. Prepare quilt top for quilting and hand-quilt as desired referring to the General Instructions. **Note:** *The quilt shown was hand-quilted 1/4" from seams in all D, G and H pieces and in a 1" diagonal grid on the wide border strips using cream hand-quilting thread.*

Step 7. Prepare 5 1/2 yards self-made straight-grain binding from dark green tone-on-tone and apply to the quilted top to finish referring to the General Instructions. ✦

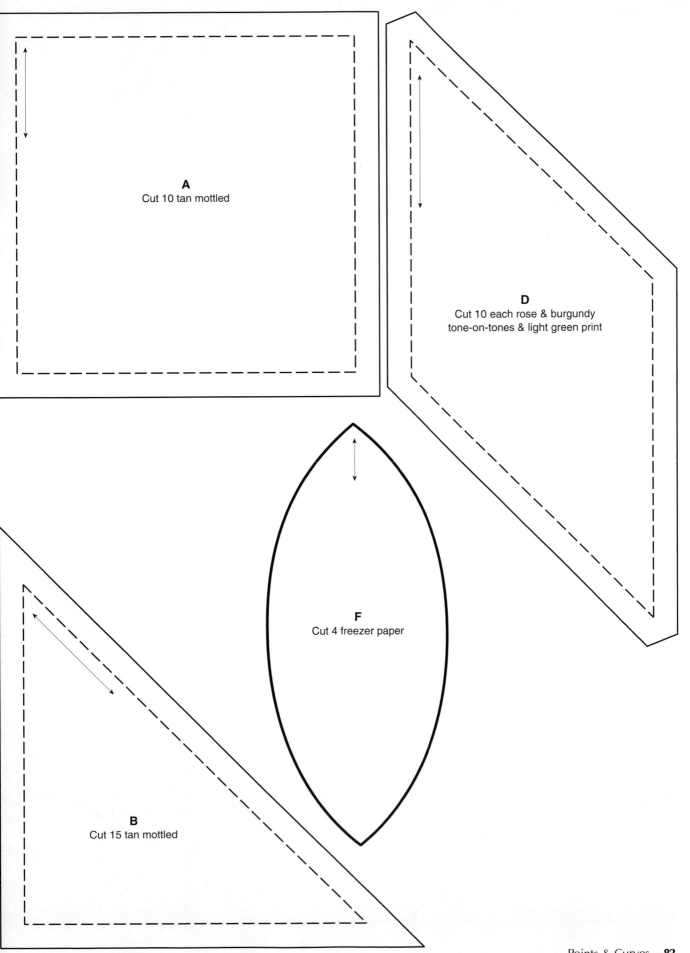

A
Cut 10 tan mottled

D
Cut 10 each rose & burgundy
tone-on-tones & light green print

F
Cut 4 freezer paper

B
Cut 15 tan mottled

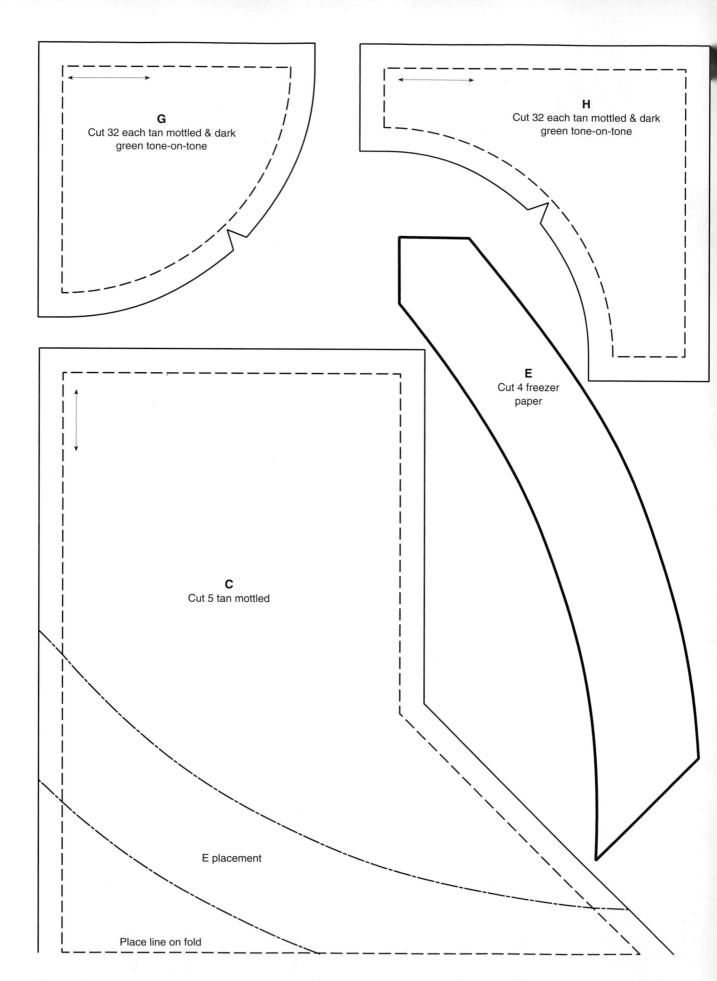

G
Cut 32 each tan mottled & dark
green tone-on-tone

H
Cut 32 each tan mottled & dark
green tone-on-tone

E
Cut 4 freezer
paper

C
Cut 5 tan mottled

E placement

Place line on fold

Granddaughter's Flower Garden

By Connie Kauffman

Center tiny motifs in the hexagon shapes to create an "I spy" kind of quilt for kids.

Project Notes

The traditional Grandmother's Flower Garden quilt with its hexagon motifs makes the perfect showcase for fussy cutting small motifs to create "flowers" with interesting designs. Each flower shape is made with six hexagons with the same design centered in each hexagon.

To test a motif for use in this quilt, cut the A and B templates from see-through template material. Carry the template with you to audition fabrics for the pieces. Place the template on the chosen fabric, centering a motif from the chosen fabric. If the motif runs into the seam allowance, it is too big. If the motif fits inside the design area, isolate six motifs to cut from the fabric.

The sample shown uses many different motifs. Included are snowmen, Tigger, hearts, apples, keys, chickens, rabbits, houses, teapots, boats and more.

Any small child would have fun finding the motifs on this pretty little quilt.

Project Specifications

Skill Level: Intermediate

Quilt Size: 38" x 38"

Block Size: 8" x 8"

Number of Blocks: 9

Materials

✦ Assorted prints with small motifs to fit inside the A and B templates

✦ Assorted coordinating scraps

✦ 1/2 yard lime green mottled

✦ 1 yard yellow/orange stripe

✦ 5/8 yard white-on-white print

✦ Backing 42" x 42"

✦ Batting 42" x 42"

✦ Neutral color all-purpose thread

✦ White hand-quilting thread

✦ Fabric glue stick

✦ Basic sewing tools and supplies, see-through template material, and plain white paper

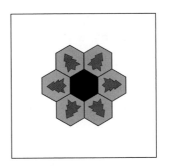

Flower Garden A
8" x 8" Block

Instructions

Step 1. Cut nine 8 1/2" x 8 1/2" squares white-on-white print for block backgrounds. Fold and crease to mark centers; set aside.

Step 2. Prepare templates for A and B using see-through template material.

Step 3. Make 9 copies of the A full-size drawing and 16 copies of the B full-size drawing. Cut out the shapes on the lines, separate A and B pieces and place in separate zipper bags.

Step 4. For each hexagon motif, cut either six A or B pieces, centering motifs with bottom of the design parallel with one flat seam in each piece referring to Figure 1. Cut one each coordinating A or B piece for the center of each hexagon motif. You will need a total of 9 A motifs and 16 B motifs.

Figure 1
Center motifs with bottom
of the design parallel with
1 flat seam in each piece.

Step 5. To piece one A motif, add a small dab of fabric glue stick to one side of an A paper. Center the paper on the wrong side of an A fabric patch as shown in Figure 2. Fold the fabric over the paper and baste in place through fabric and paper as shown in Figure 3. Repeat on all sides; repeat for six centered-motif A pieces and one coordinating fabric A piece.

Figure 2
Center the paper on
the wrong side of an
A fabric patch.

Figure 3
Fold the fabric over the
paper and baste in place
through fabric and paper.

Step 6. Place two matching A pieces right sides together with sides of design touching as shown in Figure 4. Start stitching by inserting needle under at end of seam between the paper and the folded seam as shown in Figure 5. Make tiny whipstitches along the seam, making a small slipstitch at the end of each seam. Open the two A pieces to see an invisible seam. Next, add the center A piece to the stitched unit as shown in Figure 6. Continue sewing pieces together until the A motif is complete as shown in Figure 7. Repeat for nine A motifs and 16 B motifs.

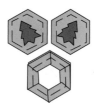

Figure 4
Place 2 matching A pieces
right sides together with
sides of design touching.

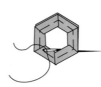

Figure 5
Start stitching by inserting
needle under at end of
seam between the paper
and the folded seam.

Figure 6
Add the center A
piece to the
stitched unit.

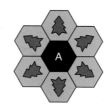

Figure 7
Continue sewing
pieces together until
the A motif is complete.

Step 7. Center an A motif on one background square as shown in Figure 8; hand-stitch in place all around the motif. Repeat for 9 A blocks.

8 1/2" x 8 1/2"

Figure 8
Center an A motif on 1
background square.

Step 8. Remove basting stitches from each A motif. Clip into the background fabric behind each appliqué motif as shown in Figure 9. Trim excess background

away to 1/4" from appliqué seam as shown in Figure 10. Remove paper pieces.

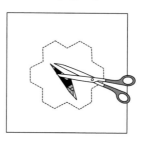

Figure 9
Clip into the background
fabric behind each
appliqué motif.

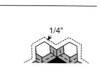

1/4"

Figure 10
Trim excess
background away
to 1/4" from
appliqué seam.

Step 9. Cut one 8 1/2" by fabric width strip lime green mottled; subcut strip into 2" segments to make 12 C sashing strips.

Step 10. Arrange the A blocks in three rows of three blocks each. When satisfied with the positioning, join three blocks from one row with four C sashing strips to make a row as shown in Figure 11; repeat for three rows. Press seams toward C.

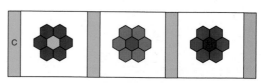

Figure 11
Join 3 blocks from 1 row with 4 C
sashing strips to make a row.

Step 11. Cut four 2" x 30 1/2" strips lime green mottled for D. Join the rows with the D strips, beginning and ending with D. Press seams toward D.

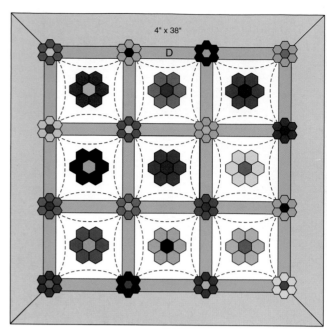

Granddaughter's Flower Garden
Placement Diagram
38" x 38"

Step 12. Cut four 4 1/2" x 38 1/2" strips yellow/orange stripe. Center and sew a strip to each side of the completed center, mitering corners. Trim excess seams at mitered corners to 1/4"; press seams open.

Step 13. Center a B motif on the intersection of C and D sashing strips and border strips referring to the

Placement Diagram; hand-stitch in place. Remove basting stitches and paper as in Step 8.

Step 14. Prepare quilt top for quilting and hand-quilt as desired referring to the General Instructions. **Note:** *The quilt shown was hand-quilted using the pattern given in the background blocks, with a purchased butterfly design* in the outer border, in the ditch of C and D seams and borders and around each A and B motif using white hand-quilting thread.

Step 15. Prepare 4 1/2 yards self-made straight-grain binding from yellow/orange stripe and apply to the quilted top to finish referring to the General Instructions. ✦

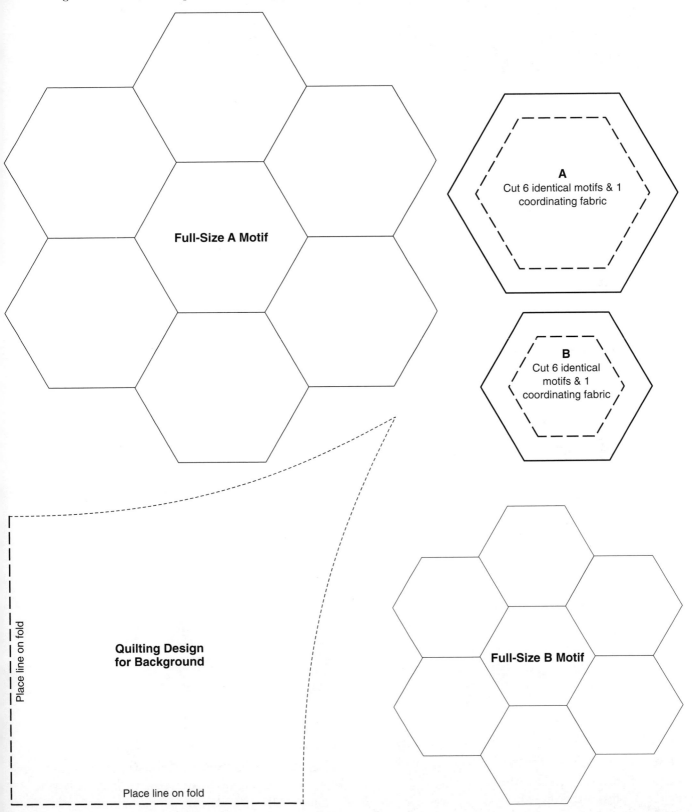

Full-Size A Motif

A
Cut 6 identical motifs & 1
coordinating fabric

B
Cut 6 identical
motifs & 1
coordinating fabric

Place line on fold

**Quilting Design
for Background**

Place line on fold

Full-Size B Motif

All Points Lead Home

By Sandra L. Hatch

Bright colors point toward the center square in each block and for some, that means home.

Project Specifications

Skill Level: Intermediate

Quilt Size: 52" x 52"

Block Size: 12" x 12"

Number of Blocks: 9

Materials

+ 1/3 yard navy print
+ 1 yard yellow mottled
+ 1 1/2 yards white print
+ 1 1/2 yards navy floral
+ 1 3/4 yards pink mottled
+ Backing 56" x 56"
+ Batting 56" x 56"
+ Neutral color all-purpose thread
+ Pink and yellow hand-quilting thread
+ Basic sewing tools and supplies

All Points Lead Home
12" x 12" Block

Instructions

Step 1. Prepare templates using pattern pieces given; cut as directed on each piece.

Step 2. To piece one block, sew B and BR to A as shown in Figure 1; repeat for four A-B units. Press seams away from A.

Figure 1
Sew B and BR to A.

Step 3. Sew ER to CR; press seam toward ER. Sew to an A-B unit as shown in Figure 2; repeat for four A-B-C-E units. Press seams away from A-B units.

Step 4. Sew E to C to D as shown in Figure 3; press seams away from C.

Figure 2
Sew the ER-CR unit to an A-B unit.

Sew the E-C-D unit to an A-B-C-E unit as shown in Figure 4. Repeat for four A-E units. Press seams toward the E-C-D units.

Figure 3
Sew E to C to D.

Figure 4
Sew the E-C-D unit to an A-B-C-E unit.

Step 5. Sew H to G to F as shown in Figure 5; repeat for four units. Press seams away from G.

Figure 5
Sew H to G to F.

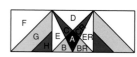

Figure 6
Join 2 H-G-F units with 1 A-E unit to make a row.

Step 6. Join two H-G-F units with one A-E unit to make a row as shown in Figure 6; repeat for two rows. Press seams away from the A-E unit.

Step 7. Sew J between two A-E units to make a row as shown in Figure 7; press seams toward J.

Figure 7
Sew J between 2 A-E units to make a row.

Step 8. Join the rows to complete one block as shown in Figure 8; repeat for nine blocks.

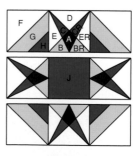

Figure 8
Join the rows to complete 1 block.

Step 9. Join three blocks to make a row; press seams in one direction. Repeat for three rows. Join the rows to complete the pieced center; press seams in one direction.

Step 10. Cut two strips each 2 1/2" x 36 1/2" and 2 1/2" x 40 1/2" pink mottled. Sew the shorter strips to opposite sides and longer strips to the top and bottom of the pieced center; press seams toward strips.

Step 11. To make border strips, sew B and BR to A as in Step 2. Repeat for 40 A-B units.

Step 12. Join 10 A-B units with 11 K pieces to make a border strip as shown in Figure 9; press seams toward K. Repeat for four border strips.

Figure 9
Join 10 A-B units with 11 K pieces to make a border strip.

Step 13. Sew a border strip to each side of the pieced center, stitching corner seams after adding strips. Press seams toward pink mottled strips.

Step 14. Cut two strips each 4 1/2" x 44 1/2" and 4 1/2" x 52 1/2" along the length of the navy floral. Sew the shorter strips to opposite sides and longer strips to the top and bottom; press seams toward strips.

Step 15. Prepare the quilt top for quilting referring to the General Instructions. *Note: The quilt shown was hand-quilted in the ditch of all seams, echo-quilted in the larger areas, and in the J squares and around flowers in the navy floral border strips with either pink or yellow hand-quilting thread.*

Step 16. Prepare 6 1/4 yards straight-grain binding from pink mottled and bind referring to the General Instructions. ✦

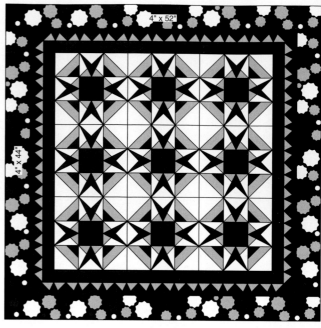

All Points Lead Home
Placement Diagram
52" x 52"

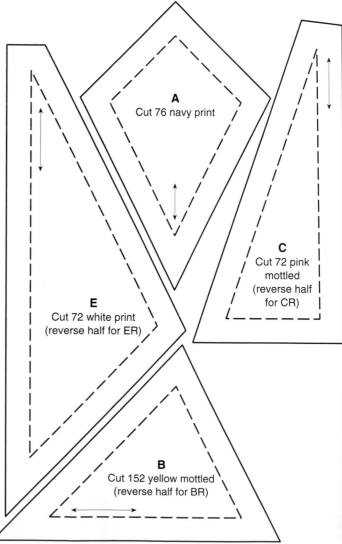

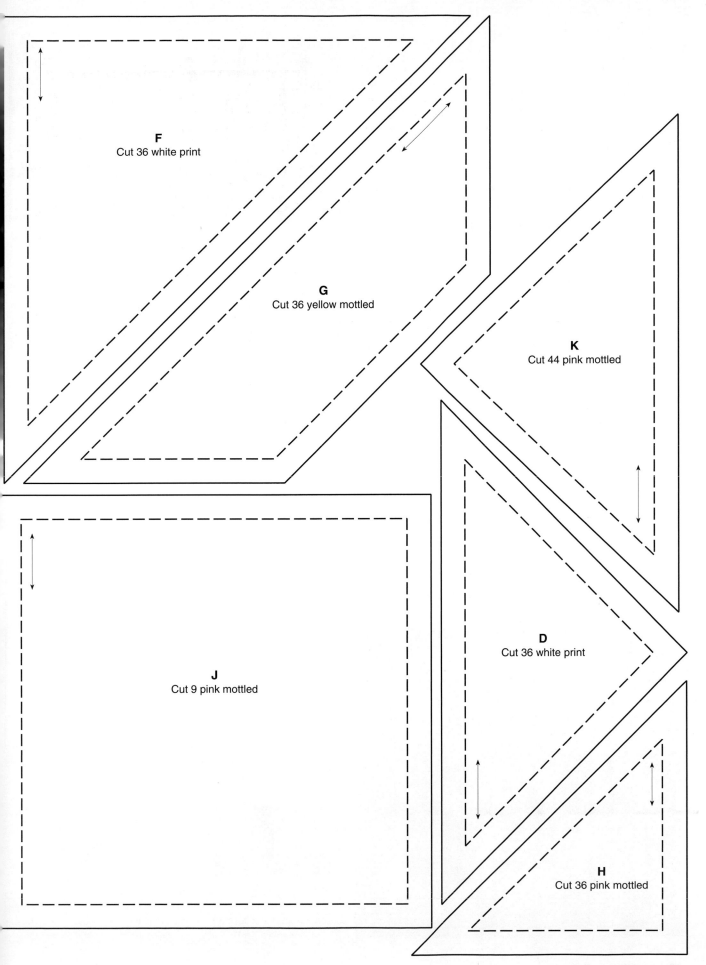

F
Cut 36 white print

G
Cut 36 yellow mottled

K
Cut 44 pink mottled

J
Cut 9 pink mottled

D
Cut 36 white print

H
Cut 36 pink mottled

Summer Sunset

By Peg Johnson

Make a small abstract landscape quilt without templates using lots of different scraps.

Project Notes

When making an abstract landscape quilt, the first step should be choosing a size. The instructions given suggest sizes to correspond with those used in the sample, but you may enlarge or reduce the design.

The appliqué is done on a muslin base, which should be cut 1" larger all around than the appliqué area without added borders.

Choose a piece of fabric for the sky. The sample shown was made with hand-painted sky fabrics. Remember the "Rule of Thirds" as applied to photography. The sky should be about 1/3 the depth of the landscape, in this case, about 4".

Select fabrics for other landscape features such as water, valleys, mountains, flowers, etc. Before cutting the fabrics, layer them on the muslin to see how you like the flow. I call this process auditioning fabrics. I usually follow the colors in the sky. In the sample shown, the sky fabric has shades of blue, pink, red, gray and purple—colors in a sunset sky. My other fabrics coordinate with those colors.

Once fabrics are chosen, start cutting. Do not sew anything onto the muslin base until all pieces are cut and arranged. Cut pieces in hill and valley shapes. These pieces are somewhat curved, rather than sharply curved.

If the valley is cut too deep, it will be difficult to turn under the top edge and have the fabric lie flat when stitched down. Remember to allow 1/4" extra at both the top and bottom edge of each piece. The top edge will be turned under before being appliquéd; the bottom edge will be under the next layer that is stitched.

A very narrow strip of contrasting color helps determine the horizon. In other words, if you use a burgundy or other dark color for mountains, a small strip of gold or red at the foot of the mountains helps to differentiate the mountains from the next stitched layer as shown in Figure 1.

Figure 1
Select a contrasting fabric for a horizon and sew at the foot of the mountains to differentiate the mountains from the next stitched layer.

In order for the mountains to lie flat when stitched down, you may have to clip slightly into the top edge of each valley in one or two places. If you have ever made a garment with set-in sleeves, you remember having to clip the underarm seam allowance so that it would lie flat.

It is important to note that the fabric pieces should be cut so that they do not all meet in the center. Try to have some of them overlap at different places as shown in Figure 2. Some may go all the way across from the left edge to the right edge. With the exception of pieces that do go all the way across from edge to edge, all pieces must be cut so that they slope down on the inside edge as shown in Figure 3—they cannot be cut as rectangles because they won't blend into each other.

Figure 2
Overlap pieces in the center area in different places as shown.

Figure 3
With the exception of pieces that do go all the way across from edge to edge, all pieces must be cut so that they slope down on the inside edge.

After all pieces are cut, lay them on the muslin to see how they look and fit. If you are happy with the layout, you may begin sewing. It is advisable to pin three or four of the bottom layers together, lift them off the muslin and set them aside. Then pin three or four more of the middle layers and set them aside, keeping them in the correct order. This makes it possible to handle only one or two layers at a time while keeping the pieces in order.

As each piece is appliquéd onto the piece above it, all raw edges must be covered. Each edge must be overlapped with the new piece being added. After sewing each piece on, lift it up and trim excess off the previous piece as shown in Figure 4. This helps to eliminate any extra bulk, and makes it easier to hand-sew through the layers.

When stitching, using a No. 50 or higher (finer) thread and the smallest needle you can handle. I find a No. 10 between needle works best. I also prefer to use silk thread when possible, although it's sometimes difficult to find the right colors to match my fabrics.

To appliqué, bring the needle up from the back of the muslin through all layers into the fold at the top of the piece being stitched. Then go back down into the fabric right behind where you came up—take a 1/8"–1/4" stitch, making sure to catch all layers, again coming up into the fold; repeat until the whole piece is stitched down. The object is to keep the stitches as invisible as possible.

When the piece is finished, you should be able to see a background area (mountains or hills), a mid-ground area and a foreground area so that it looks a bit like a painting.

The appliquéd area should then be squared up to prepare for finishing.

Figure 4
Trim excess away
under pieces.

Project Specifications

Skill Level: Intermediate

Quilt Size: 18" x 15"

Materials

+ Fat eighths, fat quarters or scrap fabrics to represent sky, water, grass, mountains, etc.
+ 4 1/2" x 17" strip fabric for back sleeve for hanging
+ 16" x 13" piece of muslin for appliqué base
+ 1/3 yard blue mottled for borders and binding
+ Backing 22" x 19"
+ Batting 22" x 19"
+ Silk thread to match fabrics
+ Basic sewing tools and supplies

Instructions

Step 1. Cut a piece of sky fabric 4 1/2" x 16". Pin to the muslin base as shown in Figure 5.

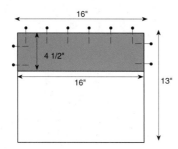

Figure 5
Pin sky fabric to the muslin base.

Step 2. Cut fabric pieces for moutains, valleys, rivers, grass, flowers, etc., from fabrics as suggested in the Project Notes.

Step 3. Arrange the pieces in order on the muslin. When

Summer Sunset
Placement Diagram
18" x 15"

satisfied with the arrangement, apply pieces and complete the appliqué as suggested in the Project Notes.

Step 4. Trim appliquéd background to 14 1/2" x 11 1/2".

Step 5. Cut two strips each 2 1/2" x 14 1/2" and 2 1/2" x 15 1/2" blue mottled. Sew the shorter strips to the top and bottom and longer strips to opposite sides of the appliquéd center; press seams toward strips.

Step 6. Prepare finished top for quilting and finish referring to the General Instructions. **Note:** *The quilt shown was quilted in the ditch of appliqué seams using silk thread to match fabrics.*

Step 7. Prepare 2 yards blue mottled straight-grain binding and apply referring to the General Instructions.

Step 8. Prepare a hanging sleeve and apply to the back top using sleeve fabric and referring to the General Instructions to finish. ✦

Quilting Tote Along

By Jill Reber

Choose two blocks from your unfinished-project stash or make the star blocks given here to make yourself a handy tote for your quilting.

Project Specifications

Skill Level: Beginner
Tote Size: 13" x 14" closed; 26" x 14" open
Block Size: 12" x 12"
Number of Blocks: 2

Materials

+ Two 9" x 11 1/2" pieces white felt
+ 1/8 yard medium blue solid
+ 1/8 yard light blue print
+ 1/8 yard light blue solid
+ 1/4 yard medium blue print
+ 3/8 yard dark blue solid
+ 5/8 yard blue print
+ Muslin backing 30" x 16"
+ Batting 30" x 16"
+ All-purpose thread to match fabrics
+ 3/4" button with shank
+ 4 yards blue elastic cord
+ 2 (1-gallon) plastic zipper bags
+ 2 (3/4" x 4") pieces hook-and-loop tape
+ 2 (20") zippers
+ Basic sewing tools and supplies

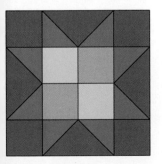

Four-Patch Star
12" x 12" Block

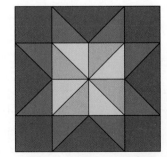

Pinwheel Star
12" x 12" Block

Instructions

Making Blocks

Step 1. From dark blue solid, cut eight 3 1/2" x 3 1/2" squares for A and eight 3 1/2" x 6 1/2" rectangles for C.

Step 2. Cut 16 squares medium blue print 3 1/2" x 3 1/2" for B; draw a line from corner to corner on the wrong side of each B square.

Step 3. Cut two squares each light blue print and light blue solid 3 7/8" x 3 7/8"; cut each square in half on one diagonal to make D triangles.

Step 4. Cut two squares each light and medium blue solids 3 1/2" x 3 1/2" for E.

Step 5. To piece one Pinwheel Star block, lay a B square on a C rectangle and stitch on the marked line as shown in Figure 1; trim seam allowance to 1/4" and press B to the right side, again referring to Figure 1.

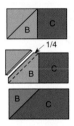

Figure 1
Lay a B square on a C rectangle; stitch on the marked line. Trim seam allowance to 1/4"; press B to the right side.

Step 6. Place a second B on C referring to Figure 2; stitch, trim and press as in Step 5 to complete a B-C unit, again referring to Figure 2. Repeat for four units.

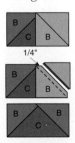

Figure 2
Place a second B on C; stitch, trim and press to complete a B-C unit.

Step 7. Sew a light blue print D to a light blue solid D as shown in Figure 3; repeat for four D units. Press seams toward darker fabric.

Figure 3
Sew a light blue print D to a light blue solid D.

Step 8. Join four D units as shown in Figure 4; press seams in one direction.

Figure 4
Join 4 D units.

Figure 5
Sew a B-C unit to opposite sides of the pieced D unit.

Step 9. Sew a B-C unit to opposite sides of the pieced D unit as shown in Figure 5; press seams toward the B-C units.

Step 10. Sew an A square to each short end of the remaining B-C units; press seams toward A. Sew the A-B-C units to the remaining sides of the B-C-D unit to complete the block as shown in Figure 6.

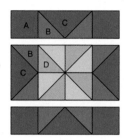

Figure 6
Sew the A-B-C units to the remaining sides of the B-C-D unit to complete 1 block.

Step 11. To piece one Four-Patch Star block, complete four B-C units referring to Steps 5 and 6.

Step 12. Sew a light blue solid E to a medium blue solid E; repeat. Join the E units to complete the block center.

Step 13. Join the block center with four A squares and the B-C units to complete the block as shown in Figure 7.

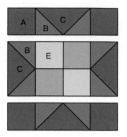

Figure 7
Complete the Four-Patch Star block as shown.

Making the Tote

Step 1. Join the two pieced blocks; press seam open.

Step 2. Cut two strips each 1 1/2" x 14 1/2" and 1 1/2" x 24 1/2" blue print. Sew the longer strips to opposite long sides and the shorter strips to the short ends of the pieced section referring to Figure 8; press seams toward strips.

1 1/2" x 14 1/2"   1 1/2" x 24 1/2"

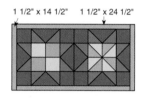

Figure 8
Sew the longer strips to opposite long sides and shorter strips to the short ends of the pieced section.

Step 3. Sandwich the batting between the pieced block section and the muslin backing; pin or baste layers to hold flat.

Step 4. Quilt as desired by hand or machine. **Note:** *The project shown was machine-quilted close to seams on all A, C and E pieces and on the darker D pieces using all-purpose thread to match fabrics.*

Step 5. When quilting is complete, remove pins or basting; trim batting and backing edges even with the pieced top.

Step 6. Open one zipper. Starting at the center of one long side, sew one zipper to the outside of the tote, matching raw edge of tote to edge of zipper as shown

in Figure 9, ending at the center of each end. Repeat on the opposite side with the second zipper.

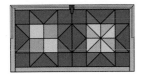

Figure 9
Starting at the center of 1 side,
sew 1 zipper to the outside of
the tote matching raw edge of
tote to edge of zipper.

Step 7. Cut a 14 1/2" x 26 1/2" rectangle blue print for tote lining.

Step 8. Cut four each 6 1/2" x 7 1/2" and 5 1/2" x 7 1/2" rectangles dark blue solid for pockets. Place two same-size pocket pieces right sides together; stitch all around, leaving a 3" opening on one side. Clip corners; turn right side out through opening. Press flat; hand-stitch opening closed. Repeat for all pocket pieces.

Step 9. Press under 1/2" along the 7" edge of each pocket piece.

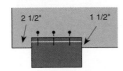

Figure 10
Pin the edge of the pressed
end of the smaller pocket 1 1/2"
from 1 long edge and 2 1/2"
from the end of the lining piece.

Step 10. Pin the edge of the pressed end of the smaller pocket 1 1/2" from one long edge and 2 1/2" from the end of the lining piece as shown in Figure 10; machine-stitch close to edge to hold in place.

Step 11. Fold the pocket to the right side, keeping the pressed edge flat on the top side to make a pleat at the bottom of the pocket to allow for shapes being fit inside referring to Figure 11. Stitch close to side edges, securing stitching at the beginning and end. Divide the pocket into three sections as desired and mark; stitch on marked lines, securing stitching at the beginning and end. Repeat with second smaller pocket on opposite end of lining piece.

Figure 11
Fold the pocket to the right side,
keeping the pressed edge flat on
the top side to make a pleat at the
bottom of the pocket.

Figure 12
Place a loop strip 2 3/4"
from the top long side
and 4" from the end.

Step 12. Stitch the loop strip of one hook-and-loop tape piece 2 3/4" from the long edge and 4" from the end of the lining piece as shown in Figure 12. Center and sew the hook strip 1/4" from one 7" edge of a larger pocket piece.

Step 13. Repeat Steps 10 and 11, leaving 1 1/2" between the top edge of the smaller pocket and the stitching line for the bottom of the larger pocket referring to Figure 13, except do not divide pocket into sections. Repeat with second pocket on opposite end of lining.

Figure 13
Place the large pocket, leaving 1 1/2" between the top edge of the smaller pocket and the stitching line for the bottom of the larger pocket.

Step 14. Place the lining piece right sides together with the quilted top. Sew all around on the zipper stitching line, leaving a 5" opening on one end. Trim corners; turn right side out. Press; hand-stitch opening closed.

Step 15. Lay the felt and plastic zipper bags along center of lining; stitch in place twice to secure as shown in Figure 14.

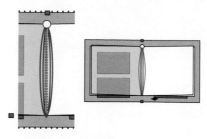

Figure 14
Lay the felt and plastic zipper bags over fold in the center; stitch in place twice to secure. Add button and elastic pieces.

Step 16. Stitch the button at the center edge of one long side on the inside of the tote. Cut blue elastic cord into two equal lengths. Tie each end of each piece to form a loop at each end. Tack the center of each cord piece to the side opposite the button to secure, again referring to Figure 14. Place the opposite ends of the loops over the button. **Note:** *These elastic pieces can hold a magazine or book in place inside the bag. The felt pieces are the perfect place to lay out pieces for stitching as they will not move around. Store projects in the plastic zipper bags and tools in the pockets.* ✦

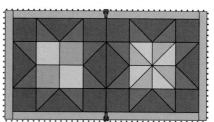

Quilting Tote Along Open
Placement Diagram
26" x 14"

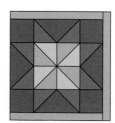

Quilting Tote Along Closed
Placement Diagram
13" x 14"

Underwater Wedding Ring

By Connie Rand

An underwater print led to this appliquéd interpretation of the traditional Double Wedding Ring pattern. You can vary the colors, number and positioning of the fish, or use scraps leftover from other projects to make your own version. Let your imagination run wild and see what happens.

Project Specifications

Skill Level: Beginner
Project Size: 54" x 54"

Materials

- Assorted bright-color scraps for fish
- 1/4 yard orange wave print
- 1/4 yard blue/green wave print
- 1 yard yellow scale print
- 1 1/4 yards blue underwater print
- 2 yards green underwater print
- Backing 58" x 58"
- Batting 58" x 58"
- All-purpose thread to match fabrics
- Yellow hand-quilting thread
- 5 assorted buttons for fish eyes
- 2 yards 3/4"-wide green lace
- 1 package green single-fold bias tape
- Basic sewing tools and supplies

Instructions

Step 1. Cut a 42 1/2" x 42 1/2" square blue underwater print for background; fold and crease to mark the center.

Step 2. Prepare templates for A and fish shapes; cut as directed on each piece. **Note**: *Use a variety of scraps to make fish parts.* Turn under seam allowance on each piece; baste in place. Baste fish parts together referring to overlap lines on patterns to make complete fish motifs. Turn under seam allowance of each basted motif; baste to hold.

Step 3. Cut twenty 2 1/2" x 2 1/2" squares each orange and blue/green wave prints for B. Turn

under edges of B squares 1/4" all around; press.

Step 4. Join the B squares referring to Figure 1 for positioning of colors; press seams in one direction.

Step 5. Sew a B unit to both ends of one A piece as shown in Figure 2; repeat. Press seams toward B units.

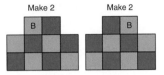

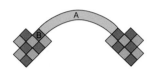

Figure 1
Join B squares as shown.

Figure 2
Sew a B unit to both ends of 1 A piece.

Step 6. Center and place the A-B units 3 1/4" from the top and bottom center edges of the background as shown in Figure 3; pin to secure.

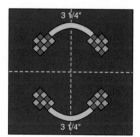

Figure 3
Center and place the A-B
units 3 1/4" from the top
and bottom center edges
of the background.

Step 7. Add remaining A pieces, centering outside A pieces 3 1/4" from the edge of the background all around and matching edge of inside A pieces to seam of B pieces; pin pieces in place to hold.

Step 8. Cut random-length segments of green single-fold bias tape and pin to A pieces, tucking ends of tape under edges of A piece and referring to the Placement Diagram for positioning suggestions.

Step 9. Cut lace into 1 1/2" segments and fold in thirds along length as shown in Figure 4. Place folded lace under edges of bias tape as shown in Figure 5; pin to hold.

Figure 4
Fold lace pieces in
thirds as shown.

Figure 5
Place folded lace
pieces under edge of
green bias tape.

Step 10. Referring to the Placement Diagram for positioning, arrange basted fish motifs on the pinned top, placing some motifs under the pinned A pieces.

Step 11. When satisfied with the positioning of all pieces, hand-stitch in place referring to the General Instructions for hand-appliqué.

Step 12. Sew a button to each fish for an eye.

Step 13. Cut (and piece) two strips each 2" x 42 1/2" and 2" x 45 1/2" yellow scale print. Sew the shorter strips to the top and bottom and longer strips to opposite sides of the appliquéd center; press seams toward strips.

Step 14. Cut and piece two strips green underwater print 5" x 45 1/2" across width of the fabric. **Note:** *The fabric used in the sample was a directional print, and strips must be cut both across the width and along the length to keep the fish in an upright position.* Sew these strips to the top and bottom of the appliquéd center; press seams toward strips.

Step 15. Cut two 5" x 54 1/2" strips green underwater print along the length of the fabric. Sew a strip to opposite long sides of the appliquéd center; press seams toward strips.

Step 16. Prepare quilt top for quilting and quilt referring to the General Instructions. **Note:** *The quilt shown was hand-quilted in a meandering design using yellow hand-quilting thread.*

Step 17. Prepare 6 1/2 yards straight-grain binding from yellow scale print and apply referring to the General Instructions to finish. ✦

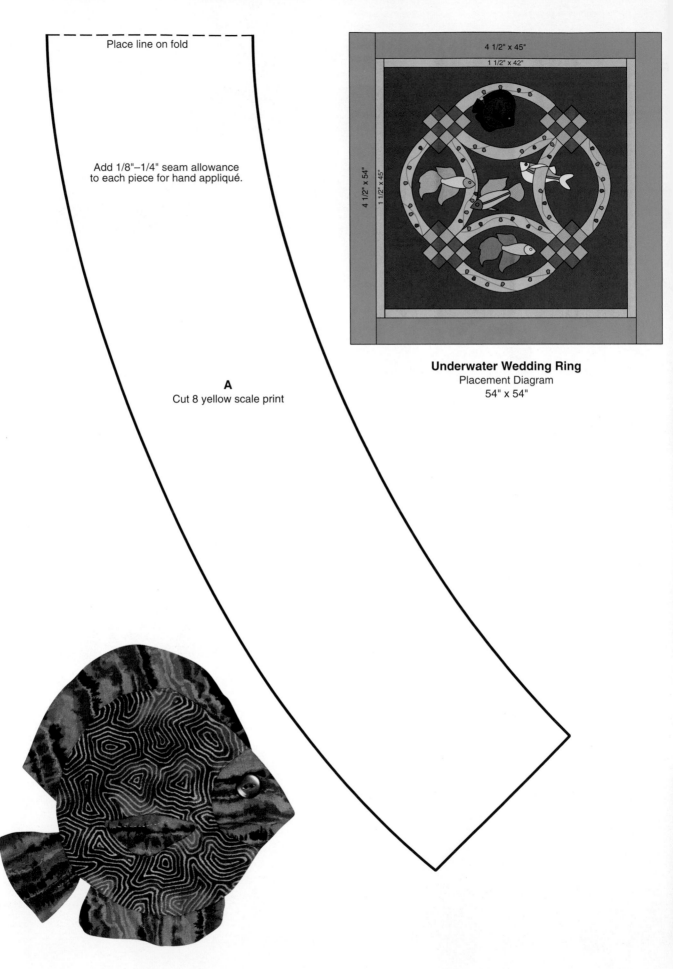

Place line on fold

Add 1/8"–1/4" seam allowance
to each piece for hand appliqué.

A
Cut 8 yellow scale print

4 1/2" x 45"

1 1/2" x 42"

4 1/2" x 54"

1 1/2" x 45"

Underwater Wedding Ring
Placement Diagram
54" x 54"

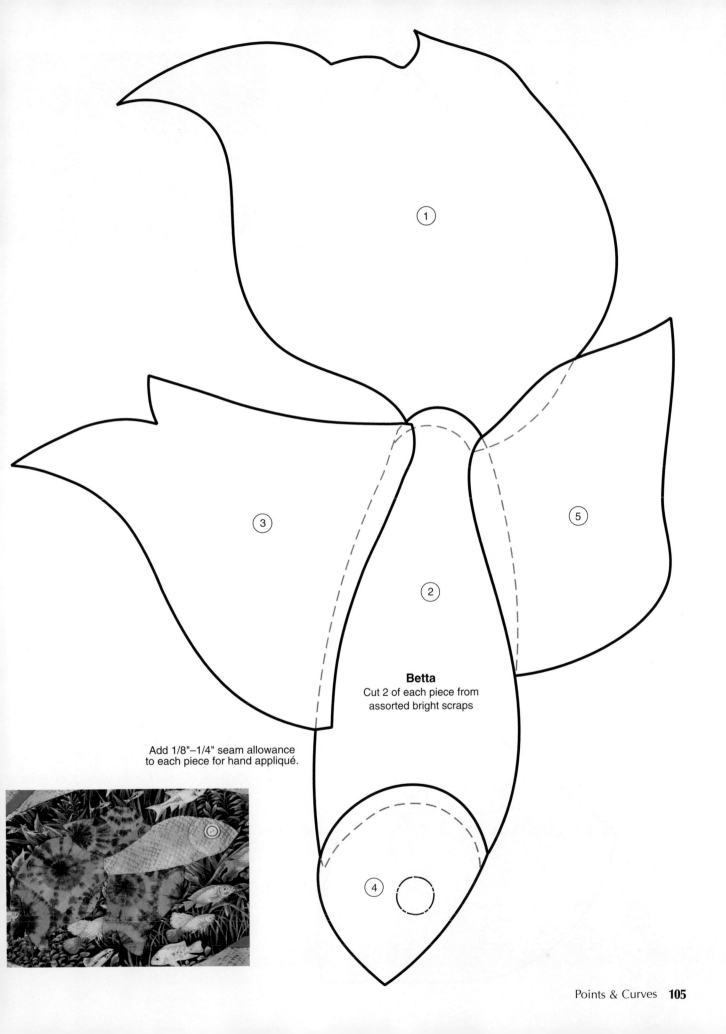

1

3

5

2

4

Betta
Cut 2 of each piece from
assorted bright scraps

Add 1/8"–1/4" seam allowance
to each piece for hand appliqué.

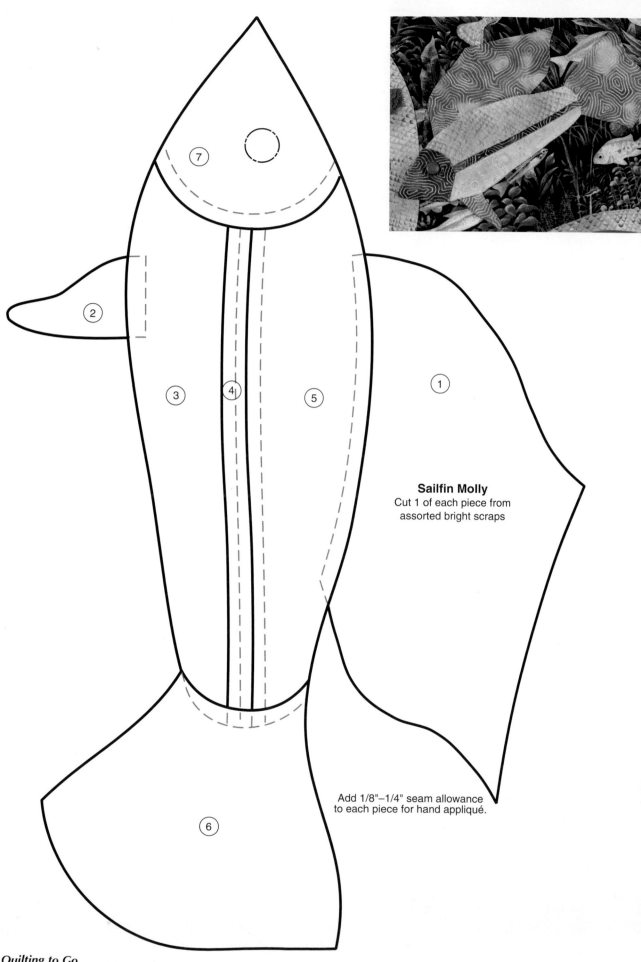

Sailfin Molly
Cut 1 of each piece from
assorted bright scraps

Add 1/8"–1/4" seam allowance
to each piece for hand appliqué.

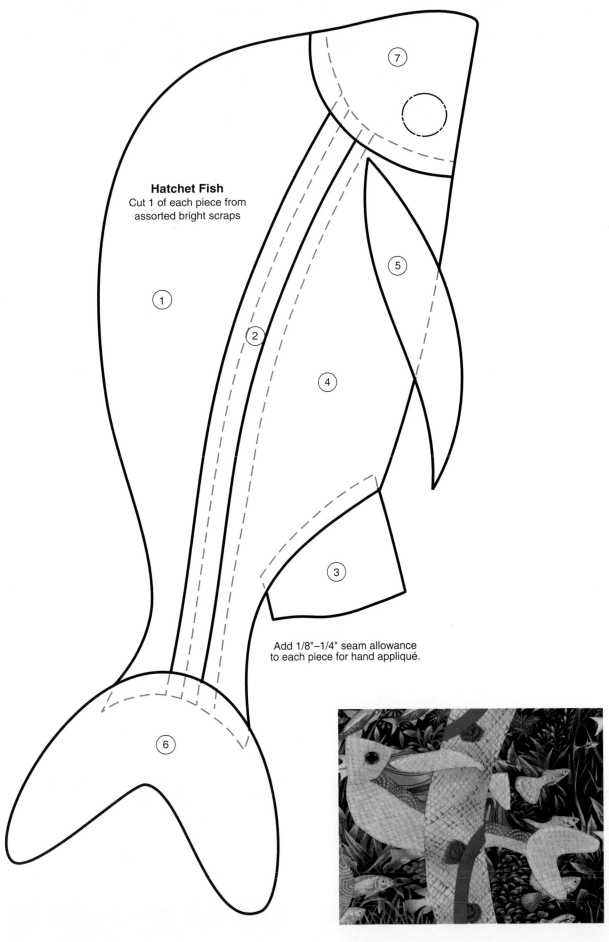

Hatchet Fish
Cut 1 of each piece from assorted bright scraps

① ② ③ ④ ⑤ ⑥ ⑦

Add 1/8"–1/4" seam allowance
to each piece for hand appliqué.

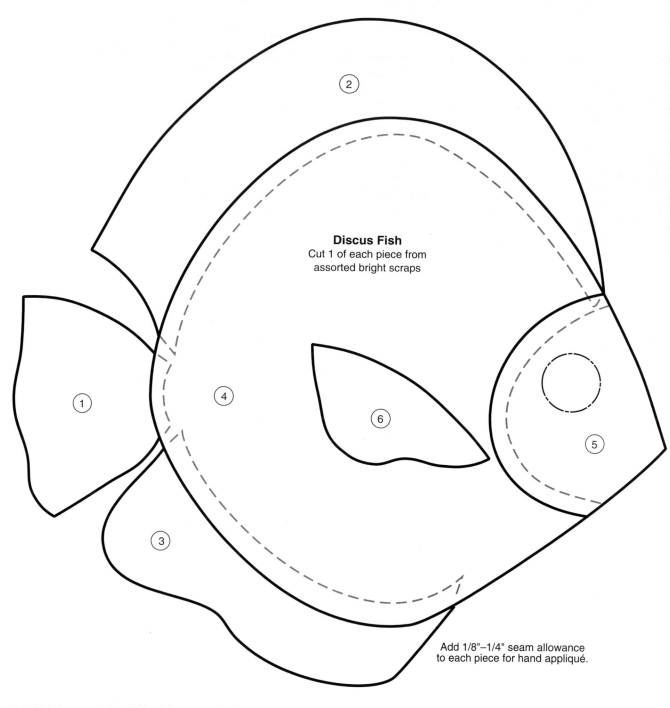

Discus Fish
Cut 1 of each piece from
assorted bright scraps

① ② ③ ④ ⑤ ⑥

Add 1/8"–1/4" seam allowance
to each piece for hand appliqué.

Fancy Threads

The wonderful threads available today
will inspire you to try something new.
Stitching them by hand provides a relaxing
time while watching your children.

Winter Door Banner

By Connie Kauffman

Fabric snowflakes are fused and stitched to create this welcome banner for the winter season.

Project Specifications

Skill Level: Beginner
Quilt Size: 12" x 21"

Materials

+ 1/8 yard each blue/lavender and purple mottleds
+ 1/4 yard white-on-white print
+ 3/8 yard snowflake print
+ Backing 13" x 22"
+ Batting 13" x 22"
+ Navy all-purpose thread
+ Silver-metallic holographic thread
+ Silver metallic thread
+ 1/2 yard fusible transfer web
+ Basic sewing tools and supplies

Instructions

Step 1. Cut a 12 1/2" x 21 1/2" rectangle snowflake print. Fold and crease rectangle to mark the center. Fold both bottom corners at the center mark and crease to make an angle as shown in Figure 1; cut along crease lines to make angled corners, again referring to Figure 1.

12 1/2"

21 1/2"

Figure 1
Fold both bottom corners at the
center mark and crease to make
an angle; cut along crease lines
to make angled corners.

Step 2. Prepare templates for appliqué shapes using patterns given; trace shapes onto the paper side of the fusible web. Cut out shapes, leaving a margin around each one.

Step 3. Fuse shapes to the wrong side of the white-on-white print; cut out shapes on marked lines. Remove paper backing.

Step 4. Arrange the snowflake shapes on the background rectangle referring to the Placement Diagram for positioning. **Note:** *There are two versions (second version on page 112) of the Placement Diagram. You may arrange your shapes as shown in either one or in a totally different version.* When satisfied with the placement, fuse shapes in place.

Step 5. Trace one set of the large letters and two sets of the small letters given on page 10 with the *Summer Door Banner* on the paper side of the fusible transfer web. Cut out shapes, leaving a margin around each one. Fuse one set of the small letters to the wrong side of the purple mottled, the second set of small letters on the wrong side of the white-on-white print, and the large letters on the wrong side of the blue/lavender mottled. Cut out letters on traced lines; remove paper backing.

Step 6. Arrange the large letters on the diagonal of the background referring to the Placement Diagram for positioning; fuse in place. Layer the white letters and then purple letters on the fused large letters; fuse in place.

Step 7. Lay the batting on a flat surface; place the

Winter Door Banner
Placement Diagram
12" x 21"

Snowflake 3
Cut 1 white-on-white print

Snowflake 2
Cut 1 white-on-white print

backing on the batting with right side up. Place the stitched top right sides together with the backing piece; pin layers together to hold.

Step 8. Machine-stitch around edges of the stitched top using a 1/4" seam allowance, leaving a 3" opening on one side. Trim excess backing and batting even with the stitched top; trim corner points.

Step 9. Turn the stitched unit right side out through the opening; press to make seam edges flat. Hand-stitch the opening closed.

Step 10. Using a machine buttonhole stitch and silver-metallic holographic thread, stitch around each white-on-white print letter and snowflake. **Note:** *This type of thread will melt upon contact with an iron.* Repeat with the silver metallic thread around remaining letters.

Step 11. Machine-stitch 1/4" from edge all around using navy all-purpose thread.

Step 12. Cut a 3 1/2" x 11 1/2" strip any leftover fabric. Fold under each short end of the strip 1/4" and press; press under 1/4" again and stitch to hem ends.

Step 13. Fold the strip with right sides together along length; stitch along length to make a tube. Turn the tube right side out; press with seam centered to complete a hanging sleeve.

Step 14. Hand-stitch the hanging sleeve to the top backside of the banner, being careful that stitches do not show on the right side. ✦

Winter Door Banner
(Alternate Placement)
Placement Diagram
12" x 21"

Snowflake 1
Cut 1 white-on-white print

Crazy-Quilted Wall Quilt & Pillow

By Marian Shenk

Scraps in a variety of rich colors and fabrics combine with an assortment of embroidery stitches to create an antique look in this wall quilt with matching pillow.

Project Specifications

Quilt Size: 24" x 24"

Pillow Size: 18" x 18"

Block Size: 10" x 10" and 14" x 14"

Number of Blocks: 4 and 1

Materials

+ Assorted scraps satin, brocade, suede, silk and velour in deep, rich colors
+ 1 square of muslin 14 1/2" x 14 1/2"
+ 4 squares muslin 10 1/2" x 10 1/2"
+ 1/4 yard black velour
+ 1/4 yard navy velour
+ 1 square each backing 18 1/2" x 18 1/2" and 26" x 26"
+ 1 square each batting 20" x 20" and 26" x 26"
+ Neutral color all-purpose thread
+ Hand-quilting thread to match some fabrics
+ Assorted colors and white 6-strand embroidery floss to match and contrast with fabrics
+ 2 1/2 yards navy 3/8"-wide cord
+ 1 package polyester fiberfill
+ 1 package assorted-color seed beads
+ 1 package black single-fold bias tape
+ Basic sewing tools and supplies

Crazy Patch
10" x 10" Block

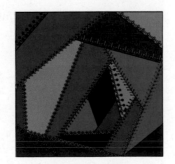

Crazy Patch
14" x 14" Block

Making the Wall Quilt

Step 1. Choose a scrap of fabric for the center patch 1; pin to the center of one 10 1/2" x 10 1/2" muslin square as shown in Figure 1.

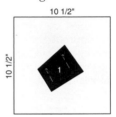

Figure 1
Pin a scrap of fabric to the center of a muslin square.

Step 2. Choose a second fabric for patch 2 to cover one end of the pinned scrap and pin with right sides together as shown in Figure 2. Stitch across edge of the two pieces, again referring to Figure 2.

Step 3. Using a lower heat setting on your iron, press patch 2 to the right side referring to Figure 3.

Figure 2
Pin a second scrap to the
center scrap and stitch.

Figure 3
Press patch 2
to the right side.

Step 4. Choose another scrap large enough to cover the patch 1–2 seam; stitch and press referring to Figure 4.

Figure 4
Choose another scrap large
enough to cover the patch 1-2
seam; stitch and press.

Step 5. Continue to choose scraps to cover seams of stitched areas, stitch and press until the entire muslin area is covered. Trim excess patch fabrics even with muslin base square to complete one block; repeat for four blocks.

Step 6. Choose an embroidery stitch from those given for first embroidery embellishment. Choose embroidery floss in desired colors for the stitch; cut an 18" length of floss. Separate into two 3-strand lengths. Separate one of the 3-strand lengths before threading the needle; thread each strand separately. Stitch along seam allowance between two pieces covering one entire seam using one type of stitch as shown in Figure 5 and photos. Repeat with a

variety of stitches and embroidery floss colors to cover all seams. Repeat for all blocks.

Figure 5
Stitch along entire seam
using a decorative stitch.

Step 7. Add French knots to the tips or center of stitches to make flowers or at the ends of buttonhole stitches using 2 strands of any color embroidery floss.

Step 8. Join two blocks to make a row; repeat for two

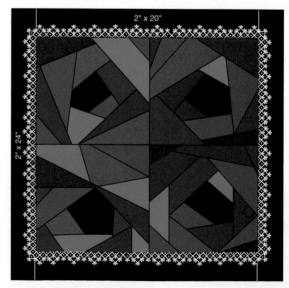

Crazy-Quilted Wall Quilt
Placement Diagram
24" x 24"

rows. Press seams open. Join the rows to complete the quilt center; press seams open.

Step 9. Cut two strips each 2 1/2" x 20 1/2" and 2 1/2" x 24 1/2" black velour. Sew the shorter strips to the top and bottom, and longer strips to the opposite sides; press seams open.

Step 10. Mark the border embroidery pattern on the border strips.

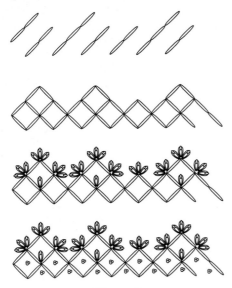

Figure 6
Stitch marked border design using
2 strands of white embroidery floss
in the order shown.

Step 11. Stitch marked border design using 2 strands of white embroidery floss and referring to Figure 6 for stitch details.

Step 12. Sandwich the 26" x 26" batting square

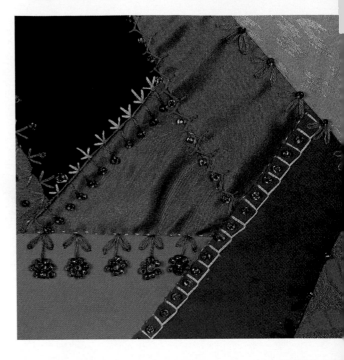

between the stitched top and 26" x 26" prepared backing square; baste to hold. Hand-quilt in the ditch of some seams using hand-quilting thread to match fabrics, trying to keep stitches invisible.

Step 13. When quilting is complete, trim edges even and bind with black single-fold bias tape to finish.

Making the Pillow

Step 1. Using the 14 1/2" x 14 1/2" muslin square, prepare a crazy-patchwork block and embroider along seams referring to Steps 1–6 for wall quilt.

Step 2. Add seed beads to make flowers and along other stitched areas using 1 strand of embroidery floss to match seed beads or embroidery stitches as shown in Figure 7.

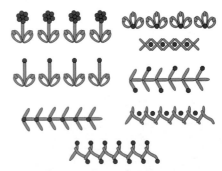

Figure 7
Add seed beads to make flowers and
along other stitched areas using 1
strand of embroidery floss to match
seed beads or embroidery stitches.

Step 3. Cut two strips each 2 1/2" x 14 1/2" and 2 1/2" x 18 1/2" navy velour. Sew the shorter strips to two opposite sides and the longer strips to the remaining sides; press seams toward strips. **Note:** *Be very careful of seed beads on the right side when pressing.*

Step 4. Add the cretan stitch between the border seams all around.

Step 5. Pin the 20" x 20" batting square to the wrong side of the stitched pillow top; baste layers to hold. Hand-quilt in the ditch of some seams using hand-quilting thread to match fabrics, trying to keep stitches invisible. When quilting is complete, trim batting even with pillow top edges.

Step 6. Pin and baste the navy cord around the outside edges of the pillow, clipping into the woven edge

of the cord seam at corners to turn; machine-stitch in place using a zipper foot.

Step 7. Place the 18 1/2" x 18 1/2" backing square right sides together with the completed pillow top; stitch all around, leaving an 8" opening on one side.

Step 8. Turn right side out through opening. Stuff polyester fiberfill through opening to create desired fullness; hand-stitch opening closed to finish. ✦

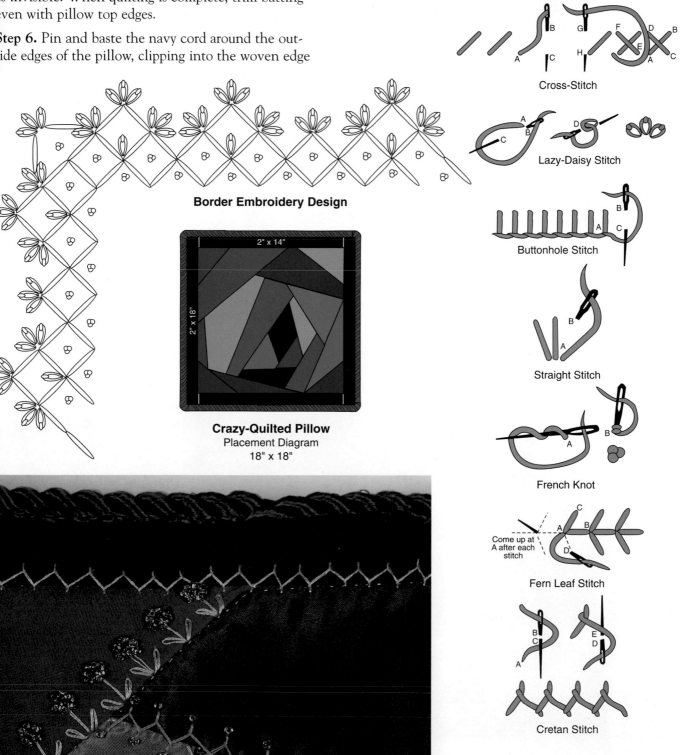

Border Embroidery Design

Crazy-Quilted Pillow
Placement Diagram
18" x 18"

2" x 14"

2" x 18"

Stitch Diagrams

Cross-Stitch

Lazy-Daisy Stitch

Buttonhole Stitch

Straight Stitch

French Knot

Come up at A after each stitch

Fern Leaf Stitch

Cretan Stitch

Miniature Whole-Cloth Quilt

By Connie Kauffman

If you have never made a whole-cloth quilt, a miniature is a great way to start.

Project Notes

Whole-cloth quilting is easy—choose a design, mark it on the fabric, sandwich with batting and backing, and quilt! There are no seams to interfere with the design or stitches. It is a good way to showcase nice, even stitches and a rather quick project since it requires no piecing or appliqué.

The project shown uses a cream mottled fabric to create some texture, and is stitched using a variegated cream-to-brown hand-quilting thread. You may consider using a darker fabric with a light-colored thread to create a totally different look.

If you enjoy hand quilting and want to showcase your talents, whole-cloth quilts are the perfect medium.

Project Specifications

Skill Level: Intermediate

Quilt Size: 15 1/2" x 15 1/2" (includes binding)

Materials

+ 3/4 yard cream mottled
+ Batting 18" x 18"
+ Cream all-purpose thread
+ Cream-to-brown variegated hand-quilting thread

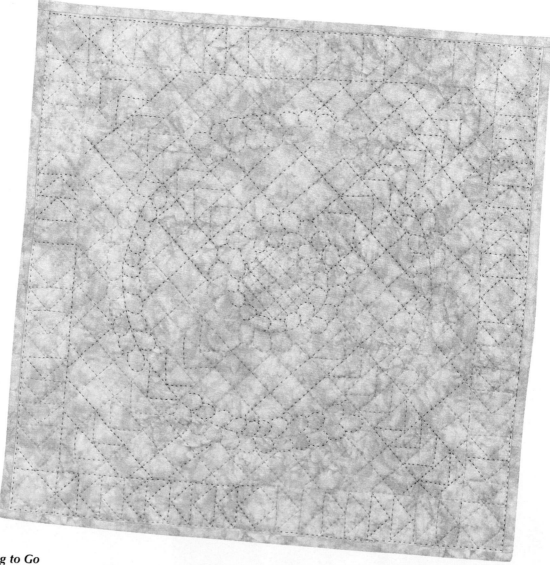

Miniature Whole-Cloth Quilt
Placement Diagram
15 1/2" x 15 1/2" (includes binding)

◆ Water-erasable marker

◆ Basic sewing tools and supplies

Instructions

Step 1. Cut two 18" x 18" squares cream mottled; fold and crease to mark the center of one square.

Step 2. Make four copies of the quilting design given; tape the copies together to complete the whole design.

Step 3. Tape the design to a window; center the creased square right side up over the taped pattern. Tape the fabric to the window, matching creased lines on fabric with center of pattern. Trace the design onto the fabric using the water-erasable marker.

Step 4. Sandwich the batting square between the marked and unmarked fabric squares; baste layers together to hold flat.

Step 5. Hand-quilt on marked lines, starting in the center and working to the outside edges.

Step 6. When quilting is complete, trim to 15 1/2" x 15 1/2".

Step 7. Prepare 2 yards cream mottled straight-grain binding and bind quilt edges referring to the General Instructions.

Step 8. When binding is complete, immerse finished quilt in cold water to remove marked lines. ✦

Quilting Pattern
1/4 of the design is given

Grandmother's Floral Bouquet

By Marian Shenk

Make 3-D flower petals and stuff the flower centers to make this beautiful fabric bouquet.

Project Specifications

Skill Level: Intermediate
Quilt Size: 25" x 41"

Materials

+ 6" x 6" scrap large butterfly print
+ 4" x 12" scrap gold tone-on-tone
+ 9" x 9" square gray mottled
+ 1 fat quarter pink tone-on-tone
+ 1/2 yard green metallic dot
+ 1/2 yard deep rose mottled
+ 2/3 yard white-on-white print
+ 4-yard length of 2 1/2"-wide border stripe
+ Backing 29" x 45"
+ Batting 29" x 45"
+ 4 1/4 yards self-made or purchased burgundy binding
+ All-purpose thread to match fabrics
+ White hand-quilting thread
+ 1 1/2 yards 1/4"-wide green bias tape
+ 1 yard 1/4"-wide gold lamé fusible bias
+ 1 handful of polyester fiberfill
+ Basic sewing tools and supplies, and card stock

Instructions

Step 1. Cut an 18 1/2" x 34 1/2" rectangle white-on-white print for appliqué background. Fold and crease background to find the horizontal, vertical and diagonal centers.

Step 2. Prepare templates using pattern pieces given; cut as directed on each piece, adding a 1/4" seam allowance all around each piece when cutting for hand appliqué.

Step 3. Cut pieces of 1/4"-wide gold lamé fusible bias to cover the lines as marked on the vase; fuse in place on vase piece in numerical order as shown in Figure 1.

Figure 1
Fuse in place in numerical
order as shown.

Step 4. Turn under seam allowance on vase piece; baste. Center and pin the vase piece to the background 2 1/4" from bottom edge as shown in Figure 2; hand-stitch in place, leaving top edge unstitched.

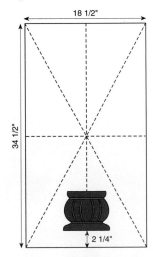

Figure 2
Center and pin the vase
piece to the background
2 1/4" from bottom edge.

Step 5. Cut the following lengths from the 1/4"-wide green bias tape for stems: 16 1/2" (A), 13" (B), 10 1/2" (C) and two 3" (D). Center the longest piece under the unstitched top edge of the vase, pin and stitch in place. Repeat with the remaining stem pieces, referring to Figure 3 and the Placement Diagram for positioning of pieces.

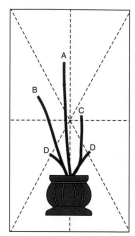

Figure 3
Arrange stem
pieces as shown.

Step 6. Prepare the large leaves for appliqué. Place one edge of each leaf under the unstitched top edge of the vase; stitch in place. Stitch the top edge of the vase in place.

Step 7. Join six hexagon pieces as shown in Figure 4; turn under outside seam allowance and baste to hold. Repeat to complete three hexagon flower shapes.

Figure 4
Join 6 hexagons.

Step 8. Arrange the hexagon flowers at the ends of the three longest stems and the small leaves along stems and under flower edges referring to the Placement Diagram for positioning; hand-stitch in place.

Step 9. Prepare three flower motifs with small and large buds for appliqué; pin, baste and stitch a flower motif at the end of each short stem and one in the center above the vase.

Step 10. To complete one petal, place two petal shapes right sides together; stitch around curved edges. Trim seams to 1/8"; clip curves. Turn right side out; press to smooth edges. Repeat for 18 petals.

Step 11. Thread and knot an 18" length of all-purpose thread to match petals in a hand-sewing needle. Starting inside the 1/4" seam allowance, sew a line of basting stitches along one petal; connect a second petal with the same thread as shown in Figure 5. Continue the process until there are six petal shapes on the thread; pull thread to gather as shown in Figure 6. Fit around center of hexagon flower and adjust gathers until the petals fit; knot the thread. Pin and then hand-stitch petals in place along gathered edge to hold.

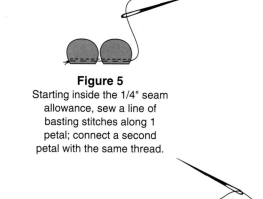

Figure 5
Starting inside the 1/4" seam
allowance, sew a line of
basting stitches along 1
petal; connect a second
petal with the same thread.

Figure 6
Pull thread to gather.

Step 12. Sew a basting stitch within seam allowance around one flower center piece. Place card-stock circle in the center of basting on the wrong side of the flower center piece. Pull stitches to gather seam allowance around card-stock circle; press seam allowance.

Step 13. Position and pin over the opening in the petal centers. Hand-stitch in place.

Step 14. Cut a slit in the wrong side of the background behind petal center; remove card-stock circle. Stuff some polyester fiberfill inside the flower center to make puffy; slip-stitch opening closed. Repeat for the three flower centers.

Step 15. Cut a butterfly motif from the square of butterfly print, leaving 1/8"–1/4" seam allowance all around for hand appliqué.

Step 16. Position butterfly shape on background referring to the Placement Diagram and photo of project for suggestions. Turn under seam allowance as you stitch the butterfly in place.

Step 17. Cut two strips each 2" x 34 1/2" and 2" x 21 1/2" deep rose mottled. Sew the longer strips to opposite sides and shorter strips to the top and bottom of the appliquéd center; press seams toward strips.

Step 18. Cut two strips each 2 1/2" x 25 1/2" and 2 1/2" x 41 1/2" from the 2 1/2"-wide border stripe yardage. Center and sew the longer strips to opposite sides and shorter strips to the top and bottom, mitering corners. Trim mitered seam to 1/4"; press seams open. Press seams toward strips.

Step 19. Prepare for quilting; quilt as desired by hand or machine referring to the General Instructions. *Note: The quilt shown was hand-quilted in diagonal rows 1 1/4" apart using white hand-quilting thread.*

Step 20. When quilting is complete trim backing and batting even with quilt top; remove pins or basting. Prepare self-made burgundy binding or use purchased binding to finish edges referring to the General Instructions. ✦

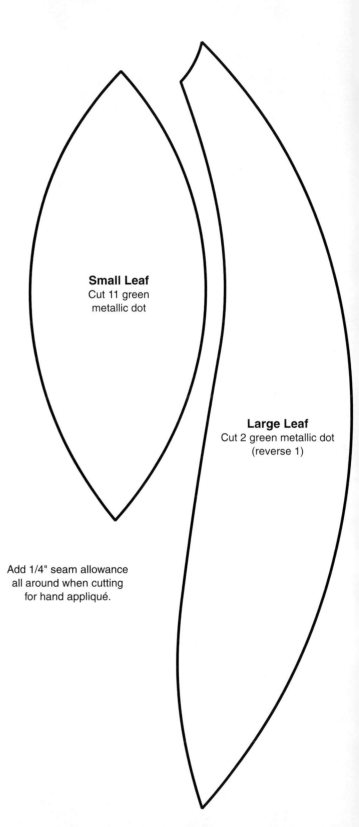

Small Leaf
Cut 11 green
metallic dot

Large Leaf
Cut 2 green metallic dot
(reverse 1)

Add 1/4" seam allowance
all around when cutting
for hand appliqué.

2" x 25"

2" x 41"

Grandmother's Floral Bouquet
Placement Diagram
25" x 41"

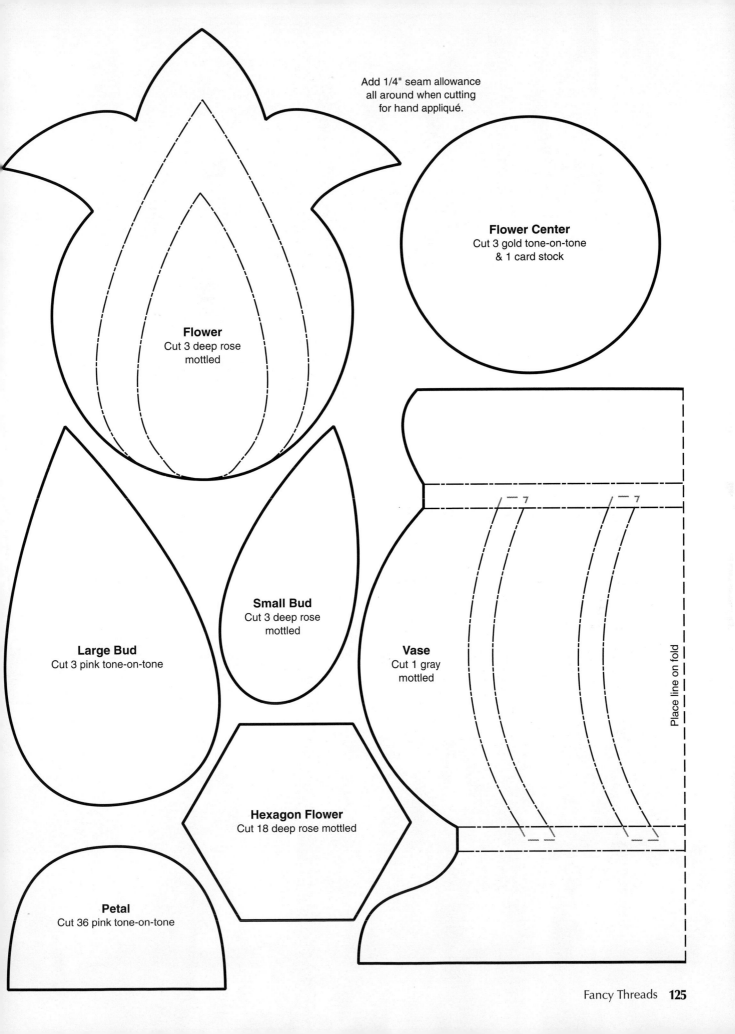

Add 1/4" seam allowance
all around when cutting
for hand appliqué.

Flower
Cut 3 deep rose
mottled

Flower Center
Cut 3 gold tone-on-tone
& 1 card stock

Large Bud
Cut 3 pink tone-on-tone

Small Bud
Cut 3 deep rose
mottled

Vase
Cut 1 gray
mottled

Place line on fold

Hexagon Flower
Cut 18 deep rose mottled

Petal
Cut 36 pink tone-on-tone

Redwork Hearts & Flowers

By Julie Weaver

Join a variety of red fabrics to make a patchwork frame for a pretty stitched redwork pattern.

Project Specifications

Skill Level: Beginner

Quilt Size: 14" x 17"

Materials

+ 12" x 14" rectangle muslin
+ 42 rectangles red scraps 1 1/2" x 2 1/2"
+ 4 squares red scraps 2 1/2" x 2 1/2"
+ 1/4 yard red print
+ Backing 18" x 21"
+ Batting 18" x 21"
+ Red all-purpose thread
+ Red and cream hand-quilting thread
+ Cream all-purpose thread
+ Red 6-strand embroidery floss
+ Basic sewing tools and supplies

Instructions

Step 1. Fold the muslin background rectangle and crease to mark the centers.

Step 2. Center and trace the embroidery design given onto the muslin background. **Note:** *Trace leaf sprig section above and below the large heart design referring to the Placement Diagram for positioning.*

Step 3. Using stem, lazy-daisy, satin, cross and French knot stitches and 2 strands red embroidery floss, stitch design on marked lines.

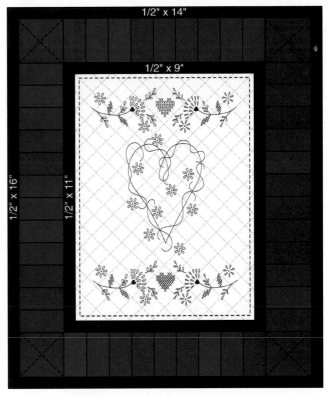

Redwork Hearts & Flowers
Placement Diagram
14" x 17"

Step 4. Trim the embroidered background to 8 1/2" x 11 1/2".

Step 5. Cut two strips each 1" x 9 1/2" and 1" x 11 1/2" red print. Sew the longer strips to opposite long sides, and shorter strips to the top and bottom of the center background; press seams away from center background.

Step 6. Choose twelve 1 1/2" x 2 1/2" red rectangles; join on the 2 1/2" sides to make one long strip as shown in Figure 1. Press seams in one direction; repeat for two strips. Sew a strip to opposite long sides of the center background; press seams toward strips.

Figure 1
Join twelve 1 1/2" x 2 1/2" red
rectangles to make a strip.

Step 7. Choose nine 1 1/2" x 2 1/2" red rectangles; join on the 2 1/2" sides to make a strip. Press seams in one direction;

repeat for two strips. Sew a 2 1/2" x 2 1/2" red square to each end of each strip; press seams toward squares.

Step 8. Sew the pieced strips to the top and bottom of the quilt top; press seams toward strips.

Step 9. Cut two strips each 1" x 14 1/2" and 1" x 16 1/2" red print. Sew the longer strips to opposite long sides and shorter strips to the top and bottom of the quilt top; press seams toward strips.

Step 10. Mark a 3/4" crosshatch design on the muslin background.

Step 11. Prepare quilt top for quilting, quilt on marked lines and as desired by hand or machine, and bind using 2 yards self-made red print straight-grain binding referring to the General Instructions.

Step 12. Stitch 1/4" from inside red borders in the background area using 2 strands red embroidery floss and a running stitch to finish. ✦

Stitch Diagrams

Lazy Daisy Stitch

Satin Stitch

Cross-Stitch

French Knot

Stem Stitch

Running Stitch

Stitching Pattern

Redwork Tote & Sewing Kit

By Pearl Louise Krush

Create a decorative pocket using hand-embroidered redwork to make this pretty tote and sewing kit.

Project Specifications

Skill Level: Beginner

Tote Size: 10" x 12" x 5"

Sewing Kit Size: 9 1/2" x 9 1/2" open;
   4 3/4" x 9 1/2" folded

Materials

- ✦ 1/4 yard each 2–3 red prints or red print scraps
- ✦ 1/3 yard cream-on-cream print
- ✦ 1 yard cream sand castle weave fabric or background fabric of choice
- ✦ 1 yard red print
- ✦ 2 squares batting 12" x 12"
- ✦ 1 square batting 9 1/2" x 9 1/2"
- ✦ Cream all-purpose thread
- ✦ Red 6-strand embroidery floss
- ✦ 7 1/2" x 9 1/2" rectangle heavy plastic
- ✦ Basic sewing tools and supplies

Making Tote

Step 1. Cut two 10 1/2" x 12 1/2" rectangles for A, two 5 1/2" x 12 1/2" rectangles for B, one 5 1/2" x 10 1/2" rectangle for C and two 2 1/2" x 22 1/2" strips for D from the background fabric.

Step 2. Cut two 4 1/2" x 10 1/2" rectangles for J, two

10 1/2" x 14" rectangles for K, two 5 1/2" x 14 1/2" rectangles for L and one 5 1/2" x 10 1/2" rectangle for M from the 1 yard red print for lining pieces.

Step 3. From the remaining red prints, cut twenty 2 1/2" x 2 1/2" squares for E, five 1 1/2" x 1 1/2" squares for F and one 1 1/2" x 12 1/2" strip for G.

Step 4. From cream-on-cream print, cut two 5 1/2" x 8" rectangles for H.

Step 5. Trace the embroidery design given for the large pocket on one H rectangle with bottom of stitching line 1/2" from one 5 1/2" edge.

Step 6. Using 2 strands of red embroidery floss, back-stitch stems, leaves and butterfly shape. Stitch French knots on butterfly antennae, inside body and in clusters on stems. Make lazy-daisy stitched flowers.

Step 7. To make a petal flower, fold each F square in half on one diagonal with wrong sides together.

Step 8. Thread a needle with a knotted double thread; sew a long basting stitch across the doubled raw edges. Add another folded square and continue stitching; repeat until there are five joined triangles on the same length of thread as shown in Figure 1. Pull the petals together and join the first and last petal to form a circle to complete a petal flower as shown in Figure 2. Tie off; clip thread and set aside.

Figure 1
Sew a long basting stitch across the doubled raw edges. Add another folded square and continue stitching; repeat until there are 5 joined triangles on the same length of thread.

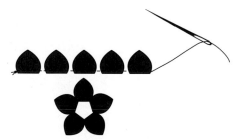

Figure 2
Pull the petals together and join the first and last petal to form a circle to complete a petal flower.

Step 9. Prepare template for circle using pattern given; cut as directed on the piece.

Step 10. Thread a needle with a knotted double thread. Fold outer edge of circle under 1/8"–1/4" and sew large gathering stitches around folded edge; pull and tie off to complete a yo-yo flower as shown in Figure 3. Repeat for four yo-yos.

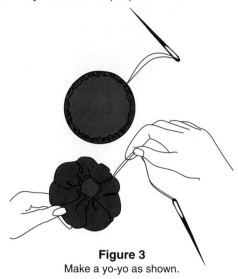

Figure 3
Make a yo-yo as shown.

Step 11. To make a ruched flower, fold the long raw edge of the G strip wrong sides together along length. Thread a needle with a knotted double thread; sew large gathering stitches in a zigzag method along the entire length of the folded strip as shown in Figure 4.

Figure 4
Sew large gathering stitches in a zigzag method along the entire length of the folded G strip.

Step 12. Referring to Figure 5, pull the thread to gather the strip. Arrange the gathered fabric strip into a circle; tack the edges together to hold the circle shape to make a ruched flower.

Figure 5
Make ruched flower as shown.

Step 13. Place a yo-yo in the center of the petal flower as shown in Figure 6; stitch around edges to hold.

Step 14. Pin and stitch the petal and ruched flowers and the three remaining yo-yos in place on the

embroidered H piece referring to the embroidery design for placement.

Figure 6
Place a yo-yo in the
center of the petal flower.

Step 15. Place the second H piece right sides together with the stitched H piece; sew all around, leaving a 2" opening on the bottom edge. Turn right side out through opening; press to flatten at seams to complete the H pocket. Set pocket aside.

Step 16. Layer and pin an A piece on top of one 12" x 12" batting square; repeat with second A piece. Using cream all-purpose thread, machine-quilt a small diagonal grid on both layered sections; when quilting is complete, trim batting even with the A pieces. **Note:** *The background fabric used on the sample has a diagonal weave which was easily used as a guide for machine quilting the grid.*

Step 17. Arrange and sew five E squares together to make a row as shown in Figure 7; press seams in one direction. Repeat for four rows. Join two rows to complete an E pocket strip as shown in Figure 8; repeat for two E pocket strips. Press seams in one direction.

Figure 7
Arrange and sew 5 E squares
together to make a row.

Figure 8
Join 2 rows to complete
an E pocket strip.

Step 18. Place a J strip right sides together with one E pocket strip; sew across one long side. Press J to the wrong side. Repeat for two E-J pockets.

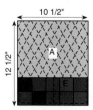

Figure 9
Place 1 E-J pocket with right J side
against 1 A piece along 1 matching
length; stitch around side and bottom
edge. Stitch down the center of the
pocket to make 2 pocket openings.

Step 19. Place one E-J pocket with right J side against one A piece along one matching length; stitch around side and bottom edge as shown in Figure 9. Stitch down the center of the pocket to make two pocket openings, again referring to Figure 9; repeat for tote back.

Step 20. Center and pin the H pocket to the A front panel 1/2" above the E-J pocket. Stitch in place around sides and across bottom 1/4" from edge.

Step 21. To piece side and bottom gusset, sew B to each short end of C as shown in Figure 10; press seams toward C.

Figure 10
To piece side and bottom gusset,
sew B to each short end of C.

Step 22. Pin the B-C side gusset to the A front panel with right sides together starting at the top edge of A and ending on the opposite top edge as shown in Figure 11; stitch. Pin to the A back panel in the same manner and stitch to complete the bag outside shell.

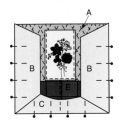

Figure 11
Pin the B-C side gusset to the A
front panel with right sides together
starting at the top edge of A and
ending on the opposite top edge.

Step 23. Join the red print lining K, L and M pieces as in Steps 21 and 22 to make lining. Fold the top edge of the lining piece under 1/4"; press. Slip lining inside bag with wrong sides together. Fold top edge of lining over top edge of bag as shown in Figure 12; hand-stitch lining in place.

Figure 12
Fold top edge of lining
over top edge of bag.

Figure 13
Fold 1 long raw edge to the
center; press. Press the
remaining long raw edge under
1/4"; press. Fold this edge over
pressed edge to cover center
raw edge; press and stitch
down the center.

Step 24. To make straps, referring to Figure 13, fold one long raw edge of D to the center; press. Press the remaining long raw edge under 1/4"; press. Fold this edge over pressed edge to cover center raw edge; press and stitch down the center to complete one strap. Repeat for two straps.

Redwork Tote
Placement Diagram
10" x 12" x 5"

Step 25. Fold under each end of each strap 1"; pin to the inside of the bag and hand-stitch to lining through bag layers but not to the right side to finish.

Making Sewing Kit

Step 1. Cut two 9 1/2" x 9 1/2" squares background fabric.

Step 2. Sandwich the 9 1/2" x 9 1/2" batting square between the two background squares; pin or baste to hold.

Step 3. Machine-quilt in a meandering design using cream all-purpose thread.

Step 4. When quilting is complete, trim edges even.

Step 5. Cut one 9 1/2" x 9 1/2" square red print for pocket; fold in half with wrong sides together and press.

Step 6. Cut one square each background and red print 4 1/4" x 4 1/4". Trace the embroidered design given for the small pocket onto the background square.

Step 7. Using 2 strands of red embroidery floss, back-stitch stems and butterfly and make lazy-daisy stitches for flowers referring to the stitch diagrams. Add French knots to butterfly antennae and body.

Step 8. Lay the red print square right sides together with the embroidered square; stitch all around, leaving a 2" opening on one side. Clip corners; turn right side out through opening. Press and hand-stitch opening closed. Topstitch 1/4" across top edge to complete the pocket.

Step 9. Center and pin the pocket to the quilted background 3/4" from one edge; stitch around sides and across bottom edge.

Step 10. Lay the folded 9 1/2" x 9 1/2" red print

square on the quilted background piece with raw edges even; machine-baste in place around sides and across bottom as shown in Figure 14.

Step 11. Fold the 7 1/2" x 9 1/2" rectangle heavy plastic in half along length; pin and stitch on the opposite side of the quilted background with folded edge toward the center referring to Figure 15.

Figure 14
Machine-baste fabric pocket in place around sides and across bottom.

Figure 15
Stitch plastic pocket to background.

Step 12. Cut one strip red print 2 1/4" by fabric width for binding. Fold the binding strip along length with wrong sides together; press. Pin to the quilted background on the side without pockets; stitch all around, overlapping at beginning and end and mitering corners referring to the General Instructions.

Step 13. Turn binding to the inside; hand-stitch in place.

Step 14. Cut two 1 1/2" x 12" strips red print; fold under

1/4" along each long raw edge of each strip and press. Fold under each end of each strip 1/4". Fold each strip in half along length with wrong sides together; stitch along folded open edge to complete ties.

Step 15. Center and stitch one end of each strip to opposite inside edges of the stitched unit to complete the sewing kit. ✦

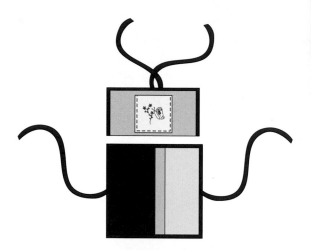

Sewing Kit
Placement Diagram
9 1/2" x 9 1/2" open
4 3/4" x 9 1/2" folded

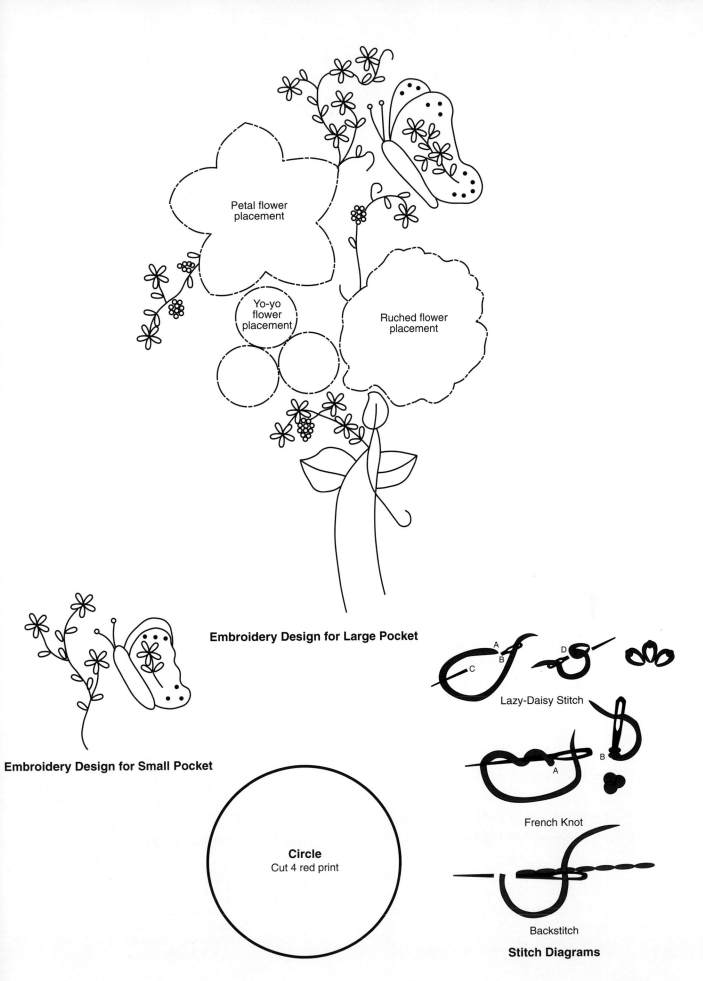

Petal flower
placement

Yo-yo
flower
placement

Ruched flower
placement

Embroidery Design for Large Pocket

Embroidery Design for Small Pocket

Circle
Cut 4 red print

Lazy-Daisy Stitch

French Knot

Backstitch

Stitch Diagrams

Kitty Blues

By Sue Harvey

Bluework-style quilting in each block echoes the kitty theme of the traditional Puss in the Corner block.

Project Specifications

Quilt Size: 39" x 39"
Block Size: 15" x 15"
Number of Blocks: 4

Materials

+ 1/8 yard teal print
+ 1/4 yard cream print
+ 1/3 yard taupe floral
+ 1/2 yard navy print
+ 2/3 yard yellow print
+ 3/4 yard kitty print
+ Batting 43" x 43"
+ Backing 43" x 43"
+ All-purpose thread to match fabrics
+ Navy No. 8 pearl cotton
+ Basic sewing tools and supplies, rotary cutter, mat and ruler

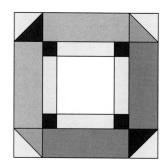

Puss in the Corner
15" x 15" Block

Instructions

Step 1. Cut four squares cream print 6 1/2" x 6 1/2" for A.

Step 2. Cut one strip yellow print 6 1/2" by fabric width; subcut into 2" segments for B. You will need 16 B segments.

Step 3. Cut one strip each teal, navy and yellow prints 3 7/8" by fabric width; subcut into 3 7/8" square segments for D. You will need four teal, six navy and 10 yellow D squares.

Step 4. Cut one strip navy print 2" by fabric width;

subcut into 2" squares for C. You will need 20 C squares.

Step 5. Cut two strips each taupe floral and kitty print 3 1/2" by fabric width; subcut each strip into 9 1/2" segments for E. You will need eight each taupe and kitty E segments. **Note:** *If using directional prints, cut four E segments along the length and four across the width of the fabric.*

Step 6. Mark a diagonal line on the wrong side of each yellow D square. Place a yellow D square right sides together with each navy D square. Stitch 1/4" on each side of the marked line as shown in Figure 1; cut apart on the marked line and press open to make navy D units, again referring to Figure 1. You will need 12 navy D units. Repeat with teal and yellow D squares to make eight teal D units.

Figure 1
Make D units as shown.

Step 7. To piece one Puss in the Corner block, sew B to opposite sides of A; press seams toward B. Sew a C square to each end of two B segments; press seams toward B. Sew a B-C unit to the remaining sides of A to complete the center unit as shown in Figure 2; press seams away from A.

Figure 2
Complete the center
unit as shown.

Step 8. Sew one taupe E and one kitty E to opposite sides of the center unit as shown in Figure 3; press seams toward E.

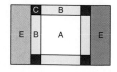

Figure 3
Sew 1 taupe E and 1
kitty E to opposite sides
of the center unit.

Make Your Own Quilting Design

The quilting patterns used in Kitty Blues were taken directly from the theme fabric. Follow these simple steps to add finishing touches to your quilt with a unique quilting design.

Step 1. Choose a motif from the fabric.

Step 2. Trace the outline and just enough detail to make the shape obvious.

Step 3. Enlarge the shape on a photocopier to fit the area to be quilted.

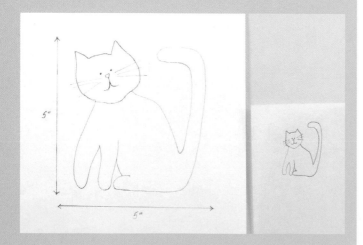

Step 9. Sew a navy D unit to one end and a teal D unit to the opposite end of a taupe E as shown in Figure 4; repeat with a kitty E, again referring to Figure 4; press seams toward E.

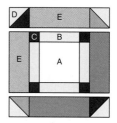

Figure 4
Sew a navy D unit to 1 end and
a teal D unit to the opposite end
of taupe and kitty E segments.

Step 10. Sew the E-D units to the remaining sides of the center unit to complete one block as shown in Figure 5; repeat for four blocks as shown in Figure 6. Press seams toward E strips.

Figure 5
Sew the E-D units to the
remaining sides of the center
unit to complete 1 block.

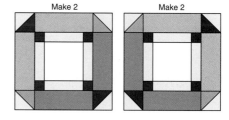

Make 2   Make 2

Figure 6
Make 2 blocks and 2 reversed blocks as shown.

Step 11. Join two blocks to make a row as shown in Figure 7; repeat for two rows. Join the rows to complete the pieced center referring to the Placement Diagram for positioning of rows.

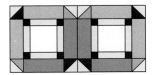

Figure 7
Join 2 blocks to make a row.

Step 12. Cut four strips yellow print 2" x 30 1/2". Sew a strip to opposite sides of the pieced center. Sew a C square to opposite ends of the remaining strips; sew to the remaining sides of the pieced center. Press seams toward strips.

Step 13. Cut four strips kitty print 3 1/2" x 33 1/2". Sew a strip to opposite sides of the pieced center. Sew a navy D unit to each end of the remaining strips referring to the Placement Diagram for positioning of the D units; sew to the remaining sides of the pieced center to complete the top. Press seams toward strips.

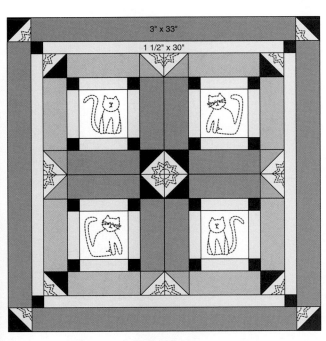

Kitty Blues
Placement Diagram
39" x 39"

Step 14. Mark the kitty A quilting pattern in two A center squares and the kitty B quilting pattern in the remaining A center squares referring to the Placement Diagram for positioning and reversing one of each. Mark the flower pattern in the center yellow D units, half of the flower pattern in the edge yellow D units and a quarter of the flower pattern in the corner yellow D units.

Step 15. Sandwich the batting between the completed top and prepared backing piece; pin or baste to hold.

Step 16. Hand-quilt on all marked lines, and 1/4" and 1" from seams using navy pearl cotton, quilting down the center of all yellow print strips. Remove pins or basting; trim edges even with the quilted top.

Step 17. Cut five strips navy print 2 1/4" by fabric width; join diagonally on short ends to make a long strip. Press in half along length with wrong sides together to make a binding strip. Bind edges of quilt to finish. ✦

**Kitty A
Quilting
Design**

**Flower
Quilting
Design**

**Kitty B
Quilting
Design**

Barrel-Bottom Purse

By Holly Daniels

Carry CDs, sewing items, jewelry and more in this patchwork drawstring purse.

Project Specifications

Skill Level: Beginner

Purse Size: 7" x 10 3/4"

Materials

- ✦ Scraps 3 different burgundy plaids
- ✦ Scraps of a variety of blue, tan, cream and red/burgundy plaids
- ✦ 6" x 23" muslin rectangle
- ✦ 1/2 yard blue/brown plaid
- ✦ Cotton batting 6" x 23" and 8" x 8"
- ✦ Neutral color all-purpose thread
- ✦ Black 6-strand embroidery floss
- ✦ Cream and navy hand-quilting thread
- ✦ 4" x 9" rectangle fusible transfer web
- ✦ 2 yards 1/4" blue cord
- ✦ 3 (5/8") assorted buttons
- ✦ Masking tape or fabric glue
- ✦ Basic sewing tools and supplies

Instructions

Step 1. Cut three 3 1/2" x 4 1/2" rectangles from cream plaid scraps for appliqué background.

Step 2. Trace the heart pattern given onto the paper side of the fusible transfer web; cut out shapes, leaving a margin around each one. Fuse paper shapes to the wrong side of the burgundy plaid scraps; cut out shapes on traced lines. Remove paper backing.

Step 3. Center and fuse a heart shape to the 3 1/2" x 4 1/2" background rectangles.

Step 4. Using 3 strands of black embroidery floss, stitch a buttonhole or blanket stitch around each heart shape.

Step 5. Cut 12 squares plaid scraps 2 1/2" x 2 1/2" for patchwork. Join four squares as shown in Figure 1 to complete a Four-Patch unit; repeat for three units and press.

Figure 1
Join 4 squares
to complete a
Four-Patch unit.

Step 6. Join the Four-Patch units and the appliquéd heart units to make a

patchwork band as shown in Figure 2; press seams away from Four-Patch units.

Figure 2
Join the Four-Patch units and
the appliquéd heart units to
make a patchwork band.

Step 7. Sandwich the 6" x 23" batting rectangle between the 6" x 23" muslin rectangle and the stitched band; pin or baste layers together to hold.

Step 8. Hand-quilt 1/8" around heart shapes using cream hand-quilting thread. Mark an X through the center of each Four-Patch unit; hand-quilt on marked lines using navy hand-quilting thread and stopping stitching 1/4" from edge as shown in Figure 3. Trim muslin and batting even with patchwork band.

Figure 3
Hand-quilt on marked lines
using navy hand-quilting
thread and stopping
stitching 1/4" from edge.

Figure 4
Stitch, catching only the
right side of the band,
leaving batting and muslin
edges unstitched.

Step 9. Fold back muslin and batting layers on short ends and pin out of the way. Fold quilted band with right sides together to make a tube; stitch, catching

only the right side of the band, leaving batting and muslin edges unstitched as shown in Figure 4.

Figure 5
Trim batting layers away
so that when flat, the ends
of the batting butt up
against each other.

1/4"

Figure 6
Turn under 1 muslin layer
1/4" and hand-stitch in
place to cover seam.

Step 10. Trim batting layers away so that when flat, the ends of the batting butt up against each other as shown in Figure 5. Flatten muslin layers over batting; turn under one muslin layer 1/4" and hand-stitch in place to cover seam as shown in Figure 6.

Step 11. Cut an 18" x 21 1/2" rectangle blue/brown plaid. Place short ends right sides together; stitch to make a tube; press seam open.

Step 12. Pin the stitched blue/brown plaid tube right sides together with the top edge of the quilted band; stitch all around. Press seam away from quilted band.

Step 13. Fold the top blue/brown plaid edge to the inside and pin to the wrong side of the bottom edge of the quilted band to create a lining. The exposed area of plaid on the outside of the bag should be approximately 6 3/4".

Step 14. Cut two strips red/burgundy scraps 1 1/2" x 10"; press 1/4" under all around. Pin strips to the bag top 1" from top folded edge and 1/2" from side seam as shown in Figure 7.

Figure 7
Pin strips to the bag top 1" from top folded edge and 1/2" from side seam.

Step 15. Using 3 strands black embroidery floss, buttonhole-stitch or blanket-stitch along long edges of each strip through all layers.

Step 16. Cut two 7 1/2" circles blue/brown plaid and one 7 1/2" circle batting. Sandwich the batting circle between the two fabric circles; baste all around.

Step 17. Turn the bag wrong side out; pin the sandwiched circle to the bottom of the bag, catching all layers of the circle and the quilted band, leaving muslin and blue/brown plaid lining free as shown in Figure 8; stitch.

Figure 8
Pin the sandwiched circle to the bottom of the bag, catching all layers of the circle and the quilted band, leaving muslin and blue/brown plaid lining free.

Step 18. Pull the muslin edge and blue/brown plaid lining over seam allowance; fold edge of blue/brown plaid lining under 1/4" and whipstitch to the bag bottom to enclose seam.

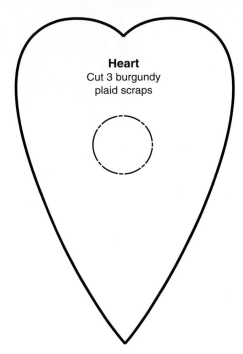

Heart
Cut 3 burgundy
plaid scraps

Step 19. Hand-quilt 1/4" above pieced band to secure layers using navy hand-quilting thread. Sew a 5/8" button in the center of each heart appliqué.

Step 20. Cut two pieces of 1/4" blue cord 36" long. Stiffen the ends of the cord by either applying masking tape to form a needle shape or applying glue to the ends.

Step 21. Insert first cord through the red/burgundy strips, completely encircling top of bag. Secure cord ends by tying a knot or whipstitching ends together as shown in Figure 9. Pull cord through so that the join is hidden under the strip. Repeat with remaining cord.

Figure 9
Whipstitch ends together as shown.

Step 22. To close bag, pull each cord from opposite directions. ✦

Barrel-Bottom Purse
Placement Diagram
7" x 10 3/4"

Baltimore Album Cross-Stitch Quilt

By Judith Sandstrom

Cross-stitched blocks may be used to create a colorful quilt.

Project Specifications

Skill Level: Intermediate

Quilt Size: 20" x 30"

Materials

+ 6 (10 1/2" x 10 1/2") squares 14-count Aida cloth
+ 1/4 yard green print
+ Backing 24" x 34"
+ Batting 24" x 34"
+ Cream all-purpose thread
+ Cream hand-quilting thread
+ Basic sewing tools and supplies

Instructions

Step 1. Fold and crease each 10 1/2" x 10 1/2" square 14-count Aida cloth to mark the center.

Step 2. Starting at the center and working to the outside, refer to the stitching charts to complete the cross-stitch embroidery on each square, including adding the border design given around each stitched center.

Step 3. Carefully straighten and press each cross-stitched block.

Step 4. Join the blocks in rows of two blocks each referring to the Placement Diagram for positioning; press seams open. Join the rows to complete the quilt top; press seams open.

Step 5. Prepare the quilt top for quilting and hand-quilt 1/2" inside of block border design and 1/4" from outside of block border design and as desired using cream hand-quilting thread.

Step 6. When quilting is complete, trim backing and batting even with quilt top.

Step 7. Prepare 3 yards straight-grain binding from green print and bind edges to finish referring to the General Instructions. ✦

Baltimore Album Cross-Stitch Quilt
Placement Diagram
20" x 30"

Floral Wreath

Floral Wreath

■	DMC 895 Dark hunter green
••	DMC 913 Medium Nile green
#	DMC 321 Red
••	DMC 742 Light tangerine

Musical Bluebirds

Musical Bluebirds

- **#** DMC 321 Red
- **··** DMC 742 Light tangerine
- **%** DMC 798 Blue
- **◇** DMC 895 Dark hunter green
- **◆◆** DMC 913 Medium Nile green
- **$** DMC 957 Pale geranium

Vase of Flowers

Vase of Flowers

⊞ DMC 321 Red
•• DMC 742 Light tangerine
⁒ DMC 798 Blue
∞ DMC 895 Dark hunter green
•• DMC 913 Medium Nile green
$ DMC 957 Pale geranium

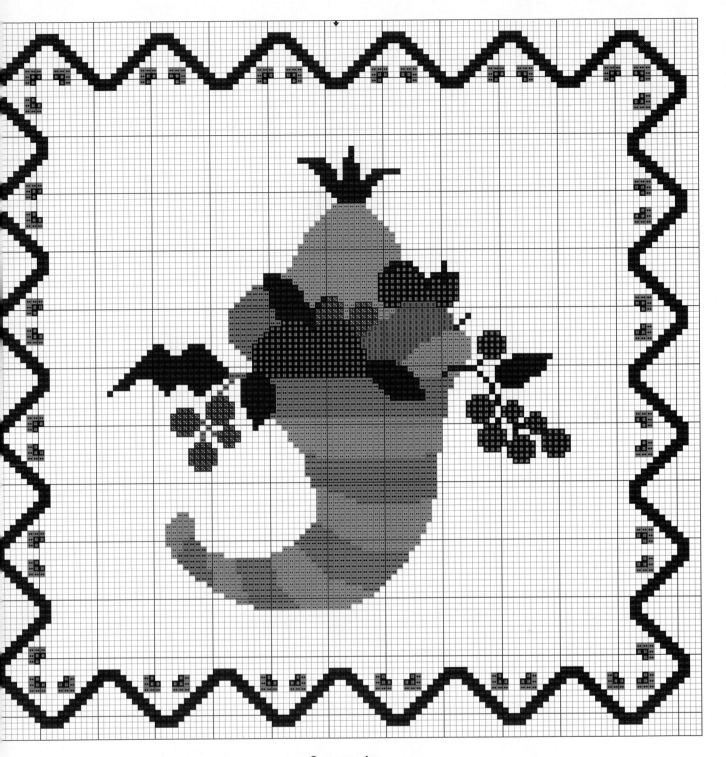

Cornucopia

Cornucopia

- ⌗ DMC 321 Red
- ⣀ DMC 742 Light tangerine
- ⧄ DMC 798 Blue
- ⬟ DMC 895 Dark hunter green
- ⬩⬩ DMC 913 Medium Nile green
- $ DMC 957 Pale geranium

Floral Maze

Floral Maze

▦	DMC 321 Red
••	DMC 742 Light tangerine
▨	DMC 798 Blue
⊠	DMC 895 Dark hunter green
◆◆	DMC 913 Medium Nile green
$	DMC 957 Pale geranium

Jacobean Flowers

Chicken Wall Quilt

By Chris Malone

Fill the pockets in this wall quilt with dried flowers, notepads or other small items.

Project Specifications

Quilt Size: 18 1/2" x 31 1/4"

Block Size: 12" x 12"

Number of Blocks: 1

Chicken
12" x 12" Block

Materials

+ Scraps white-on-white, yellow, orange, red and blue prints
+ 6" x 12" rectangle green tone-on-tone
+ 1 fat quarter lime green tone-on-tone
+ 1 fat quarter blue sky print
+ 1/4 yard black mini dot
+ 1/4 yard black-and-white chicken print
+ 1/4 yard black-and-white print
+ 1/4 yard yellow floral
+ Batting 23" x 35"
+ Backing 23" x 35"
+ All-purpose thread to match fabrics
+ Black hand-quilting thread
+ Black machine-quilting thread
+ Black, white, and light and dark green 6-strand embroidery floss
+ 1/4 yard fusible transfer web
+ 1/8 yard fusible interfacing
+ 1 (1/2") black button
+ 2 (7/8") red buttons
+ 2 (1 1/8") black buttons
+ 4 (3/8") white buttons
+ 1 1/2" x 18 1/2" x 1/4" wooden slat
+ Fabric glue and spray adhesive (optional)

+ 2 (1") sawtooth hangers
+ Basic sewing tools and supplies

Instructions

Step 1. Cut a 12 1/2" x 8" rectangle blue sky fabric and a 12 1/2" x 5" rectangle each lime green tone-on-tone and fusible transfer web.

Step 2. Reverse and trace ground line marked on the chicken pattern on the paper side of the 12 1/2" x 5" piece fusible transfer web. Continue the line in a pleasing curve to each edge as shown in Figure 1.

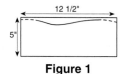

Figure 1
Continue the line in a
pleasing curve to each side.

Step 3. Fuse the marked piece of fusible transfer web to the wrong side of the lime green tone-on-tone rectangle; cut along drawn curved line. Remove paper backing.

Step 4. Place the fused rectangle over the bottom edge of the blue sky fabric rectangle; before fusing top edge of ground in place, check to be sure the unit will be 12 1/2" high after fusing; fuse in place.

Step 5. Reverse and trace the chicken pieces onto the paper side of fusible transfer web. Cut out shapes, leaving a margin around each one.

Step 6. Fuse shapes to the wrong side of fabrics as directed on each one for color; cut out shapes on traced lines. Remove paper backing.

Step 7. Arrange and fuse shapes on the background in numerical order and aligning the background line with line on chicken to help with positioning.

Step 8. Using 2 strands of embroidery floss, embroider a blanket stitch around comb, wattle, tail and body using black floss, and along edge of lime green tone-on-tone edge using light green.

Step 9. Prepare template for pocket piece; cut as directed. Trim 1/4" seam allowance from two shorter sides of each interfacing triangle. Place and fuse an interfacing triangle on wrong side of one half of each

fabric pocket with long edge of interfacing running down the center of the pocket as shown in Figure 2.

Figure 2
Place and fuse an interfacing triangle on wrong side of 1 half of each fabric pocket with long edge of interfacing running down the center of the pocket.

Step 10. Fold each pocket square in half with wrong sides together to make triangles, covering the interfacing as shown in Figure 3.

Figure 3
Fold each pocket square in half with wrong sides together to make triangles, covering the interfacing.

Step 11. Using 2 strands white embroidery floss, blanket-stitch along the folded edge of each pocket piece as shown in Figure 4.

Blanket Stitch

Figure 4
Using 2 strands white embroidery floss, blanket-stitch along the folded edge of each pocket piece.

Step 12. Cut four 6 1/2" x 6 1/2" squares black-and-white chicken print.

Step 13. Place a triangle on each square to make pocket units as shown in Figure 5; baste together along outer edges.

 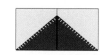

Figure 5
Place a triangle on each square.

Figure 6
Join 2 pocket units.

Step 14. Join two pocket units as shown in Figure 6; press seams open. Repeat for two units.

Step 15. Join the two pocket units as shown in Figure 7; press seam away from pocket pieces.

Step 16. Cut three 1 1/4" x 12 1/2" strips for A and two 1 1/4" x 26 3/4" strips for B black mini dot.

Figure 7
Join the 2 pocket panels.

Step 17. Referring to Figure 8, join the chicken panel and the pocket panel with the A strips; press seams toward A. Add B strips to opposite long sides; press seams toward B.

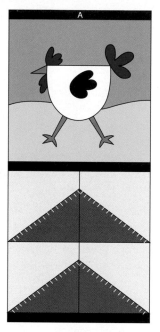

Figure 8
Join the chicken panel and the pocket panel with the A strips.

Step 18. Cut two strips each 3" x 14" for C and 3" x 31 3/4" for D yellow floral. Sew the C strips to the top and bottom, and D strips to opposite long sides of the pieced center; press seams toward strips.

Step 19. Trim batting and backing piece to fit the completed top. Place the batting piece on a flat surface; place the stitched quilt top right side up on the batting. Place the backing piece right sides together with the quilt top; pin layers together to secure.

Step 20. Stitch all around, leaving a 6" opening on one side; clip corners. Turn right side out through opening; press. Hand-stitch opening closed.

Step 21. Prepare templates for the yo-yo circle and leaf pieces using pattern pieces given. Cut yo-yo circles as directed on the pattern.

Step 22. Fold the 6" x 12" rectangle green tone-on-tone in half with right sides together along length; pin to hold. Trace six leaf motifs on the folded fabric, leaving 1/2" between pieces. Machine-stitch along marked lines through both layers, leaving bottom edge open. Cut out leaf shapes, leaving 1/8" seam allowance all around.

Step 23. Turn leaf shape right side out; press to shape.

Step 24. Using 2 strands dark green embroidery floss, make three fly stitches down the center of each leaf referring to Figure 9.

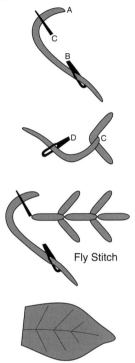

Figure 9
Make 3 fly stitches down the
center of each leaf.

Step 25. Pinch two small pleats at the open edge of each leaf; tack to secure.

Step 26. Referring to Figure 10, finger-press a 1/8" hem along the edge of each yo-yo circle. Using a

Figure 10
Make a yo-yo flower as shown.

double strand of matching all-purpose thread, stitch along the folded edge; pull to gather fabric into a tight circle and knot thread. Do not cut thread.

Step 27. Flatten gathered circles into flower shapes using your fingers. Use the same thread to sew a 3/8" white button in the center of each flower; do not cut thread.

Step 28. Place a flower on the lime green tone-on-tone background referring to the pattern and Placement Diagram for positioning. Hand-stitch in place through all layers. Repeat for the remaining yo-yo flowers.

Step 29. Hand-stitch a 7/8" red button to the top of the pocket centers and the 1/2" black button to the chicken for eye. Hand-quilt in the ditch of the borders and sashing strip using black hand-quilting thread.

Step 30. Cut two 6" x 9" rectangles black-and-white chicken print for hanging tabs. Fold each piece in half with right sides together along length; sew all around, leaving 2" open on one side. Clip corners; turn right side out through opening. Press; hand-stitch openings closed.

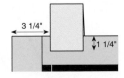
3 1/4"   1 1/4"

Figure 11
Measure and mark 3 1/4" from each
top corner edge. Fold a tab over the
top edge and overlap 1 1/4" on front
and back on marked line.

Step 31. Measure and mark 3 1/4" from each top corner edge. Fold a tab over the top edge and overlap

1 1/4" on front and back on marked line as shown in Figure 11; sew a 1 1/8" black button on the front side through all layers to secure.

Step 32. Cut a 4" x 20" strip black mini dot to cover wooden slat. Apply fabric glue or spray adhesive to one side of the wooden slat and the wrong side of the fabric strip. Center the wooden slat on wrong side of fabric, and bring fabric ends up and over short ends of slat; apply pressure to adhere fabric to wooden slat. If desired, trim off some of the corner fabric before pulling the long edges up and over wood. Fabric overlaps in back. Attach one 1" sawtooth hanger to each end on back of covered slat. Slip slat through fabric tabs to hang. ✦

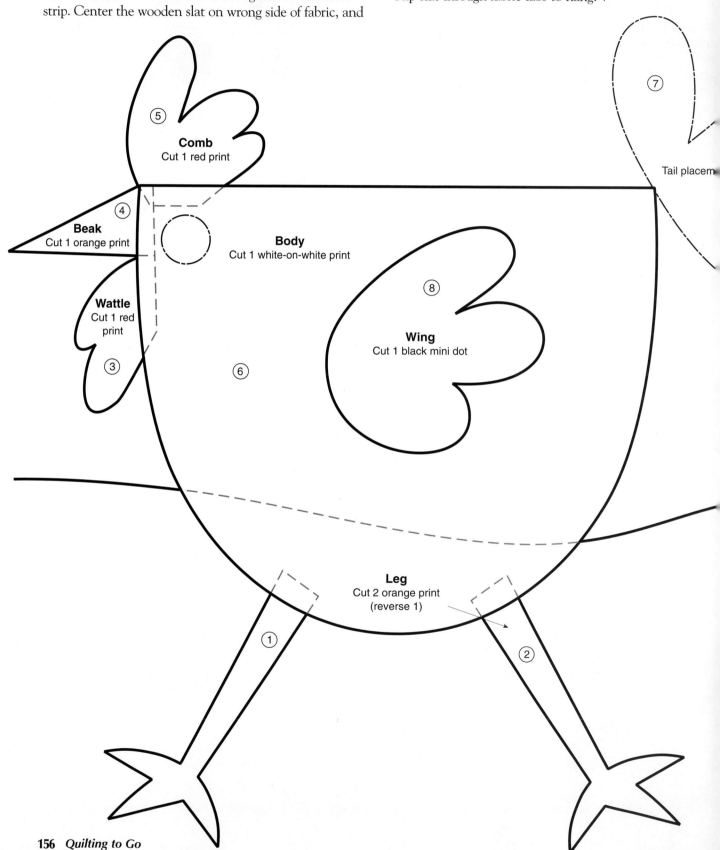

⑦

Tail placem

⑤
Comb
Cut 1 red print

④
Beak
Cut 1 orange print

Body
Cut 1 white-on-white print

⑧
Wing
Cut 1 black mini dot

Wattle
Cut 1 red print

③

⑥

Leg
Cut 2 orange print
(reverse 1)

①

②

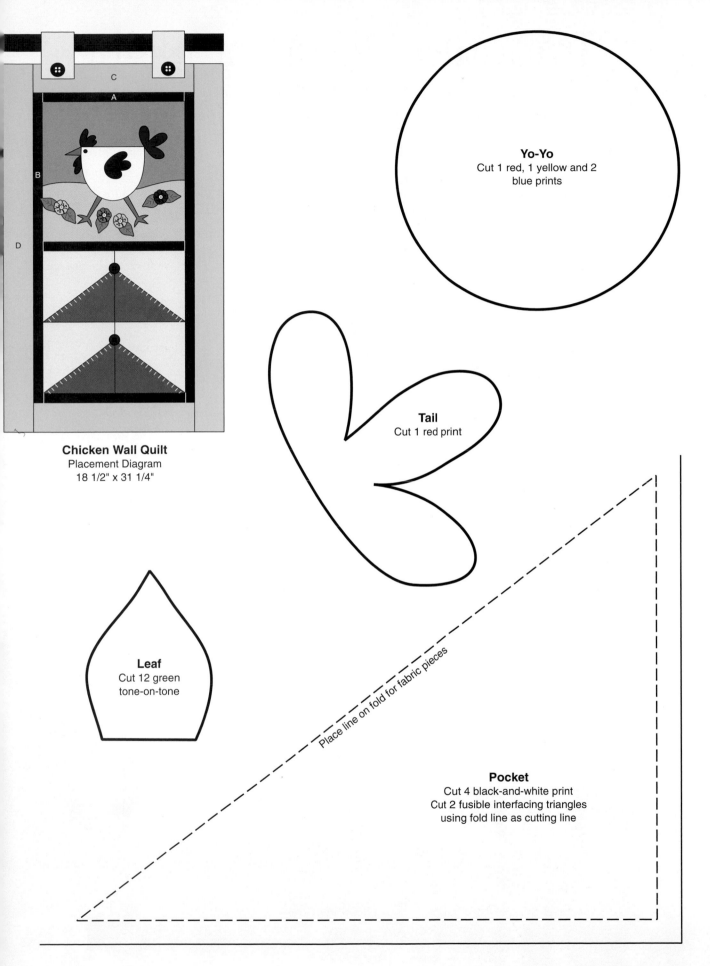

Chicken Wall Quilt
Placement Diagram
18 1/2" x 31 1/4"

Yo-Yo
Cut 1 red, 1 yellow and 2
blue prints

Tail
Cut 1 red print

Leaf
Cut 12 green
tone-on-tone

Place line on fold for fabric pieces

Pocket
Cut 4 black-and-white print
Cut 2 fusible interfacing triangles
using fold line as cutting line

Trapunto Desert at Night

By Donna Friebertshauser

Trapunto using colored yarns is a simple way to highlight a quilted design to make it stand out.

Project Notes

Traditional trapunto is white stitching on white fabric. This type of stitching creates a rich effect but the pattern is not visible from a distance. Trapunto Desert at Night uses colored threads for stitching and colored yarn for the cord to make the design visible.

There are two types of trapunto—padded or corded. The project shown uses the corded method. Both methods require two layers of fabric.

Parallel rows of running stitches are worked first. Then

4-ply yarn is inserted in the stitched channel to fill and color the channel.

Project Specifications

Skill Level: Beginner

Quilt Size: 10" x 9" (stitched area only)

Materials

+ 2 (15" x 13") rectangles white batiste
+ 15" x 13" thin white cotton batting
+ Any color all-purpose thread for basting

+ 1 skein each light, medium and dark green, tan, blue and yellow 6-strand embroidery floss
+ 4-ply worsted-type yarn in yellow, and light, medium and dark green—1/2 yard yellow, 2 yards each light and medium green, and 3 yards dark green
+ Water-soluble fabric marker
+ No. 24 tapestry needle
+ No. 7 embroidery needle
+ Basic sewing tools and supplies

Instructions

Step 1. Test the water-soluble marker on a scrap of fabric to be sure the lines will disappear when the completed trapunto is put in cold water.

Step 2. Accurately trace the design given on one fabric rectangle.

Step 3. Pin the two layers of fabric with wrong sides together. Baste from the center to the corners and sides, and around all sides to hold the layers together.

Step 4. Cut a length of any one of the floss colors; separate into 2 strands. Separate the 2 strands; thread the single strands into the embroidery needle. After threading, pull the strands back together again; knot the end of the thread.

Step 5. Begin stitching at any part of the design using the designated color embroidery floss referring to the color key and colored lines on the stitching diagram.

Step 6. Work a simple, even running stitch of

approximately 1/8" length on the front and a slightly smaller stitch on the back of the fabric. **Note:** *Remove basting stitches as design is stitched. Do not stitch over basting thread.* End stitch with a backstitch on the lining or back fabric inside of a channel. **Note:** *These stitches will be covered by yarn later. Keep parallel rows equidistant to form the channels.* Continue stitching until all lines have been stitched, using only 1 strand of floss to stitch the ground and mountains.

Step 7. To fill the channels, thread the tapestry needle with yarn of the proper color as indicated on the stitching diagram and color key for specific channel; do not knot the yarn.

Step 8. Insert the needle from the wrong side of the fabric through the lining fabric and inside of a channel. Check to be sure that you have not pierced the right side of the fabric.

Step 9. Leaving a yarn tail of approximately 1/4", slide the needle through the channel as far as you can or to the beginning of a curve or point. Bring the threaded needle out through the lining, leave a small loop of approximately 1/8"; re-enter the same hole and continue to fill the channel as shown in Figure 1. Leave a 1/4" tail at the end of the stitching. **Note:** *At a pointed section of the design, bring the needle to the very tip of the point, leave the loop and go back in the same hole.* Fill all channels.

Figure 1
Re-enter the fabric in the same
hole and continue stitching.

Step 10. When stitching is complete, immerse the entire piece in cold water to remove marked lines; rinse several times. Roll in a dry towel to remove excess water; dry flat on a second towel. Press, if desired. **Note:** *The trapunto areas will create some fabric distortion; do not try to press flat.*

Step 11. To frame the trapunto piece, you may choose to use a mat to coordinate with the stitch colors. Purchased frames with mats are available in standard sizes. Select the frame and trim the stitched piece to fit inside. Place

the batting piece on the cardboard provided with the frame and place the stitched piece on top.

Step 12. Using lacing stitches, secure the stitched piece on the padded cardboard as shown in Figure 2.

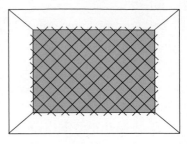

Figure 2
Secure the stitched piece
on the padded cardboard.

Step 13. Place the stitched piece in the frame without glass and secure to finish. **Note:** *The stitched piece may be used as a pillow top or the center of a bordered wall quilt.* ✦

Trapunto Desert at Night
Placement Diagram
10" x 9"
(stitched area only)

COLOR KEY
■ Dark green floss
■ Medium green floss
■ Light green floss
□ Tan floss
■ Blue floss
□ Yellow floss
■ Dark green yarn
■ Medium green yarn
□ Light green yarn
□ Yellow yarn

Full-Size Stitching Diagram
Note color key for stitch colors as marked by stitching lines.

Penny Rug Posy Table Runner

By Pearl Louise Krush

Use wool felt to make an antique-looking runner in the penny rug style.

Project Specifications

Skill Level: Beginner

Runner Size: 19" x 36" (including scallops)

Materials

- ✦ 1/4 yard light gold felt
- ✦ 1/2 yard black felt
- ✦ 1/2 yard burgundy felt
- ✦ 1 yard dark green felt
- ✦ 6–8 skeins burgundy 6-strand embroidery floss
- ✦ Basic sewing tools and supplies

Instructions

Step 1. Make complete pattern for the C and D pieces using pattern given. **Note:** *Add 6 3/4" to marked folded edge when making patterns for C and D.* Cut as directed on patterns.

Step 2. Prepare templates for pieces A and B, and flower pieces using patterns given; cut as directed on each piece.

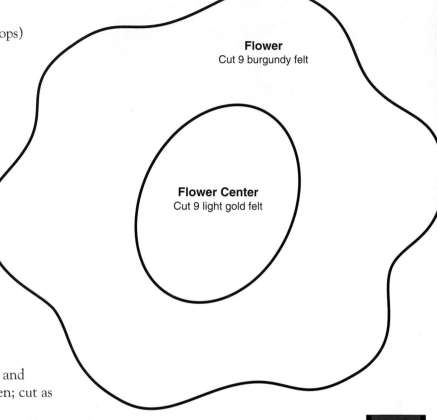

Flower
Cut 9 burgundy felt

Flower Center
Cut 9 light gold felt

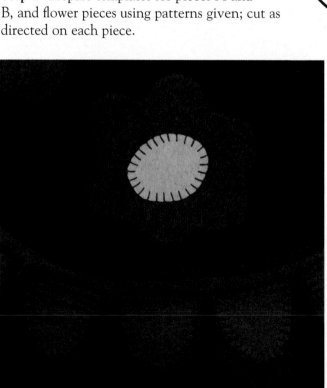

Step 3. Place a B piece on an A piece, matching straight edges as shown in Figure 1.

Step 4. Using 2 strands burgundy embroidery floss, blanket-stitch around the curved edges of the B

Figure 1
Place a B piece on an A piece, matching straight edges.

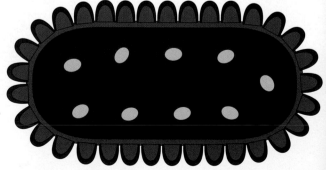

Penny Rug Posy Table Runner
Placement Diagram
19" x 36" (including scallops)

162   *Quilting to Go*

piece to secure on A; repeat to make 33 A-B units.

Step 5. Stitch a flower center to a flower as in Step 4; repeat on all flowers.

Step 6. Arrange the flowers on D referring to the Placement Diagram and photo of project for suggestions. Stitch in place as in Step 4.

Step 7. Evenly space the A-B units around the edge of C; pin in place 1/4" from edge of C. Stitch in place through all layers as in Step 4.

Step 8. Center and baste the appliquéd D layer on C; stitch in place through all layers as in Step 4. Remove basting to finish. ✦

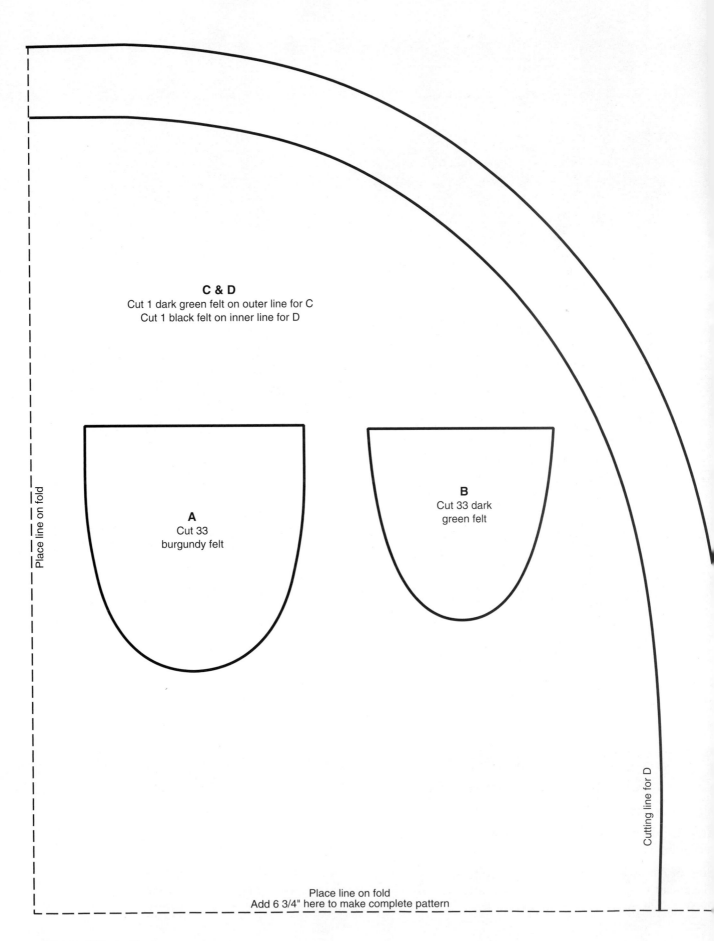

C & D
Cut 1 dark green felt on outer line for C
Cut 1 black felt on inner line for D

A
Cut 33
burgundy felt

B
Cut 33 dark
green felt

Place line on fold

Cutting line for D

Place line on fold
Add 6 3/4" here to make complete pattern

One Block at a Time

If you only have a few minutes a day to quilt, try to complete a block every week or two. You'll be surprised how quickly you can finish a quilt!

Autumn Door Banner

By Connie Kauffman

Trace and cut out the fused motifs wherever you are and finish the project when you get home.

Project Specifications

Skill Level: Beginner
Quilt Size: 12" x 21"

Materials

- Scraps gold, tan, rust, brown and green for appliqué motifs
- 1/8 yard black/gold mottled
- 1/8 yard rust mottled
- 1/4 yard green mottled
- 3/8 yard cream mottled
- Backing 13" x 22"
- Batting 13" x 22"
- Neutral color all-purpose thread
- Cream and green hand-quilting thread
- 1/2 yard fusible transfer web
- Basic sewing tools and supplies

Instructions

Step 1. Cut a 12 1/2" x 13" rectangle cream mottled and a 12 1/2" x 9" rectangle green mottled. Sew the green mottled rectangle to the cream mottled rectangle along the 12 1/2" edges; press seam toward darker fabric.

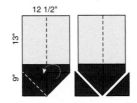

Figure 1
Fold both bottom corners at the center mark and crease to make an angle; cut along crease lines to make angled corners.

Step 2. Fold and crease stitched rectangle to mark the center. Fold both bottom green mottled corners at the center mark and crease to make an angle as shown in Figure 1; cut along crease lines to make angled corners, again referring to Figure 1.

Step 3. Prepare templates for appliqué shapes using

patterns given; trace shapes onto the paper side of the fusible transfer web. Cut out shapes, leaving a margin around each one. **Note:** *Patterns are given in reverse for fusible appliqué.*

Step 4. Fuse shapes to the wrong side of the fabric scraps as directed on patterns for color; cut out shapes on marked lines. Remove paper backing.

Step 5. Arrange the appliqué shapes on the background rectangle referring to the Placement Diagram for positioning. When satisfied with the placement, fuse shapes in place.

Step 6. Trace one set of the large letters and one set of the small letters given on page 10 with the Summer Door Banner on the paper side of the fusible transfer web. Cut out shapes, leaving a margin around each one. Fuse the set of small letters to the wrong side of the rust mottled, the large letters on the wrong side of the black/gold mottled. Cut out letters on traced lines; remove paper backing.

Step 7. Arrange the large letters on the diagonal of the background referring to the Placement Diagram for positioning; fuse in place. Layer the small letters on the fused large letters; fuse in place.

Step 8. Lay the batting on a flat surface; place the backing on the batting with right side up. Place the stitched top right sides together with the backing piece; pin layers together to hold.

Step 9. Machine-stitch around edges of the stitched top using a 1/4" seam allowance, leaving a 3" opening on one side. Trim excess backing and batting even with the stitched top; trim corner points.

Step 10. Turn the stitched unit right side out through the opening; press to make seam edges flat. Hand-stitch the opening closed.

Step 11. Hand-quilt around letters and in a meandering design in the cream mottled area using cream hand-quilting thread and in the green mottled area using green hand-quilting thread.

Step 12. Hand-quilt 1/4" from edge all around using cream hand-quilting thread in the cream mottled area and green hand-quilting thread in the green mottled area.

Step 13. Cut a 3 1/2" x 11 1/2" strip any leftover fabric. Fold under each short end of the strip 1/4" and press; press under 1/4" again and stitch to hem ends.

Step 14. Fold the strip with right sides together along length; stitch along length to make a tube. Turn the tube right side out; press with seam centered to complete a hanging sleeve.

Step 15. Hand-stitch the hanging sleeve to the top backside of the banner, being careful that stitches do not show on the right side. ✦

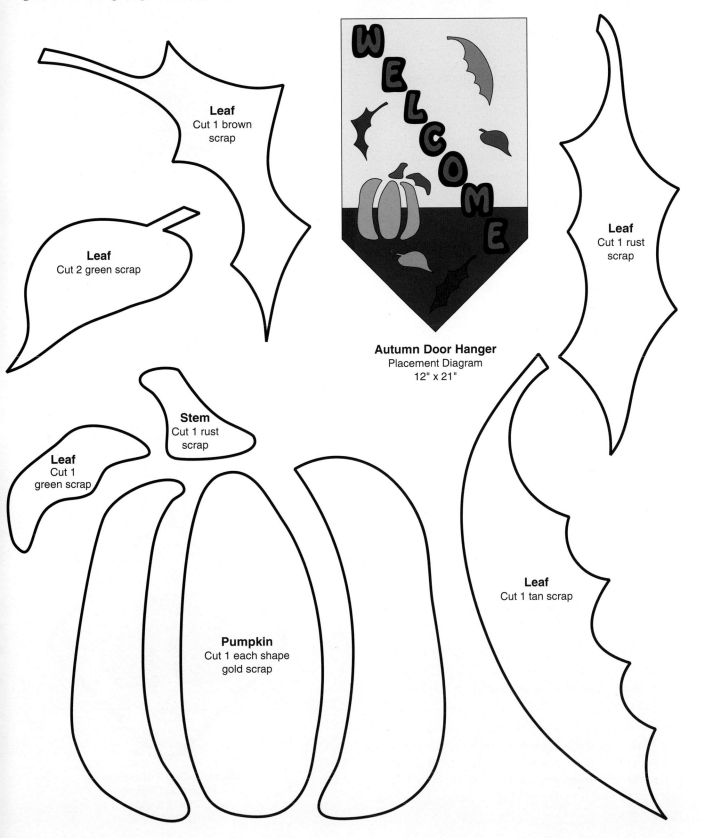

Leaf
Cut 1 brown scrap

Leaf
Cut 2 green scrap

Leaf
Cut 1 rust scrap

Autumn Door Hanger
Placement Diagram
12" x 21"

Stem
Cut 1 rust scrap

Leaf
Cut 1 green scrap

Leaf
Cut 1 tan scrap

Pumpkin
Cut 1 each shape gold scrap

Apple-a-Day Pot Holders

By Marian Shenk

They say "an apple a day keeps the doctor away"—does it work with fabric apples?

Project Specifications

Skill Level: Beginner

Pot Holder Size: 9 1/2" x 9 1/2" (includes binding)

Materials

+ Scraps green and brown
+ 8 different 6" x 6" squares beige-on-beige print scraps
+ 3 different 4" x 8" rectangles red print scraps
+ 2 squares backing 9 1/2" x 9 1/2"
+ 4 squares batting 9 1/2" x 9 1/2"
+ All-purpose thread to match fabrics
+ Cream hand-quilting thread
+ 1 package green wide bias tape
+ Basic sewing tools and supplies

Instructions

Step 1. Cut 16 squares beige-on-beige print 2 3/4" x 2 3/4"; repeat for second pot holder.

Step 2. Join four squares to make a row; press seams in one direction. Repeat for four rows. Join the rows to complete the background for one pot holder as shown in Figure 1; press seams in one direction. Repeat for second pot holder.

Figure 1
Join the rows to complete
the background.

Step 3. Prepare templates for appliqué shapes using patterns given; cut as directed on each piece, adding a 1/8" seam allowance all around when cutting for hand appliqué.

Step 4. Arrange three apple motifs in the center of one background square in numerical order referring to Figure 2. Pin, baste and hand-stitch each piece in place, turning under seam allowance as you stitch and using matching all-purpose thread. Repeat for second pot holder.

Figure 2
Arrange 3 apple motifs in
the center of a background
square in numerical order.

Step 5. Sandwich two pieces of batting between the appliquéd top and one backing square; pin or baste to hold. Hand-quilt around each appliqué motif and in the ditch of background seams using cream hand-quilting thread.

Step 6. When quilting is complete, trim edges even.

Step 7. Cut a 4" length green wide bias tape for loop; fold in half and place in the top corner of one quilted pot holder as shown in Figure 3.

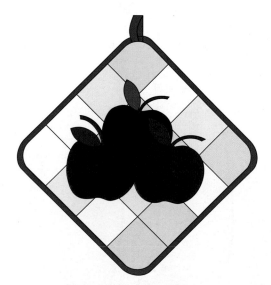

Apple-a-Day Pot Holder
Placement Diagram
9 1/2" x 9 1/2"
(includes binding)

Figure 3
Fold bias tape in half and
place in the top corner of
1 quilted pot holder.

Step 8. Bind edges using green wide bias tape, beginning
at the loop corner and overlapping binding at the beginning and end. Turn bias binding to the backside; hand-
stitch in place. Tack loop edge to the edge of the binding

to cover seam and keep loop in the hanging position as
shown in Figure 4. Repeat for second pot holder. ✦

Figure 4
Tack loop edge to the edge of the
binding to cover seam and keep
loop in the hanging postition.

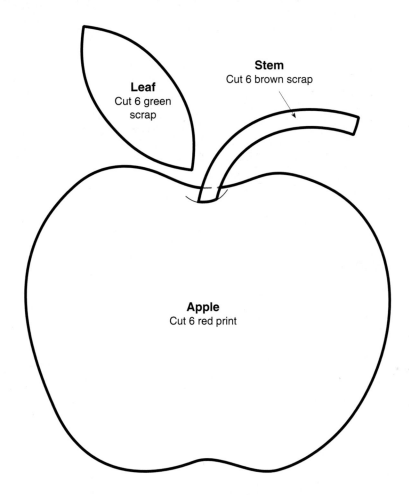

Leaf
Cut 6 green
scrap

Stem
Cut 6 brown scrap

Apple
Cut 6 red print

Add a 1/8" seam allowance all around
when cutting for hand appliqué.

Gone Fishin'

By Holly Daniels

Children in their colorful bathing suits playing at the local pool are like a school of fish in clear blue water.

Project Notes

The sample quilt was made using background C squares to connect units instead of using the B triangles to make blocks as described in the instructions. This method eliminates seams, but makes piecing a bit more complicated. If you prefer to create units instead of blocks, cut two background B squares to create triangles to use at the top and bottom of the rows and cut 21 background C squares to use between fish units.

Project Specifications

Skill Level: Beginner

Quilt Size: 50" x 55"

Block Size: 12" x 6"

Number of Blocks: 24

Materials

+ 1 fat quarter each 12 different bright prints
+ 1 1/8 yards light blue tone-on-tone
+ 2 yards blue print
+ Backing 54" x 59"
+ Batting 54" x 59"
+ Neutral color all-purpose thread
+ Blue hand-quilting thread
+ Variety of 6-strand embroidery floss
+ Basic sewing tools and supplies

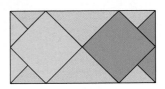

Fish
12" x 6" Block

Instructions

Step 1. Cut two 4 1/4" x 4 1/4" squares from each of the 12 different bright prints for A; cut each A square in half on both diagonals to make A triangles. You will need eight A triangles of each color.

Step 2. Cut three strips 4 1/4" by fabric width blue tone-on-tone; subcut strips into 4 1/4" squares for AA. Cut each AA square in half on both diagonals to make AA triangles. You will need 96 AA triangles.

Step 3. Cut three strips 7 1/4" x 7 1/4" by fabric width blue tone-on-tone; subcut strips into 7 1/4" x 7 1/4" squares for B. Cut each B square on both diagonals to make B triangles. You will need 48 B triangles.

Step 4. Cut four 4 3/4" x 4 3/4" squares from each of the 12 different bright prints for C.

Step 5. To piece one block, sew a bright print A to AA as shown in Figure 1; repeat for 48 A units and 48 AR units. Press seams toward darkest fabric.

Figure 1
Sew a bright print A to AA.

Step 6. Sew a same-fabric A and AR unit to a matching-fabric C square as shown in Figure 2; repeat to make a reverse unit, again referring to Figure 2. Press seams toward C.

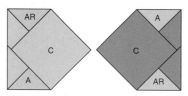

Figure 2
Sew a same-fabric A and AR unit to a matching-fabric C square.

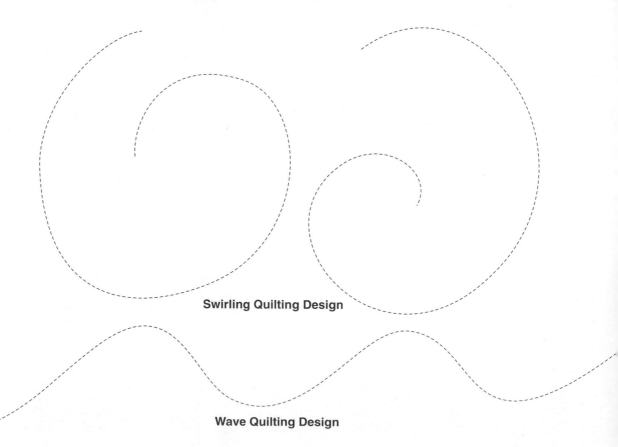

Swirling Quilting Design

Wave Quilting Design

seam open. Repeat for three identical pairs for one block. Join the pairs to create a star shape as shown in Figure 4, again ending stitches 1/4" from outer edge; press seams open. Repeat for six star shapes.

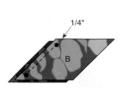

Figure 3
Join 2 identical B pieces, stopping stitching 1/4" from the outer edge.

Figure 4
Join the pairs to create a star shape.

Step 5. Turn under a 1/4" seam allowance all around each star shape; press to hold.

Step 6. Center and pin a pieced star shape on one A square aligning crease lines on A with seams on the star shape as shown in Figure 5; hand-stitch star shape in place all around. Repeat for six blocks.

Figure 5
Center and pin a pieced star shape on 1 A square aligning crease lines on A with seams on the star shape.

Step 7. Referring to Figure 6, join No. 1 and No. 2 fabric C pieces as in Step 4; repeat for six 1-2 C units. Repeat with fabrics 3 and 4, 5 and 6, and 7 and 8 to make six units of each combination. Press seams open.

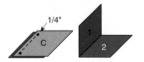

Figure 6
Join No. 1 and No. 2 fabric C pieces.

Step 8. Turn under the 1/4" seam allowance on each C unit as shown in Figure 7; press. **Note:** *Leave seam allowance of edges along right-angle corner unturned.*

Kaleidoscope Stars
Placement Diagram
40" x 60"

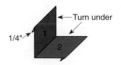

Figure 7
Turn under the 1/4" seam allowance on each C unit.

Step 9. Place a different pressed C unit on each corner of each appliquéd A square with raw edges even as shown in Figure 8; hand-appliqué C units in place to complete the blocks. **Note:** *Place each C unit in the same position on each A square.*

Figure 8
Place a different pieced C
unit on each corner of each
appliquéd A square with
raw edges even.

Step 10. Join two blocks to make a row; repeat for three rows. Press seams open. Join the rows to complete the pieced center; press seams open.

Step 11. Prepare the quilt top for quilting and quilt referring to the General Instructions. **Note:** *The quilt shown was hand-quilted 1/4" away from star points using cream hand-quilting thread.*

Step 12. Prepare 6 yards straight-grain binding from coordinating print and bind referring to the General Instructions. ✦

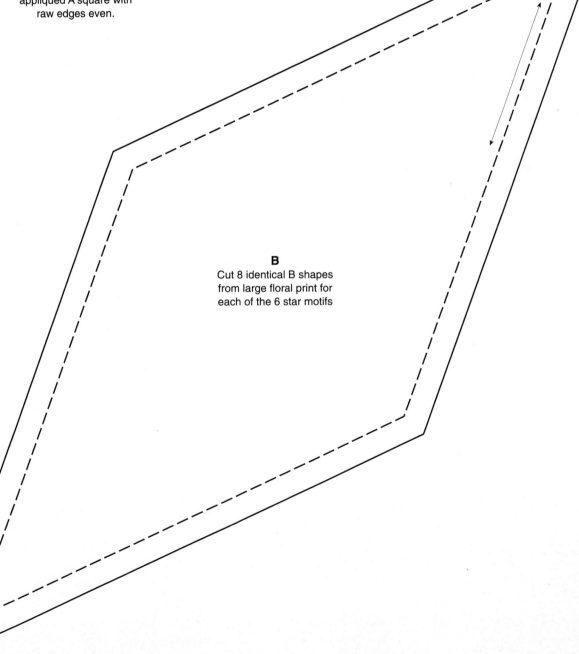

B
Cut 8 identical B shapes
from large floral print for
each of the 6 star motifs

Iris & Tulip Garden

By Judith Sandstrom

Appliquéd fabric tulips and irises make a colorful garden quilt to rival the real thing.

Project Specifications

Skill Level: Intermediate

Quilt Size: 41 1/8" x 52 1/2"

Block Size: 8" x 8"

Number of Blocks: 12

Materials

+ 1/4 yard each dark rose, pink, purple, lavender and gold tone-on-tones
+ 1/3 yard green tone-on-tone
+ 5/8 yard rose tone-on-tone
+ 2/3 yard floral print
+ 2 yards cream tone-on-tone
+ Backing 46" x 57"
+ Thin cotton batting 46" x 57"
+ All-purpose thread to match fabrics
+ Cream hand-quilting thread
+ Basic sewing tools and supplies

Tulip
8" x 8" Block

Iris
8" x 8" Block

Instructions

Step 1. Cut six 4 1/2" by fabric width strips cream tone-on-tone; subcut strips into 4 1/2" square segments for A. You will need 48 A squares.

Step 2. Cut six 8 1/2" x 8 1/2" squares cream tone-on-tone print for B.

Step 3. Cut three 12 5/8" x 12 5/8" squares cream tone-on-tone for C. Cut each square in half on both diagonals to make C triangles. You will need 10 C triangles.

Step 4. Cut two 6 5/8" x 6 5/8" squares cream tone-on-tone for D. Cut the squares in half on one diagonal to make four D triangles.

Step 5. Cut five 3/4" by fabric width strips green tone-on-tone. Subcut strips into twenty-four 4 1/2" pieces for E and twelve 6 1/2" pieces for F.

Step 6. Prepare templates for appliqué shapes using patterns given; cut as directed on each piece, adding a 1/4" seam allowance all around when cutting for hand appliqué. **Note:** *The 1/4" seam allowance has already been added to the straight sides of each piece for matching to edges of A squares.*

Step 7. To complete one Tulip block, pin and baste the raw edge of one tulip shape of each color onto an A square. Hand-stitch in place using matching all-purpose thread, clipping curves and turning under seam allowance on curved edges as you stitch.

Step 8. Press under 1/4" on both long edges of an F strip. Center and pin the F strip along the center diagonal of an A square as shown in Figure 1. Hand-stitch in place along folded edges using matching all-purpose thread; trim ends even with A.

Figure 1
Center and pin the F strip
along the center diagonal
of an A square.

Step 9. Turn under one long edge of two E strips 1/4"; align the remaining raw edge with the raw edge of the A-F unit as shown in Figure 2. Baste along raw edge; hand-stitch in place along folded edge using matching all-purpose thread. Repeat with second E strip on adjacent edge of the A-F unit.

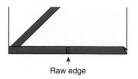

Raw edge

Figure 2
Align the raw edge
of E with the raw
edge of the A-F unit.

Step 10. Join the three tulip units with the A-F-E unit to complete one Tulip block as shown in Figure 3; repeat for six blocks.

Figure 3
Join the 3 tulip units
with the A-F-E unit to
complete 1 Tulip block.

Step 11. Repeat Steps 7–9 using one each purple, lavender and gold tone-on-tone iris shapes and appliquéing a leaf piece at the base of each iris shape as shown in Figure 4. Join the stitched units to complete one Iris block as shown in Figure 5. Repeat for six Iris blocks.

Figure 4
Appliqué a leaf
piece at the base of
each iris shape.

Figure 5
Join the stitched
units to complete
1 Iris block.

Step 12. Join three Iris blocks with two B squares, one C triangle and one D triangle

to make the center diagonal row as shown in Figure 6; press seams toward B, C or D.

Figure 6
Join 3 Iris blocks and 2 B squares with C and
D triangles to make the center diagonal row.

Step 13. Complete remaining diagonal rows with B, C and D pieces and appliquéd blocks as shown in Figure 7; press seams away from appliquéd blocks.

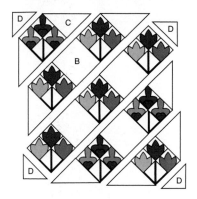

Figure 7
Complete remaining diagonal
rows with B, C and D pieces
and appliquéd blocks.

Step 14. Join the rows with the remaining D triangles to complete the quilt center; press seams in one direction.

Step 15. Cut (and piece) two strips each 4" x 34 5/8" and 4" x 53" floral print. Sew the shorter strips to the top and bottom and longer strips to opposite sides; press seams toward strips.

Step 16. Prepare the quilt top for quilting and quilt referring to the General Instructions. **Note:** *The quilt shown was hand-quilted using the quilting design given in background areas as shown in the Placement Diagram, in the ditch of border seams and 1/4" inside each appliquéd flower shape using cream hand-quilting thread.*

Step 17. Prepare 5 1/2 yards straight-grain binding from rose tone-on-tone and bind referring to the General Instructions. ✦

3 1/2" x 34 1/8"

3 1/2" x 52 1/2"

Iris & Tulip Garden
Placement Diagram
41 1/8" x 52 1/2"

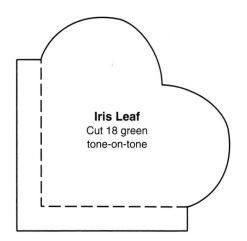

Iris Leaf
Cut 18 green
tone-on-tone

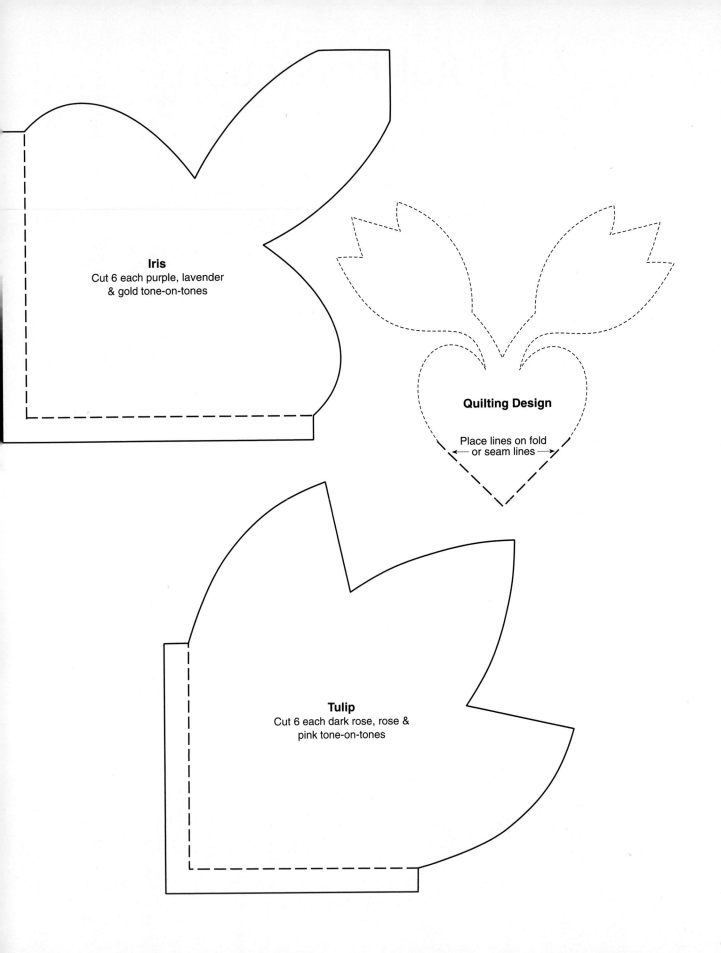

Iris
Cut 6 each purple, lavender
& gold tone-on-tones

Quilting Design

Place lines on fold
← or seam lines →

Tulip
Cut 6 each dark rose, rose &
pink tone-on-tones

Floral Reflections

By Marian Shenk

Make this autumn-look table centerpiece or change the colors to reflect any season of the year.

Project Specifications

Skill Level: Intermediate

Quilt Size: 22" x 14" (includes binding)

Materials

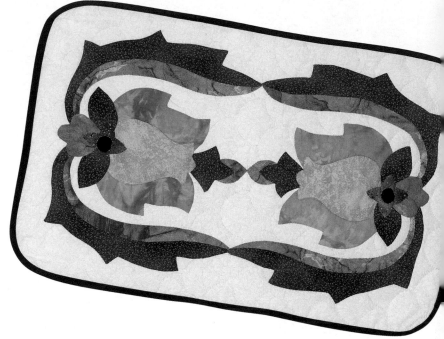

- ✦ Scraps brown solid and brown mottled
- ✦ 1 fat quarter each orange, gold, medium and dark green tone-on-tones or mottleds
- ✦ 1/2 yard cream tone-on-tone
- ✦ Backing 26" x 18"
- ✦ Batting 26" x 18"
- ✦ All-purpose thread to match fabrics
- ✦ Cream hand-quilting thread
- ✦ 1 package brown wide bias tape
- ✦ Basic sewing tools and supplies

Instructions

Step 1. Cut a 22" x 14" rectangle cream tone-on-tone for background; fold and crease to mark the center.

Step 2. Prepare templates for appliqué shapes using patterns given; cut as directed on each piece, adding a 1/8"–1/4" seam allowance all around when cutting for hand appliqué.

Step 3. Prepare fabric patches for hand appliqué referring to the General Instructions.

Step 4. Place one E piece on background with finished tip touching the exact center; continue placing pieces for each motif in numerical order referring to Figure 1; pin or baste in place.

Step 5. Hand-appliqué pieces in place in numerical order using all-purpose thread to match fabrics. Repeat for two motifs. Remove pins or basting.

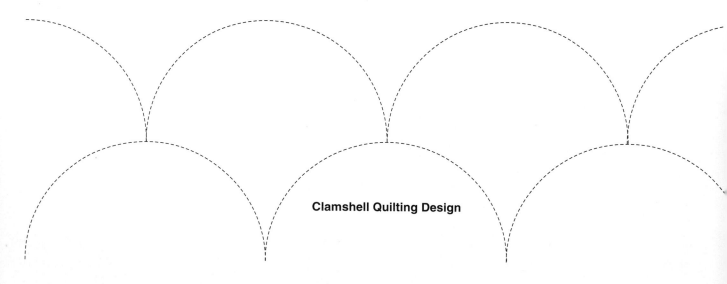

Clamshell Quilting Design

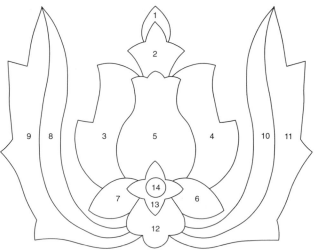

Figure 1
Appliqué pieces in place
in numerical order.

Step 6. Mark the background area with the clamshell quilting design given.

Step 7. Prepare top for quilting and quilt on marked lines and as desired referring to the General Instructions. **Note:** *The sample project was hand-quilted in the clamshell pattern and close to edges of each appliqué shape using cream hand-quilting thread.*

Step 8. When quilting is complete, remove pins or basting. Trim edges even and round corners using pattern given. Bind edges with brown wide bias tape referring to the General Instructions to finish. ✦

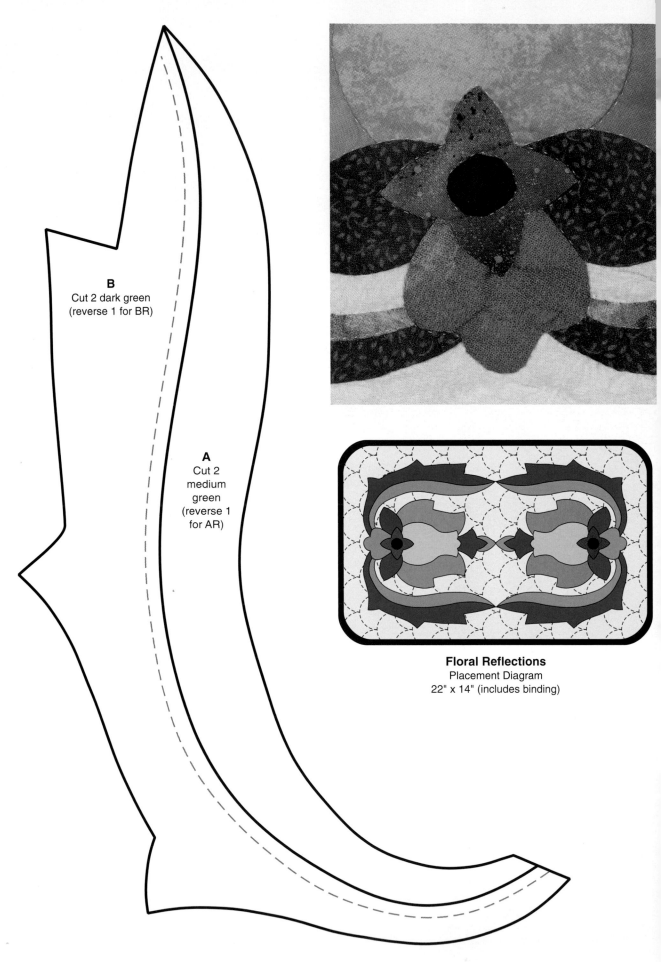

B
Cut 2 dark green
(reverse 1 for BR)

A
Cut 2
medium
green
(reverse 1
for AR)

Floral Reflections
Placement Diagram
22" x 14" (includes binding)

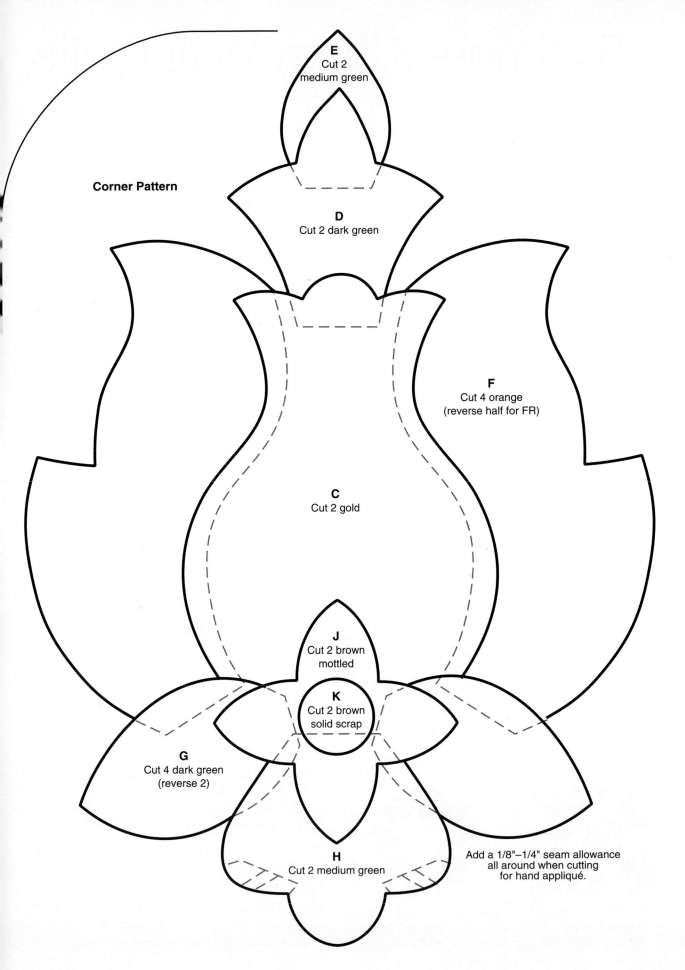

Corner Pattern

E
Cut 2
medium green

D
Cut 2 dark green

F
Cut 4 orange
(reverse half for FR)

C
Cut 2 gold

J
Cut 2 brown
mottled

K
Cut 2 brown
solid scrap

G
Cut 4 dark green
(reverse 2)

H
Cut 2 medium green

Add a 1/8"–1/4" seam allowance
all around when cutting
for hand appliqué.

Baltimore Album Wall Quilt

By Barbara Clayton

Traditional red and green fabrics are used for the appliqué on a light background in this complicated wall quilt.

Project Specifications

Skill Level: Advanced
Quilt Size: 38" x 38" without scallop borders
Block Size: 12" x 12"
Number of Blocks: 4

Materials

+ 1/8 yard gold mottled
+ 1/4 yard each light and dark red mottleds
+ 3/4 yard each 2 different white-on-white prints
+ 3/4 yard white-on-white stripe
+ 1 yard red solid
+ 1 yard green mottled
+ 1 1/2 yards white solid for backing
+ Batting 40" x 40"
+ All-purpose thread to match fabrics
+ White hand-quilting thread
+ 2 yards lightweight fusible interfacing
+ 1/4" and 3/8" bias bars

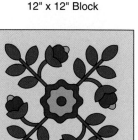

Basket
12" x 12" Block

Bow
12" x 12" Block

Ohio Rose
12" x 12" Block

Wreath
12" x 12" Block

+ Card stock
+ Basic sewing tools and supplies, and 14"-square tracing paper

Preparing Bias Stems

Step 1. Cut six 1" x 36" bias strips from green mottled.

Step 2. Fold each bias strip in half with wrong sides together; stitch 1/4" from raw edges along length. Trim seam to 1/8".

Step 3. Insert the 1/4" bias bar inside the tube, rolling seam to the back, and press as shown in Figure 1; continue pushing the bar through the tube, pressing as you go.

Figure 1
Insert the 1/4" bias bar
inside the tube, rolling seam
to the back, and press.

Step 4. Cut 1 1/4"-wide bias strips from red solid and join as shown in Figure 2 to equal 2 yards for basket and bow. Repeat Steps 2 and 3 using the 3/8" bias bar.

Figure 2
Join strips on short ends.

Preparing Pieced Border Units

Step 1. Cut four 3" x 40" strips red solid for scallop border; set aside.

Step 2. Cut three 2 3/8" by fabric width strips red solid. Cut two strips each 2 3/8" by fabric width white-on-white prints. Subcut strips into 2 3/8" segments. You will need 17 of each white-on-white print and 34 red solid squares.

Step 3. Draw a diagonal line on the wrong side of each white-on-white print square.

Step 4. Place a red solid square right sides together with a white-on-white print square. Stitch 1/4" on each side of the drawn line as shown in Figure 3; cut apart on the drawn line and press open to reveal two

triangle/square units as shown in Figure 4. You will need a total of 68 units.

Figure 3
Stitch 1/4" on each
side of the drawn line.

Figure 4
Cut apart on the drawn line
and press open to reveal 2
triangle/square units.

Step 5. Join 16 triangle/square units to make a strip as shown in Figure 5; press seams in one direction. Repeat for two 16-unit strips and two 17-unit strips.

Figure 5
Join triangle/square units to make strips.

Step 6. Sew one of the remaining units to one end of each of the 17-unit strips as shown in Figure 6; press seams in one direction.

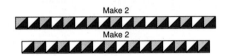

Figure 6
Sew 1 of the remaining units to 1
end of each of the 17-unit strips.

Step 7. Set aside pieced border strips.

Preparing Appliqué Pieces

Step 1. Prepare templates for each appliqué shape using full-size patterns given, except flower center.

Step 2. Trace the shapes onto the smooth side of the lightweight fusible interfacing as directed on each piece, leaving at least a 1/4" seam allowance margin between pieces when tracing.

Step 3. Cut out interfacing shapes, leaving 1/4" seam allowance around cut shapes.

Step 4. Pin the interfacing shapes with the fusible side on the right side of the fabrics as directed on each piece for number to cut of each fabric; do not cut out shapes.

Step 5. Stitch all the way around each shape except leave straight end open on the rosebud centers. Trim away excess fabric to a 1/8" seam allowance, clipping curves and trimming points as shown in Figure 7.

Figure 7
Trim away excess fabric to a
1/8" seam allowance, clipping
curves and trimming points.

Step 6. Make a small slit in the center of the interfacing side only, as shown in Figure 8; turn right side out through slit and smooth seams and points. **Note:** *Fusible side of interfacing should be on the outside of the backside of each piece.*

Figure 8
Make a small slit in
the center of the
interfacing side only.

Step 7. To prepare flower center circles, cut card-stock circles as directed on pattern. Cut eight gold mottled and six light red mottled fabric circles 1/4" larger all around using card-stock circle as pattern.

Step 8. Hand-sew a knotted basting stitch around each circle a scant 1/4" from the edge referring to Figure 9. Insert a card-stock circle and pull the thread tight. Press, cut the thread and remove the card-stock circle.

Figure 9
Hand-sew a knotted basting stitch
around each circle a scant 1/4"
from the edge. Insert a card-stock
circle and pull the thread tight.

Appliquéing Blocks

Step 1. Using patterns given, transfer complete block patterns to paper, overlapping or reversing patterns as needed. **Note:** *Each pattern is symmetrical and therefore half of each block pattern is given. Trace one half, pick up the pattern, reverse and trace the second half, connecting dashed lines in the center.*

Step 2. Cut two 12 1/2" x 12 1/2" squares from each white-on-white print for background; fold and crease to mark the centers.

Step 3. Center and pin the traced paper Ohio Rose pattern to the wrong side of one background square with drawing side touching the wrong side of the square; transfer design to the background square. Repeat with the Basket on the same-fabric background square, and the Bow and Wreath patterns on the remaining background squares.

Baltimore Album Wall Quilt
Placement Diagram
38" x 38"
(without scallop borders)

Step 4. Cut the prepared green mottled bias to lengths shown on patterns, leaving enough at each end to tuck under appliqué shapes. Pin and hand-stitch the bias stem pieces to the background blocks using matching all-purpose thread.

Step 5. Pin remaining appliqué shapes in place, placing each motif in numerical order referring to patterns for order and color of flowers. Hand-stitch in place as for bias stem pieces. **Note:** *Always use a red flower center on a gold flower shape and a gold flower center on a red flower shape.*

Step 6. For Basket block, use the red bias for the outline of the basket and the woven lines, and refer to pattern for strip lengths and placement.

Step 7. For Bow block, the bow is formed with the red bias. Cut the pieces to match the pattern. Fold the small knot piece to enclose the raw ends of the two loops. Tuck the tie ends under the bow. Fold the tie ends under on a diagonal slant and stitch in place.

Completing the Quilt Top

Step 1. Join two appliquéd blocks to make a row referring to the Placement Diagram for positioning; repeat for two rows. Press seams open.

Step 5. Sew two border strips to opposite sides of the quilt center; press seams toward strips. Sew a corner square to each end of the remaining strips, positioning fabric squares as shown in the Placement Diagram; press seams toward corner squares. Sew these strips to the remaining sides of the quilt center; press seams toward strips.

Step 6. Center and arrange bias stem pieces in a curving design along each border strip referring to the Placement Diagram for positioning; pin and stitch in place.

Step 7. Appliqué leaves, rosebud and corner flower shapes in place, again referring to the Placement Diagram for positioning of pieces. *Note: Use light red mottled rosebuds and dark red mottled large flowers for border appliqué.*

Step 2. Join the rows to complete the center; press seams open.

Step 3. Sew a 16-unit border strip to the top and bottom and the 18-unit strips to opposite sides referring to Figure 10 for positioning of strips. Press seams toward strips.

Figure 10
Sew a 16-unit border strip to the top and bottom and the 18-unit strips to opposite sides.

Step 4. Cut four 6" x 27 1/2" strips white-on-white stripe. Cut two 6" x 6" squares from each white-on-white print for border corners.

Finishing

Step 1. Fold each previously cut 3" x 40" strip red solid in half along length with right sides together; press.

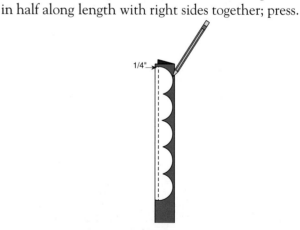

Figure 11
Align the straight edge of the template with the raw edges of 1 strip, leaving a 1/4" seam allowance at the end; trace the scallops, moving the template along.

Step 2. Prepare template for scallop piece using pattern given. Align the straight edge of the template with the raw edges of one strip, leaving a 1/4" seam allowance at the end; trace the scallops, moving the template along as shown in Figure 11 and tracing until there are 19 scallops on the strip. Leave a 1/4" seam allowance at the end of the strip and trim excess strip; repeat for four strips.

Step 3. Stitch along the marked line through both fabric layers as shown in Figure 12. Trim a 1/8" seam allowance, clipping into inverted points almost to the stitching line and clipping into curved areas as shown in Figure 13.

Figure 12
Stitch along the marked line
through both fabric layers.

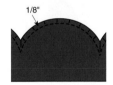

Figure 13
Trim a 1/8" seam allowance, clipping into
inverted points almost to the stitching
line and clipping into curved areas.

Step 4. Turn the strip right side out. Smooth out curved scallops at seams; press to make smooth edges. Repeat for four scallop strips.

Step 5. Pin a scallop strip to each side of the quilt top as shown in Figure 14; machine-baste in place 1/8" from edge.

Figure 14
Pin a scallop strip to each
side of the quilt top.

Step 6. Cut a backing piece from white solid using finished top as a pattern. Pin the backing square right sides together with the completed top. Pin the batting square to the wrong side of the quilt top; trim batting

even with stitched top. Stitch all around through all layers, leaving a 6" opening on one side.

Step 7. Trim corners; turn right side out through opening. Flatten scallop borders; press entire top flat. Turn in seam allowance at opening; hand-stitch opening closed.

Step 8. Quilt as desired by hand or machine. **Note:** *The sample project was hand-quilted in the ditch of all seams, around each appliqué shape, 1/4" from border seams, 1/4" from each border appliqué shape and in a 3/4" diagonal grid in the background of the blocks as shown in Figure 15 using white hand-quilting thread.* ✦

Figure 15
Mark a 3/4" diagonal grid on the
background blocks as shown.

Add a 1/8"–1/4"
seam allowance
all around when cutting
for hand appliqué.

1/2 Ohio Rose Block Pattern
Use light red mottled rosebuds, gold
mottled small flower and dark red
mottled large flower. Place each
rosebud and leaf motif in the order
shown, then the flower motif.

dark red

gold

light red

Place line on fold

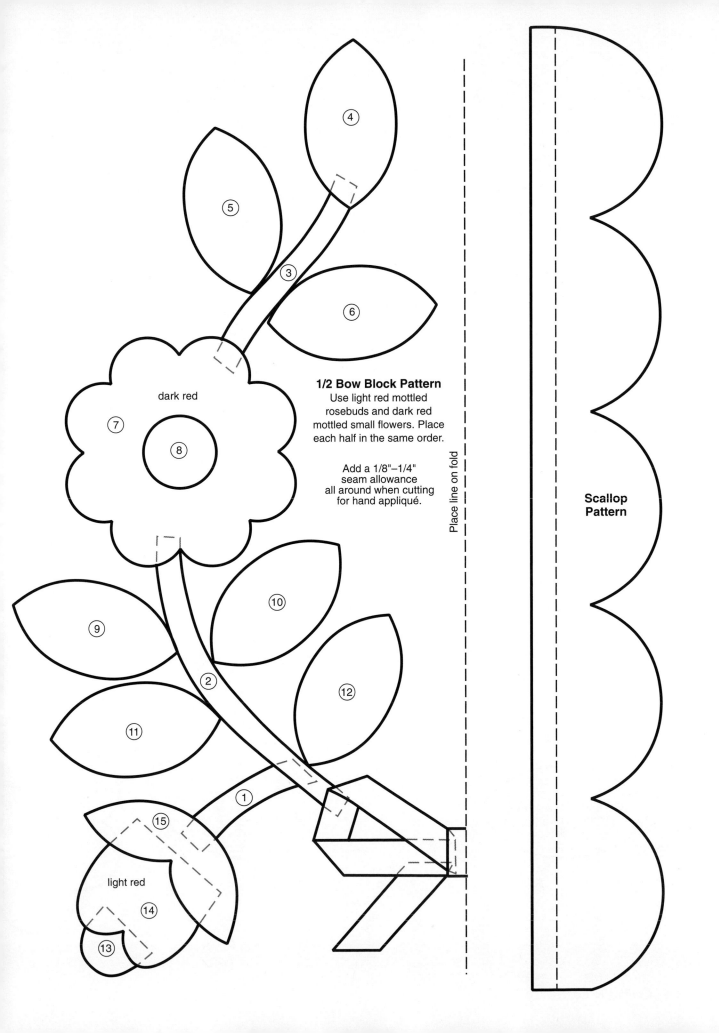

1/2 Bow Block Pattern
Use light red mottled
rosebuds and dark red
mottled small flowers. Place
each half in the same order.

Add a 1/8"–1/4"
seam allowance
all around when cutting
for hand appliqué.

Place line on fold

dark red

light red

Scallop Pattern

Small Flower
Cut 14 lightweight interfacing, 2
dark red mottled & 6 each light red
and gold mottleds

Flower Center
Cut 14 card stock

dark red

1/2 Wreath Block Pattern
Use dark red mottled small flowers.
Place each half in the same order.

Add a 1/8"–1/4"
seam allowance
all around when cutting
for hand appliqué.

Place line on fold

Leaf
Cut 155 each lightweight
interfacing & green
mottled

1/2 Basket Block Pattern

Use dark red mottled rosebuds, 1 gold and 2 light red mottled small flowers and a dark red mottled large flower. Place each half in the same order with the large flower motif last.

dark red

Add a 1/8"–1/4" seam allowance all around when cutting for hand appliqué.

light red

dark red

gold

Place line on fold

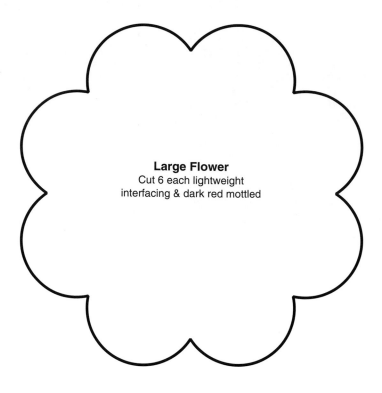

Large Flower
Cut 6 each lightweight
interfacing & dark red mottled

Add a 1/8"–1/4"
seam allowance
all around when cutting
for hand appliqué.

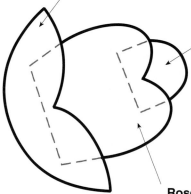

Double Leaf
Cut 28 each lightweight
interfacing & green mottled

Rosebud Center
Cut 28 each lightweight
interfacing & gold mottled

Rosebud
Cut 28 lightweight interfacing, 2 dark
red mottled & 26 light red mottled

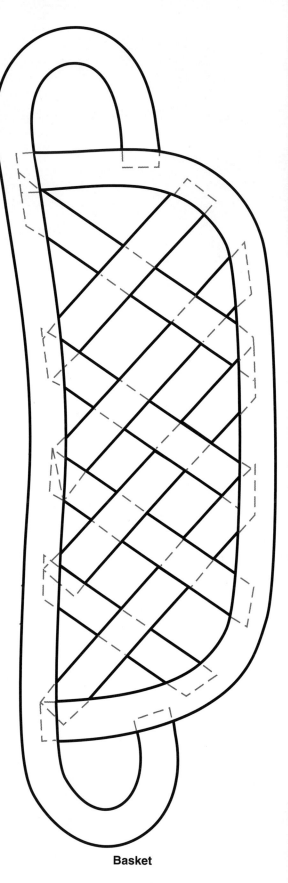

Basket

Spring Bouquet Pillow

By Marian Shenk

Shadow appliqué creates a soft, pastel look in this pretty pillow design.

Project Specifications

Skill Level: Intermediate
Pillow Size: 16" x 16" without ruffle

Materials

✦ Scraps tan, blue, bright pink, orchid and yellow solids
✦ 1 fat quarter bright green solid
✦ 1/2 yard blue moiré
✦ 1 yard white voile
✦ 13 1/2" x 13 1/2" square bleached muslin
✦ All-purpose thread to match fabrics
✦ Purple, gold, yellow, pink and green 6-strand embroidery floss
✦ 16" x 16" pillow form
✦ 2 1/2 yards 1/8"-wide blue satin ribbon
✦ 2 yards 1 1/2"-wide white lace
✦ Fabric glue stick
✦ Basic sewing tools and supplies, tracing paper and marking pen

Instructions

Step 1. Using the half pattern on page 202, prepare full-size drawing of the appliqué motif as shown in Figure 1.

Figure 1
Prepare a full-size drawing of the appliqué motif repeating the floral unit.

Step 2. Center and transfer the full-size pattern to the bleached muslin square.

Step 3. Prepare templates for appliqué shapes as directed on patterns; do not add a seam allowance.

Step 4. Place a dab of fabric glue on each cut patch. Lay the cut patches on the marked square in numerical order referring to Figure 1. Apply pressure to secure glue stick areas.

Step 5. Cut a 13 1/2" x 13 1/2" square white voile. Center the square on the bleached muslin square with glued patches being careful not to move any of the pieces. Carefully pin the voile in place; baste to hold and remove pins.

Step 6. Making stitches small and even, stitch close to the edge of each fabric shape using 2 strands of embroidery floss to match the fabric to secure each shape in place referring to Figure 2. Remove basting; press.

Figure 2
Stitch close to the edge of each fabric shape using 2 strands of embroidery floss to match the fabric to secure each shape in place.

Step 7. Referring to patterns for placement, add buttonhole stitches around the flower centers and straight stitches to flower centers using 2 strands gold embroidery floss. Add straight stitches around flower centers using 2 strands of embroidery floss to match flower fabric. Add straight stitches to buds and leaves using 2 strands of matching embroidery floss.

Step 8. Cut two 16 1/2" x 16 1/2" squares blue moiré. Center the stitched section on one of the squares; turn under raw edges of stitched section and hand-stitch to the blue moiré square.

Step 9. Place the 1 1/2"-wide white lace over the

stitched edge, pleating corners; machine-stitch in place all around, beginning and ending at a corner with a pleat to hide ends.

Step 10. Cut a 53" length 1/8"-wide blue satin ribbon and place on the stitched lace over stitched line; zigzag the ribbon in place with matching all-purpose thread as shown in Figure 3, and beginning and ending at a corner.

Figure 3
Zigzag the ribbon in place with
matching all-purpose thread.

Step 11. Cut four 8" pieces 1/8"-wide blue satin ribbon; tie each length into a small bow. Hand-stitch a bow in place at each corner referring to Figure 4.

Figure 4
Hand-stitch a bow in
place at each corner.

Step 12. Cut three 5" by fabric width strips white voile; join strips on short ends to make one long length. Press seams open. Press strip in half along length with wrong sides together to make a double-layer for ruffle.

Step 13. Sew a double line of large machine gathering stitches inside the 1/4" seam allowance all around the ruffle tube. Divide the tube into four equal sections and place a pin at each division. Pull threads to gather, matching pins with corners of stitched top. Distribute gathers evenly; machine-baste ruffle in place.

Spring Bouquet Pillow
Placement Diagram
16" x 16"
(without ruffle)

Step 14. Place the second 16 1/2" x 16 1/2" square blue moiré right sides together with the pinned pillow top; stitch all around, leaving an 8" opening on one side.

Step 15. Turn right side out through opening, pushing out corners and flattening edges; insert pillow form.

Step 16. Hand-stitch opening closed to finish. ✦

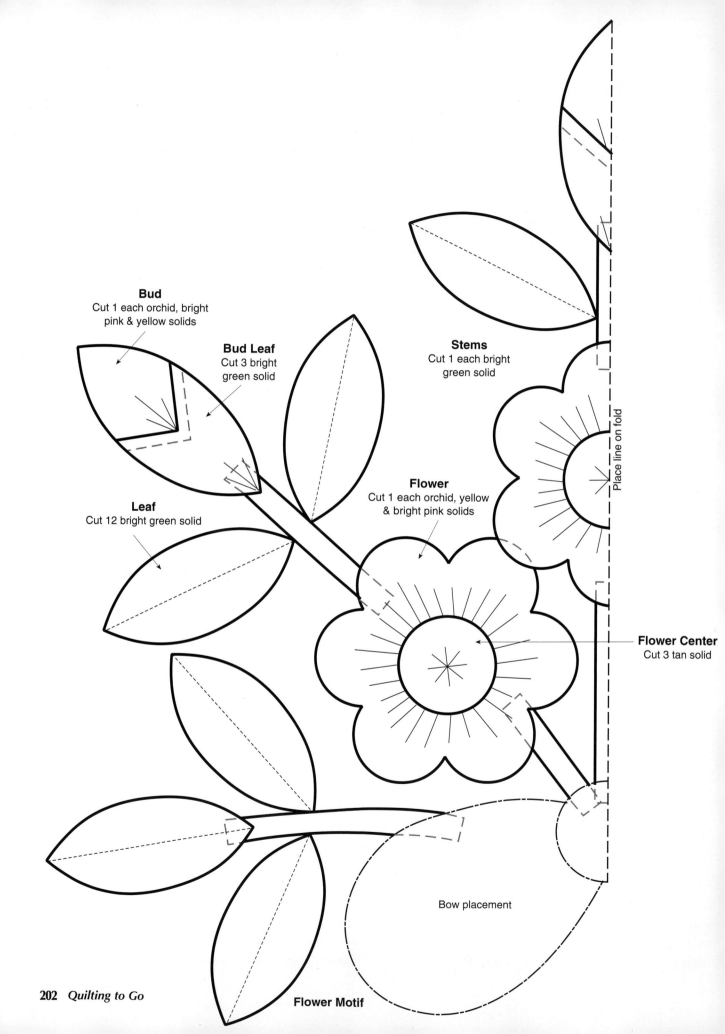

Bud
Cut 1 each orchid, bright
pink & yellow solids

Bud Leaf
Cut 3 bright
green solid

Stems
Cut 1 each bright
green solid

Leaf
Cut 12 bright green solid

Flower
Cut 1 each orchid, yellow
& bright pink solids

Place line on fold

Flower Center
Cut 3 tan solid

Bow placement

Flower Motif

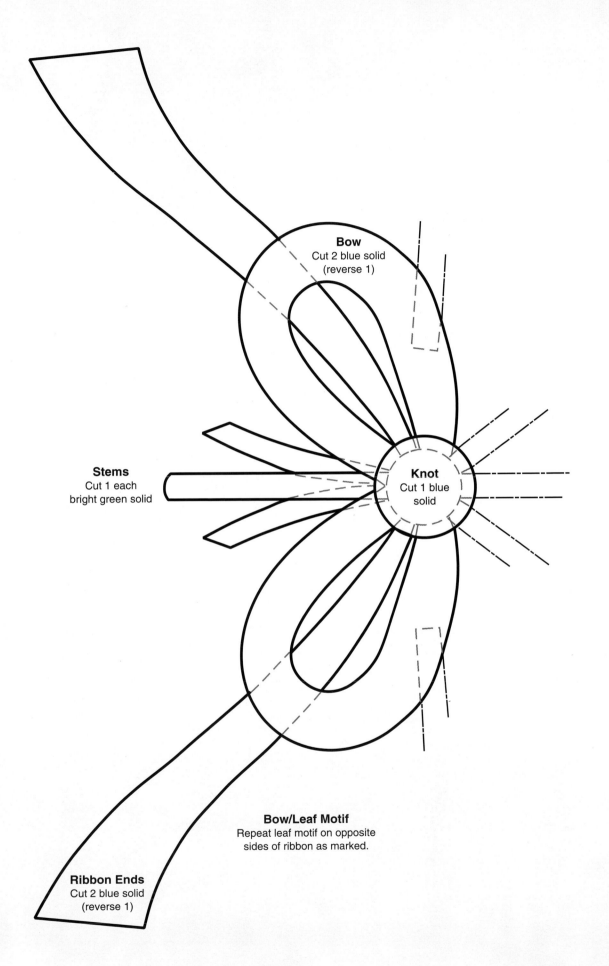

Bow
Cut 2 blue solid
(reverse 1)

Knot
Cut 1 blue
solid

Stems
Cut 1 each
bright green solid

Bow/Leaf Motif
Repeat leaf motif on opposite
sides of ribbon as marked.

Ribbon Ends
Cut 2 blue solid
(reverse 1)

Baltimore Album Flower Basket

By Marian Shenk

Tackle Baltimore-Album-style appliqué in a small wall quilt.

Project Specifications

Skill Level: Advanced
Quilt Size: 28" x 28"

Materials

- Scraps light, medium and dark greens for leaves
- Scraps yellow, gold, lavender and purple for flowers
- Scraps tan and rust for basket
- 1 fat quarter dark green solid for stems
- 1/4 yard each medium and dark rose mottleds
- 1 1/4 yards gray tone-on-tone
- 6 yards 1 1/4"-wide stripe for framing
- Backing 32" x 32"
- Batting 32" x 32"
- All-purpose thread to match fabrics
- Cream hand-quilting thread
- Yellow, brown, green and gold 6-strand embroidery floss
- 2 packages green wide bias tape
- Basic sewing tools and supplies

Instructions

Note: Use all-purpose thread to match fabrics for all hand appliqué.

Step 1. Cut a 16 1/2" x 16 1/2" square gray tone-on-tone for background; fold and crease to mark the center.

Step 2. Prepare templates for appliqué shapes using patterns given; cut as directed on each piece, adding a 1/8"–1/4" seam allowance all around when cutting for hand appliqué.

Step 3. Prepare fabric patches for hand appliqué referring to the General Instructions.

Step 4. To prepare basket for appliqué, cut slits in the basket as marked on the pattern; turn under all around to make four 3/8" openings. Lay the rust insert piece under the openings and baste in place as shown in Figure 1. Hand-stitch around openings to secure.

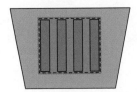

Figure 1
Lay the rust insert piece under the openings and baste in place.

Step 5. Center the basket motif 1 1/4" from edge of background as shown in Figure 2; baste in place, leaving top edges open.

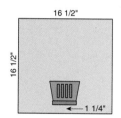

Figure 2
Center the basket motif 1 1/4" from
bottom edge of background; baste
in place, leaving top edges open.

Step 6. Prepare 1 yard 3/8"-wide bias strips from dark green solid. Fold under 1/8" on the long edges of the strip and press to make a 1/8"-wide stem strip. Cut stem pieces from strip referring to the full-size pattern for lengths.

Step 7. Arrange stem pieces above basket shape, tucking one end inside basket top referring to the full-size pattern for placement; hand-stitch stems and then basket shape in place.

Step 8. Arrange appliqué shapes on stems in numerical order, starting with the center floral motif and placing a side flower motif on each side; baste in place. Hand-stitch pieces in place in numerical order.

Step 9. Cut four 18" strips from the 1 1/4"-wide border stripe. Center and sew a strip to each side of the appliquéd center, mitering corners. Press seams toward strips. Trim excess seam at miters; press corner seams open.

Step 10. Cut four 5" x 27" strips gray tone-on-tone. Center and sew a strip to each side of the stitched center, mitering corners. Press seams toward strips. Trim excess seam at miters; press corner seams open.

Step 11. Arrange and baste border corner and center flower and swag motifs on border strips in numerical order, with center of swag pieces 2" from border seams as shown in Figure 3. Hand-stitch in place.

Figure 3
Center swag pieces 2"
from border seams.

Step 12. Center and baste a side flower motif on each strip in numerical order referring to placement lines on swag pieces for positioning; hand-stitch in place.

Step 13. Cut four 28 1/2" strips from the 1 1/4"-wide border stripe. Center and sew a strip to each side of the appliquéd center, mitering corners. Press seams toward strips. Trim excess seam at miters; press corner seams open.

Step 14. Using 1 strand of embroidery floss, straight-stitch the gold tulip centers in green, the bell flower centers in yellow, the corner flower centers in gold and the gold flower centers in brown referring to patterns for placement. Using 2 strands green embroidery floss, stem-stitch stem sections referring to patterns for placement.

Step 15. Remove basting from all stitched areas.

Step 16. Mark the background area in a 1 1/4" diagonal grid referring to Figure 4.

Figure 4
Mark the background area
in a 1 1/4" diagonal grid,

Step 17. Prepare top for quilting and quilt on marked lines and as desired referring to the General Instructions. ***Note:*** *The sample project was hand-quilted on the marked lines, around each appliqué shape, on leaf veins and in an echo pattern of swag shapes using cream hand-quilting thread.*

Step 18. When quilting is complete, remove pins or

basting. Bind edges with green wide bias tape referring to the General Instructions to finish. ✦

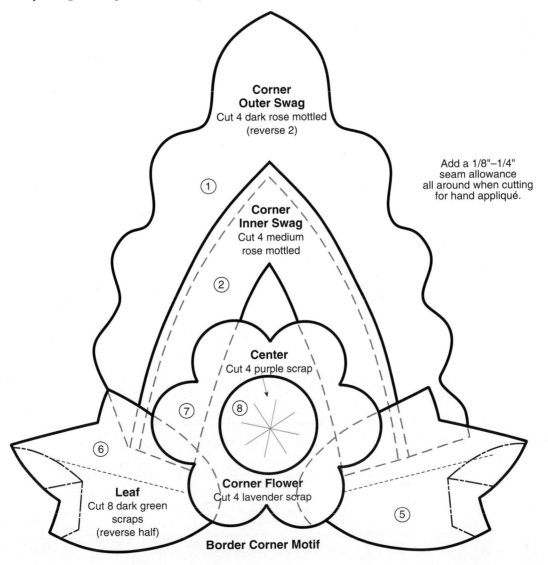

Corner Outer Swag
Cut 4 dark rose mottled
(reverse 2)

Corner Inner Swag
Cut 4 medium rose mottled

Add a 1/8"–1/4"
seam allowance
all around when cutting
for hand appliqué.

Center
Cut 4 purple scrap

Corner Flower
Cut 4 lavender scrap

Leaf
Cut 8 dark green scraps
(reverse half)

Border Corner Motif

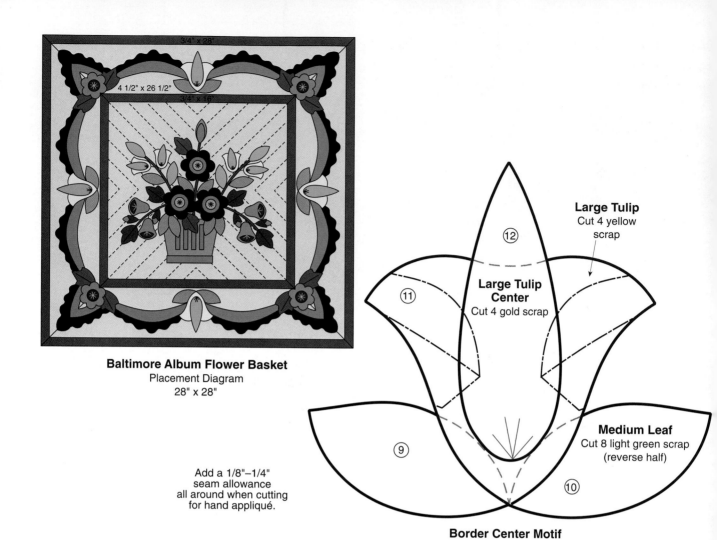

Baltimore Album Flower Basket
Placement Diagram
28" x 28"

3/4" x 28"

4 1/2" x 26 1/2"

3/4" x 16"

Large Tulip
Cut 4 yellow
scrap

⑫

**Large Tulip
Center**
Cut 4 gold scrap

⑪

Add a 1/8"–1/4"
seam allowance
all around when cutting
for hand appliqué.

⑨

Medium Leaf
Cut 8 light green scrap
(reverse half)

⑩

Border Center Motif

Basket
Cut 1 tan
scrap

Insert
Cut 1 rust scrap

Basket Base
Cut 1 rust scrap

Basket Motif

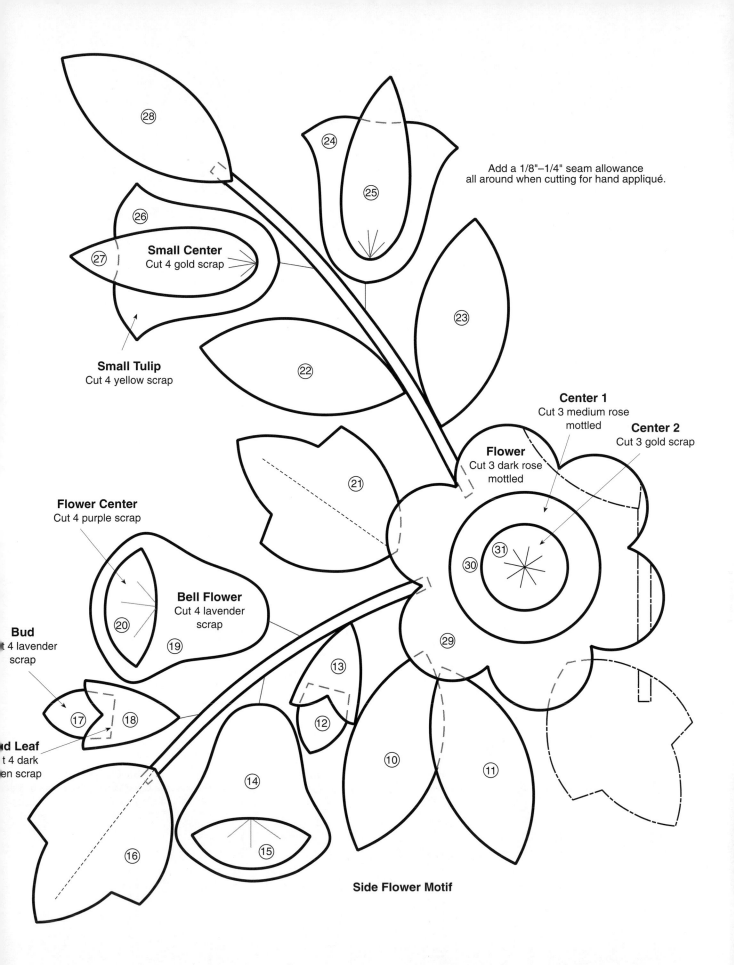

Add a 1/8"–1/4" seam allowance
all around when cutting for hand appliqué.

Small Center
Cut 4 gold scrap

Small Tulip
Cut 4 yellow scrap

Center 1
Cut 3 medium rose
mottled

Center 2
Cut 3 gold scrap

Flower
Cut 3 dark rose
mottled

Flower Center
Cut 4 purple scrap

Bell Flower
Cut 4 lavender
scrap

Bud
t 4 lavender
scrap

d Leaf
t 4 dark
en scrap

Side Flower Motif

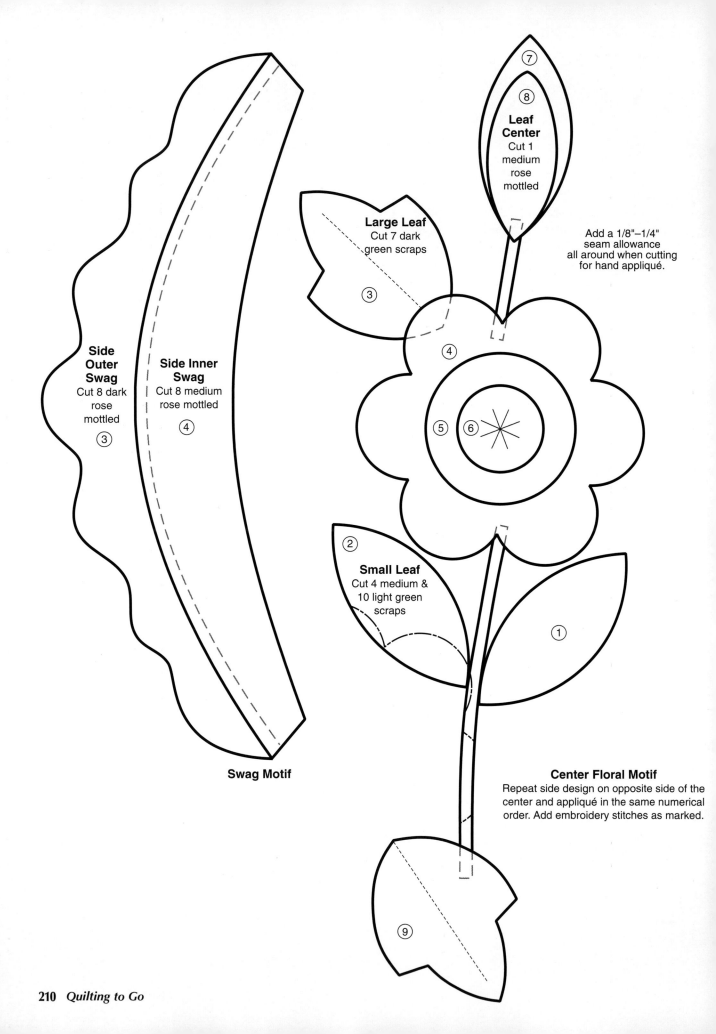

Leaf Center
Cut 1
medium
rose
mottled

⑦

⑧

Large Leaf
Cut 7 dark
green scraps

③

Add a 1/8"–1/4"
seam allowance
all around when cutting
for hand appliqué.

**Side
Outer
Swag**
Cut 8 dark
rose
mottled

③

**Side Inner
Swag**
Cut 8 medium
rose mottled

④

④

⑤ ⑥

②

Small Leaf
Cut 4 medium &
10 light green
scraps

①

Swag Motif

Center Floral Motif
Repeat side design on opposite side of the
center and appliqué in the same numerical
order. Add embroidery stitches as marked.

⑨

Quiltmaking Basics

Materials & Supplies

Fabrics

Fabric Choices. Quilts and quilted projects combine fabrics of many types, depending on the project. It is best to combine same-fiber-content fabrics when making quilted items.

Buying Fabrics. One hundred percent cotton fabrics are recommended for making quilts. Choose colors similar to those used in the quilts shown or colors of your own preference. Most quilt designs depend more on contrast of values than on the colors used to create the design.

Preparing the Fabric for Use. Fabrics may be prewashed or not, depending on your preference. Whether you do or don't, be sure your fabrics are colorfast and won't run onto each other when washed after use.

Fabric Grain. Fabrics are woven with threads going in a crosswise and lengthwise direction. The threads cross at right angles—the more threads per inch, the stronger the fabric.

The crosswise threads will stretch a little. The lengthwise threads will not stretch at all. Cutting the fabric at a 45-degree angle to the crosswise and lengthwise threads produces a bias edge that stretches a great deal when pulled (Figure 1).

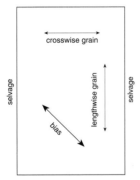

Figure 1
Drawing shows lengthwise, crosswise and bias threads.

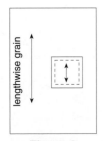

Figure 2
Place the template with marked arrow on the lengthwise grain of the fabric.

If templates are given with patterns in this book, pay careful attention to the grain lines marked with arrows. These arrows indicate that the piece should be placed on the lengthwise grain with the arrow running on one thread. Although it is not necessary to examine the fabric and find a thread to match to, it is important to try to place the arrow with the lengthwise grain of the fabric (Figure 2).

Thread

For most piecing, good-quality cotton or cotton-covered polyester is the thread of choice. Inexpensive polyester threads are not recommended because they can cut the fibers of cotton fabrics.

Choose a color thread that will match or blend with the fabrics in your quilt. For projects pieced with dark and light color fabrics choose a neutral thread color, such as a medium gray, as a compromise between colors. Test by pulling at a stitched sample seam from the right side.

Batting

Batting is the material used to give a quilt loft or thickness. It also adds warmth.

Batting size is listed in inches for each pattern to reflect the size needed to complete the quilt according to the instructions. Purchase the size large enough to cut the size you need for the quilt of your choice.

Some qualities to look for in batting are drapeability, resistance to fiber migration, loft and softness.

If you are unsure which kind of batting to use, purchase the smallest size batting available in the type you'd like to try. Test each sample on a small project. Choose the batting that you like working with most and that will result in the type of quilt you need.

Tools & Equipment

There are few truly essential tools and little equipment required for quiltmaking. The basics include needles (hand-sewing and quilting betweens), pins (long, thin sharp pins are best), sharp scissors or shears, a thimble, template materials (plastic or cardboard), marking tools (chalk marker, water-erasable pen and a No. 2 pencil are a few) and a quilting frame or hoop. For piecing and/or quilting by machine, add a sewing machine to the list.

Other necessary sewing basics are a seam ripper, pincushion, measuring tape and an iron. For choosing colors or quilting designs for your quilt, or for designing your own quilt, it is helpful to have graph paper, tracing paper, colored pencils or markers and a ruler on hand.

For making strip-pieced quilts, a rotary cutter, mat and specialty rulers are often used. We recommend an ergonomic rotary cutter, a large self-healing mat and several rulers. If you can choose only one size, a 6" x 24" marked in 1/8" or 1/4" increments is recommended.

Construction Methods

Templates

Traditional Templates. While many quilt instructions in this book use rotary-cut strips and quick-sewing methods, a few patterns require templates. Templates are like the pattern pieces used to sew a garment. They are used to cut the fabric pieces that make up the quilt top. There are two types—templates that include a 1/4" seam allowance and those that don't.

Choose the template material and the pattern. Transfer the pattern shapes to the template material with a sharp No. 2 lead pencil. Write the pattern name, piece letter or number, grain line and number to cut for one block or whole quilt on each piece as shown in Figure 3.

Figure 3
Mark each template with the pattern
name and piece identification.

Some patterns require a reversed piece (Figure 4). These patterns are labeled with an R after the piece letter; for example, A and AR. To reverse a template, first cut it with the labeled side up and then with the labeled side down. Compare these to the right and left fronts of a blouse. When making a garment, you accomplish reversed pieces when cutting the pattern on two layers of fabric placed with right sides together. This can be done when cutting templates as well.

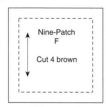

Figure 4
This pattern uses reversed pieces.

If cutting one layer of fabric at a time, first trace the template onto the backside of the fabric with the marked side down; turn the template over with the marked side up to make reverse pieces.

Appliqué patterns given in this book do not include a seam allowance. Most designs are given in one drawing rather than individual pieces. This saves space while giving you the complete design to trace on the background block to help with placement of the pieces later. Make templates for each shape using the drawing for exact size. Remember to label each piece as for piecing templates.

For hand appliqué, add a seam allowance when cutting pieces from fabric. You may trace the template with label side up on the right side of the fabric if you are careful to mark lightly. The traced line is then the guide for turning the edges under when stitching.

If you prefer to mark on the wrong side of the fabric, turn the template over if you want the pattern to face the same way it does on the page.

For machine appliqué, a seam allowance is not necessary. Trace template onto the right side of the fabric with label facing up. Cut around shape on the traced line.

Piecing

Hand-Piecing Basics. When hand-piecing it is easier to begin with templates that do not include the 1/4" seam allowance. Place the template on the wrong side of the fabric lining up the marked grain line with lengthwise or crosswise fabric grain. If the piece does not have to be reversed, place with labeled side up. Trace around shape; move, leaving 1/2" between the shapes, and mark again.

When you have marked the appropriate number of pieces, cut out pieces, leaving 1/4" beyond marked line all around each piece.

To piece, refer to assembly drawings to piece units and blocks, if provided. To join two units, place the patches with right sides together. Stick a pin in at the beginning of the seam through both fabric patches, matching the beginning points (Figure 5); for hand-piecing, the seam begins on the traced line, not at the edge of the fabric (see Figure 6).

Figure 5
Stick a pin through
fabrics to match the
beginning of the seam.

Figure 6
Begin hand-piecing at seam,
not at the edge of the fabric.
Continue stitching along
seam line.

Thread a sharp needle; knot one strand of the thread at the end. Remove the pin and insert the needle in the hole; make a short stitch and then a backstitch right over the first stitch.

Continue making short stitches with several stitches on the needle at one time. As you stitch, check the back piece often to assure accurate stitching on the seam line. Take a stitch at the end of the seam; backstitch and knot at the same time as shown in Figure 7.

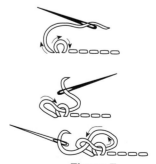

Figure 7
Make a loop in a backstitch to make a knot.

Seams on hand-pieced fabric patches may be finger-pressed toward the darker fabric.

To sew units together, pin fabric patches together, matching seams. Sew as above except where seams meet; at these intersections, backstitch, go through seam to next piece and backstitch again to secure seam joint.

Not all pieced blocks can be stitched with straight seams or in rows. Some patterns require set-in pieces. To begin a set-in seam on a star pattern, pin one side of the square to the proper side of the star point with right sides together, matching corners. Start stitching at the seam line on the outside point; stitch on the marked seam line to the end of the seam line at the center referring to Figure 8.

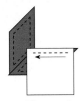

Figure 8
To set a square into a diamond point, match seams and stitch from outside edge to center.

Bring around the adjacent side and pin to the next star point, matching seams. Continue the stitching line from the adjacent seam through corners and to the outside edge of the square as shown in Figure 9.

Figure 9
Continue stitching the adjacent side of the square to the next diamond shape in 1 seam from center to outside as shown.

Machine-Piecing. If making templates, include the 1/4" seam allowance on the template for machine-piecing. Place template on the wrong side of the fabric as for hand-piecing except butt pieces against one another when tracing.

Set machine on 2.5 or 12–15 stitches per inch. Join pieces as for hand-piecing for set-in seams; but for other straight seams, begin and end sewing at the end of the fabric patch sewn as shown in Figure 10. No backstitching is necessary when machine-stitching.

Figure 10
Begin machine-piecing at the end of the piece, not at the end of the seam.

Join units as for hand-piecing referring to the piecing diagrams where needed. Chain piecing (Figure 11—sewing several like units before sewing other units) saves time by eliminating beginning and ending stitches.

When joining machine-pieced units, match seams against

each other with seam allowances pressed in opposite directions to reduce bulk and make perfect matching of seams possible (Figure 12).

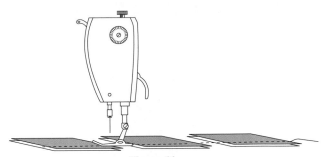

Figure 11
Units may be chain-pieced to save time.

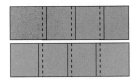

Figure 12
Sew machine-pieced units with seams pressed in opposite directions.

Cutting

Quick-Cutting. Quick-cutting and piecing strips are recommended for making many of the projects in this book. Templates are completely eliminated; instead, a rotary cutter, plastic ruler and mat are used to cut fabric pieces.

When rotary-cutting strips, straighten raw edges of fabric by folding fabric in fourths across the width as shown in Figure 13. Press down flat; place ruler on fabric square with edge of fabric and make one cut from the folded edge to the outside edge. If strips are not straightened, a wavy strip will result as shown in Figure 14.

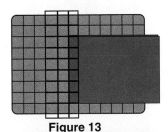

Figure 13
Fold fabric and straighten as shown.

Figure 14
Wavy strips result if fabric is not straightened before cutting.

Always cut away from your body, holding the ruler firmly with the non-cutting hand. Keep fingers away from the edge of the ruler as it is easy for the rotary cutter to slip and jump over the edge of the ruler if cutting is not properly done.

For many strip-pieced blocks two strips are stitched together as shown in Figure 15. The strips are stitched, pressed and cut into segments as shown in Figure 16.

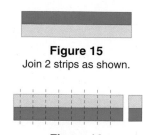

Figure 15
Join 2 strips as shown.

Figure 16
Cut segments from the stitched strip set.

The cut segments are arranged as shown in Figure 17 and stitched to complete, in this example, one Four-Patch block. Although the block shown is very simple, the same methods may be used for more complicated patterns.

Figure 17
Arrange cut segments to
make a Four-Patch block.

The direction to press seams on strip sets is important for accurate piecing later. The normal rule for pressing is to press seams toward the darker fabric to keep the colors from showing through on lighter colors later. For joining segments from strip sets, this rule doesn't always apply.

It is best if seams on adjacent rows are pressed in opposite directions. When aligning segments to stitch rows together, if pressed properly, seam joints will have a seam going in both directions as shown in Figure 18.

Figure 18
Seams go in both
directions at seam joints.

If a square is required for the pattern, it can be subcut from a strip as shown in Figure 19.

Figure 19
If cutting squares, cut proper-width strip into same-width
segments. Here, a 2" strip is cut into 2" segments to create
2" squares. These squares finish at 1 1/2" when sewn.

If you need right triangles with the straight grain on the short sides, you can use the same method, but you need to figure out how wide to cut the strip. Measure the finished size of one short side of the triangle. Add 7/8" to this size for seam allowance. Cut fabric strips this width; cut the strips into the same increment to create squares. Cut the

squares on the diagonal to produce triangles. For example, if you need a triangle with a 2" finished height, cut the strips 2 7/8" by the width of the fabric. Cut the strips into 2 7/8" squares. Cut each square on the diagonal to produce the correct-size triangle with the grain on the short sides (Figure 20).

Figure 20
Cut 2" (finished size) triangles from
2 7/8" squares as shown.

Triangles sewn together to make squares are called half-square triangles or triangle/squares. When joined, the triangle/square unit has the straight of grain on all outside edges of the block.

Another method of making triangle/squares is shown in Figure 21. Layer two squares with right sides together; draw a diagonal line through the center. Stitch 1/4" on both sides of the line. Cut apart on the drawn line to reveal two stitched triangle/squares.

Figure 21
Mark a diagonal line on the square; stitch
1/4" on each side of the line. Cut on line
to reveal stitched triangle/squares.

If you need triangles with the straight of grain on the diagonal, such as for fill-in triangles on the outside edges of a diagonal-set quilt, the procedure is a bit different.

To make these triangles, a square is cut on both diagonals; thus, the straight of grain is on the longest or diagonal side (Figure 22). To figure out the size to cut the square, add 1 1/4" to the needed finished size of the longest side of the triangle. For example, if you need a triangle with a 12" finished diagonal, cut a 13 1/4" square.

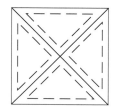

Figure 22
Add 1 1/4" to the finished size of the
longest side of the triangle needed
and cut on both diagonals to make a
quarter-square triangle.

If templates are given, use their measurements to cut fabric strips to correspond with that measurement. The template may be used on the strip to cut pieces quickly. Strip cutting works best for squares, triangles, rectangles and diamonds. Odd-shaped templates are difficult to cut in multiple layers using a rotary cutter.

Foundation Piecing

Foundation Piecing. Paper or fabric foundation pieces are used to make very accurate blocks, provide stability for weak fabrics, and add body and weight to the finished quilt.

Temporary foundation materials include paper, tracing paper, freezer paper and removable interfacing. Permanent foundations include utility fabrics, nonwoven interfacing, flannel, fleece and batting.

Methods of marking foundations include basting lines, pencils or pens, needle punching, tracing wheel, hot-iron transfers, copy machine, premarked, stamps or stencils.

There are two methods of foundation piecing—under-piecing and top-piecing. When under-piecing, the pattern is reversed when tracing. We have not included any patterns for top-piecing. **Note:** *All patterns for which we recommend paper piecing are already reversed in full-size drawings given.*

To under-piece, place a scrap of fabric larger than the lined space on the unlined side of the paper in the No. 1 position. Place piece 2 right sides together with piece 1; pin on seam line, and fold back to check that the piece will cover space 2 before stitching.

Stitch along line on the lined side of the paper—fabric will not be visible. Sew several stitches beyond the beginning and ending of the line. Backstitching is not required as another fabric seam will cover this seam.

Remove pin; finger-press piece 2 flat. Continue adding all pieces in numerical order in the same manner until all pieces are stitched to paper. Trim excess to outside line (1/4" larger all around than finished size of the block).

Tracing paper can be used as a temporary foundation. It is removed when blocks are complete and stitched together. To paper-piece, copy patterns using a copy machine or trace each block individually. Measure the finished paper foundations to insure accuracy in copying.

Tips & Techniques

If you cannot see the lines on the backside of the paper when paper-piecing, draw over lines with a small felt-tip marker. The lines should now be visible on the backside to help with placement of fabric pieces.

Appliqué

Appliqué is the process of applying one piece of fabric on top of another for decorative or functional purposes.

Making Templates. Most appliqué designs given here are shown as full-size drawings for the completed designs. The drawings show dotted lines to indicate where one piece overlaps another. Other marks indicate placement of embroidery stitches for decorative purposes such as eyes, lips, flowers, etc.

For hand appliqué, trace each template onto the right side of the fabric with template right side up. Cut around shape, adding a 1/8"–1/4" seam allowance.

Before the actual appliqué process begins, cut the background block and prepare it for stitching. Most appliqué designs are centered on the block. To find the center of the background square, fold it in half and in half again; crease with your fingers. Now unfold and fold diagonally and crease; repeat for other corners referring to Figure 23. Center-line creases help position the design. If centering the appliqué design is important, an X has been placed on each drawing to mark the center of the design. Match the X with the creased center of the background block when placing pieces.

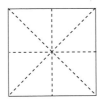

Figure 23
Fold background to mark centers as shown.

If you have a full-size drawing of the design, as is given with most appliqué designs in this book, it might help you to draw on the background block to help with placement. Transfer the design to a large piece of tracing paper. Place the paper on top of the design; use masking tape to hold in place. Trace design onto paper.

If you don't have a light box, tape the pattern on a window; center the background block on top and tape in place. Trace the design onto the background block with a water-erasable marker or chalk pencil. This drawing will mark exactly where the fabric pieces should be placed on the background block.

Hand Appliqué. Traditional hand appliqué uses a template made from the desired finished shape without seam allowance added.

After fabric is prepared, trace the desired shape onto the right side of the fabric with a water-erasable marker, light lead or chalk pencil. Leave at least 1/2" between design motifs when tracing to allow for the seam allowance when cutting out the shapes.

When the desired number of shapes needed has been drawn on the fabric pieces, cut out shapes leaving 1/8"–1/4" all around drawn line for turning under.

Turn the shape's edges over on the drawn or stitched line. When turning the edges under, make sharp corners sharp and smooth edges smooth. The fabric patch should retain the shape of the template used to cut it.

When turning in concave curves, clip to seams and baste the seam allowance over as shown in Figure 24.

Figure 24
Concave curves should be
clipped before turning as shown.

During the actual appliqué process, you may be layering one shape on top of another. Where two fabrics overlap, the underneath piece does not have to be turned under or stitched down.

If possible, trim away the underneath fabric when the block is finished by carefully cutting away the background from underneath and then cutting away unnecessary layers to reduce bulk and avoid shadows from darker fabrics showing through on light fabrics.

For hand appliqué, position the fabric shapes on the background block and pin or baste them in place. Using a blind stitch or appliqué stitch, sew pieces in place with matching thread and small stitches. Start with background pieces first and work up to foreground pieces. Appliqué the pieces in place on the background in numerical order, if given, layering as necessary.

Machine Appliqué. There are several products available to help make the machine-appliqué process easier and faster.

Fusible transfer web is a commercial product similar to iron-on interfacings except it has two sticky sides. It is used to adhere appliqué shapes to the background with heat. Paper is adhered to one side of the web.

To use, dry-iron the sticky side of the fusible product onto the wrong side of the chosen fabric. Draw desired shapes onto the paper and cut them out. Peel off the paper and dry-iron the shapes in place on the background fabric. The shape will stay in place while you stitch around it. This process adds a little bulk or stiffness to the appliquéd shape and makes hand quilting through the layers difficult.

For successful machine appliqué a tear-off stabilizer is recommended. This product is placed under the background fabric while machine appliqué is being done. It is torn away when the work is finished. This kind of stabilizer keeps the background fabric from pulling during the machine-appliqué process.

During the actual machine-appliqué process, you will be layering one shape on top of another. Where two fabrics overlap, the underneath piece does not have to be turned under or stitched down.

Thread the top of the machine with thread to match the fabric patches or with threads that coordinate or contrast with fabrics. Rayon thread is a good choice when a sheen is desired on the finished appliqué stitches. Do not use rayon thread in the bobbin; use all-purpose thread.

Set your machine to make a zigzag stitch and practice on scraps of similar weight to check the tension. If you can see the bobbin thread on the top of the appliqué, adjust your machine to make a balanced stitch. Different-width stitches are available; choose one that will not overpower the appliqué shapes. In some cases these appliqué stitches will be used as decorative stitches as well and you may want the thread to show.

If using a stabilizer, place this under the background fabric and pin or fuse in place. Place shapes as for hand-appliqué and stitch all around shapes by machine.

When all machine work is complete, remove stabilizer from the back referring to the manufacturer's instructions.

Transferring Embroidery Designs

When transferring embroidery designs to a background fabric, fold the background fabric to find the center; crease to mark. Find the center of the embroidery design, if not marked, by folding and creasing in the same manner.

If you do not have a light box as a light source, tape the transfer design to a window. Center the background piece over the center of the design; tape in place.

Use a water-erasable marker or pencil to trace the lines from the pattern onto the background. If the project will be stitched over a long period of time, a light pencil might make a better choice as water-erasable markers do disappear with humidity.

Putting It All Together

Many steps are required to prepare a quilt top for quilting, including setting the blocks together, adding borders, choosing and marking quilting designs, layering the top, batting and backing for quilting, quilting or tying the layers and finishing the edges of the quilt.

As you begin the process of finishing your quilt top, strive for a neat, flat quilt with square sides and corners, not for perfection—that will come with time and practice.

Finishing the Top

Settings. Most quilts are made by sewing individual blocks together in rows which, when joined, create a design. There are several other methods used to join blocks. Sometimes the setting choice is determined by the block's design. For

example, a house block should be placed upright on a quilt, not sideways or upside down.

Plain blocks can be alternated with pieced or appliquéd blocks in a straight set. Making a quilt using plain blocks saves time; half the number of pieced or appliquéd blocks are needed to make the same-size quilt as shown in Figure 1.

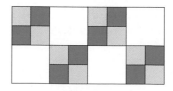

Figure 1
Alternate plain blocks with
pieced block to save time.

Adding Borders. Borders are an integral part of the quilt and should complement the colors and designs used in the quilt center. Borders frame a quilt just like a mat and frame do a picture.

If fabric strips are added for borders, they may be mitered or butted at the corners as shown in Figures 2 and 3.

Figure 2
Mitered corners
look like this.

Figure 3
Butted corners
look like this.

To determine the size for butted-border strips, measure across the center of the completed quilt top from one side raw edge to the other side raw edge. This measurement will include a 1/4" seam allowance. Cut two border strips that length by the chosen width of the border. Sew these strips to the top and bottom of the pieced center referring to Figure 4. Press the seam allowance toward the border strips.

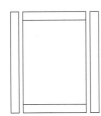

Figure 4
Sew border strips to opposite
sides; sew remaining 2 strips
to remaining sides to make
butted corners.

Measure across the completed quilt top at the center, from top raw edge to bottom raw edge, including the two border strips already added. Cut two border strips that length by the chosen width of the border. Sew a strip to each of the two remaining sides as shown in Figure 4. Press the seams toward the border strips.

To make mitered corners, measure the quilt as before. To this add twice the width of the border and 1/2" for seam allowances to determine the length of the strips. Repeat for opposite sides. Center and sew on each strip, stopping stitching 1/4" from corner, leaving the remainder of the strip dangling.

Tips & Techniques

Before machine-piecing fabric patches together, test your sewing machine for positioning an accurate 1/4" seam allowance. There are several tools to help guarantee this. Some machine needles may be moved to allow the presser-foot edge to be a 1/4" guide.

A special foot may be purchased for your machine that will guarantee an accurate 1/4" seam. A piece of masking tape can be placed on the throat plate of your sewing machine to mark the 1/4" seam. A plastic stick-on ruler may be used instead of tape with the same results.

Press corners at a 45-degree angle to form a crease. Stitch from the inside quilt corner to the outside on the creased line. Trim excess away after stitching and press mitered seams open (Figures 5–7).

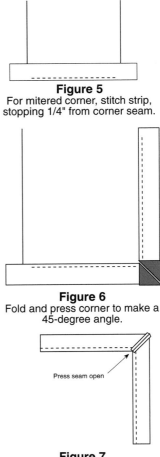

Figure 5
For mitered corner, stitch strip,
stopping 1/4" from corner seam.

Figure 6
Fold and press corner to make a
45-degree angle.

Press seam open

Figure 7
Trim away excess from
underneath when stitching is
complete. Press seams open.

Carefully press the entire quilt top. Avoid pulling and stretching while pressing, which would distort shapes.

Getting Ready to Quilt

Choosing a Quilting Design. If you choose to hand- or machine-quilt your finished top, you will need to choose a design for quilting.

There are several types of quilting designs, some of which may not have to be marked. The easiest of the unmarked designs is in-the-ditch quilting. Here the quilting stitches are placed in the valley created by the seams joining two pieces together or next to the edge of an appliqué design. There is no need to mark a top for in-the-ditch quilting. Machine quilters choose this option because the stitches are not as obvious on the finished quilt (Figure 8).

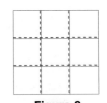

Figure 8
In-the-ditch quilting is done
in the seam that joins 2
pieces.

Outline-quilting 1/4" or more away from seams or appliqué shapes is another no-mark alternative (Figure 9) which prevents having to sew through the layers made by seams, thus making stitching easier.

Figure 9
Outline-quilting 1/4" away from seam is a popular choice for quilting.

If you are not comfortable eyeballing the 1/4" (or other distance), masking tape is available in different widths and is helpful to place on straight-edge designs to mark the quilting line. If using masking tape, place the tape right up against the seam and quilt close to the other edge.

Meander or free-motion quilting by machine fills in open spaces and doesn't require marking. It is fun and easy to stitch as shown in Figure 10.

Figure 10
Machine meander quilting fills in large spaces.

Marking the Top for Quilting or Tying. If you choose a fancy or allover design for quilting, you will need to transfer the design to your quilt top before layering with the backing and batting. You may use a sharp medium-lead or silver pencil on light background fabrics. Test the pencil marks to guarantee that they will wash out of your quilt top when quilting is complete; or be sure your quilting stitches cover the pencil marks. Mechanical pencils with very fine points may be used successfully to mark quilts.

Manufactured quilt-design templates are available in many designs and sizes and are cut out of a durable plastic template material that is easy to use.

To make a permanent quilt-design template, choose a template material on which to transfer the design. See-through plastic is the best as it will let you place the design while allowing you to see where it is in relation to your quilt design without moving it. Place the design on the quilt top where you want it and trace around it with your marking tool. Pick up the quilting template and place again; repeat marking.

No matter what marking method you use, remember—the marked lines should never show on the finished quilt. When the top is marked, it is ready for layering.

Preparing the Quilt Backing. The quilt backing is a very important feature of your quilt. In most cases, the materials list for each quilt in this book gives the size requirements for the backing, not the yardage needed. Exceptions to this are when the backing fabric is also used on the quilt top and yardage is given for that fabric.

A backing is generally cut at least 4" larger than the quilt top or 2" larger on all sides. For a 64" x 78" finished quilt, the backing would need to be at least 68" x 82".

To avoid having the seam across the center of the quilt backing, cut or tear one of the right-length pieces in half and sew half to each side of the second piece as shown in Figure 11.

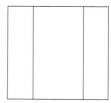

Figure 11
Center 1 backing piece with a piece on each side.

Quilts that need backing more than 88" wide may be pieced in horizontal pieces as shown in Figure 12.

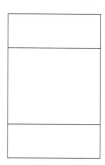

Figure 12
Horizontal seams may be used on backing pieces.

Layering the Quilt Sandwich. Layering the quilt top with the batting and backing is time-consuming. Open the batting several days before you need it and place over a bed or flat on the floor to help flatten the creases caused from its being folded up in the bag for so long.

Iron the backing piece, folding in half both vertically and horizontally and pressing to mark centers.

If you will not be quilting on a frame, place the backing right side down on a clean floor or table. Start in the center and push any wrinkles or bunches flat. Use masking tape to tape the edges to the floor or large clips to hold the backing to the edges of the table. The backing should be taut.

Place the batting on top of the backing, matching centers using fold lines as guides; flatten out any wrinkles. Trim the batting to the same size as the backing.

Fold the quilt top in half lengthwise and place on top of the batting, wrong side against the batting, matching centers. Unfold quilt and, working from the center to the outside edges, smooth out any wrinkles or lumps.

To hold the quilt layers together for quilting, baste by hand or use safety pins. If basting by hand, thread a long thin needle with a long piece of unknotted white or off-white hread. Starting in the center and leaving a long tail, make 4"–6" stitches toward the outside edge of the quilt top, smoothing as you baste. Start at the center again and work toward the outside as shown in Figure 13.

Figure 13
Baste from the center to the outside edges.

If quilting by machine, you may prefer to use safety pins for holding your quilt sandwich together. Start in the center of the quilt and pin to the outside, leaving pins open until all are placed. When you are satisfied that all layers are smooth, close the pins.

Quilting

Hand Quilting. Hand quilting is the process of placing stitches through the quilt top, batting and backing to hold them together. While it is a functional process, it also adds beauty and loft to the finished quilt.

To begin, thread a sharp between needle with an 18" piece of quilting thread. Tie a small knot in the end of the thread. Position the needle about 1/2" to 1" away from the starting point on quilt top. Sink the needle through the top into the batting layer but not through the backing. Pull the needle up at the starting point of the quilting design. Pull the needle and thread until the knot sinks through the top into the batting (Figure 14).

Figure 14
Start the needle through the top layer
of fabric 1/2"–1" away from quilting
line with knot on top of fabric.

Some stitchers like to take a backstitch at the beginning while others prefer to begin the first stitch here. Take small, even running stitches along the marked quilting line (Figure 15). Keep one hand positioned underneath to feel the needle go all the way through to the backing.

Figure 15
Make small, even running stitches on marked quilting line.

Machine Quilting. Successful machine quilting requires practice and a good relationship with your sewing machine.

Prepare the quilt for machine quilting in the same way as for hand quilting. Use safety pins to hold the layers together instead of basting with thread.

Presser-foot quilting is best used for straight-line quilting because the presser bar lever does not need to be continually lifted.

Set the machine on a longer stitch length (three or eight to 10 stitches to the inch). Too tight a stitch causes puckering and fabric tucks, either on the quilt top or backing. An even-feed or walking foot helps to eliminate the tucks and puckering by feeding the upper and lower layers through the machine evenly. Before you begin, loosen the amount of pressure on the presser foot.

Special machine-quilting needles work best to penetrate the three layers in your quilt.

Decide on a design. Quilting in the ditch is not quite as visible, but if you quilt with the feed dogs engaged, it means turning the quilt frequently. It is not easy to fit a rolled-up quilt through the small opening on the sewing machine head.

Meander quilting is the easiest way to machine quilt—and it is fun. Meander quilting is done using an appliqué or darning foot with the feed dogs dropped. It is sort of like scribbling. Simply move the quilt top around under the foot and make stitches in a random pattern to fill the space. The same method may be used to outline a quilt design. The trick is the same as in hand quilting; you are striving for stitches of uniform size. Your hands are in complete control of the design.

If machine quilting is of interest to you, there are several very good books available at quilt shops that will help you become a successful machine quilter.

Tips & Techniques

Knots should not show on the quilt top or back. Learn to sink the knot into the batting at the beginning and ending of the quilting thread for successful stitches.

When you have nearly run out of thread, wind the thread around the needle several times to make a small knot and pull it close to the fabric. Insert the needle into the fabric on the quilting line and come out with the needle 1/2" to 1" away, pulling the knot into the fabric layers the same as when you started. Pull and cut thread close to fabric. The end should disappear inside after cutting. Some quilters prefer to take a backstitch with a loop through it for a knot to end.

Making 12–18 stitches per inch is a nice goal, but a more realistic goal is seven to nine stitches per inch. If you cannot accomplish this right away, strive for even stitches—all the same size—that look as good on the back as on the front.

You will perfect your quilting stitches as you gain experience, your stitches will get better with each project and your style will be uniquely your own.

Tied Quilts, or Comforters. Would you rather tie your quilt layers together than quilt them? Tied quilts are often referred to as comforters. The advantage of tying is that it takes so much less time and the required skills can be learned quickly.

If a top will be tied, choose a thick, bonded batting—one that will not separate during washing. For tying, use pearl cotton, embroidery floss, or strong yarn in colors that match or coordinate with the fabrics in your quilt top.

Decide on a pattern for tying. Many quilts are tied at the corners and centers of the blocks and at sashing joints. Try to tie every 4"–6". Special designs can be used for tying, but most quilts are tied in conventional ways. Begin tying in the center and work to the outside edges.

To make the tie, thread a large needle with a long thread (yarn, floss or crochet cotton); do not knot. Push the needle through the quilt top to the back, leaving a 3"–4" length on top. Move the needle to the next position without cutting thread. Take another stitch through the layers; repeat until thread is almost used up.

Cut thread between stitches, leaving an equal amount of thread on each stitch. Tie a knot with the two thread ends. Tie again to make a square knot referring to Figure 16. Trim thread ends to desired length.

Figure 16
Make a square knot as shown.

Finishing the Edges

After your quilt is tied or quilted, the edges need to be finished. Decide how you want the edges of your quilt finished before layering the backing and batting with the quilt top.

Without Binding—Self-Finish. There is one way to eliminate adding an edge finish. This is done before quilting. Place the batting on a flat surface. Place the pieced top right side up on the batting. Place the backing right sides together with the pieced top. Pin and/or baste the layers together to hold flat referring to page 218.

Begin stitching in the center of one side using a 1/4" seam allowance, reversing at the beginning and end of the seam. Continue stitching all around and back to the beginning side. Leave a 12" or larger opening. Clip corners to reduce excess. Turn right side out through the opening. Slipstitch the opening closed by hand. The quilt may now be quilted by hand or machine.

The disadvantage to this method is that once the edges are sewn in, any creases or wrinkles that might form during the quilting process cannot be flattened out. Tying is the preferred method for finishing a quilt constructed using this method.

Bringing the backing fabric to the front is another way to finish the quilt's edge without binding. To accomplish this, complete the quilt as for hand or machine quilting. Trim the batting only even with the front. Trim the backing 1" larger than the completed top all around.

Turn the backing edge in 1/2" and then turn over to the front along edge of batting. The folded edge may be machine-stitched close to the edge through all layers, or blind-stitched in place to finish.

The front may be turned to the back. If using this method, a wider front border is needed. The backing and batting are trimmed 1" smaller than the top and the top edge is turned under 1/2" and then turned to the back and stitched in place.

One more method of self-finish may be used. The top and backing may be stitched together by hand at the edge. To accomplish this, all quilting must be stopped 1/2" from the quilt-top edge. The top and backing of the quilt are trimmed even and the batting is trimmed to 1/4"–1/2" smaller. The edges of the top and backing are turned in 1/4"–1/2" and blind-stitched together at the very edge.

These methods do not require the use of extra fabric and save time in preparation of binding strips; they are not as durable as an added binding.

Binding. The technique of adding extra fabric at the edges of the quilt is called binding. The binding encloses the edges and adds an extra layer of fabric for durability.

To prepare the quilt for the addition of the binding, trim the batting and backing layers flush with the top of the quilt using a rotary cutter and ruler or shears. Using a walking-foot attachment (sometimes called an even-feed foot attachment), machine-baste the three layers together all around approximately 1/8" from the cut edge.

The list of materials given with each quilt in this book often includes a number of yards of self-made or purchased binding. Bias binding may be purchased in packages and in many colors. The advantage to self-made binding is that you can use fabrics from your quilt to coordinate colors.

Double-fold, straight-grain binding and double-fold, bias-grain binding are two of the most commonly used types of binding.

Double-fold, straight-grain binding is used on smaller projects with right-angle corners. Double-fold, bias-grain binding is best suited for bed-size quilts or quilts with rounded corners.

To make double-fold, straight-grain binding, cut 2"-wide strips of fabric across the width or down the length of the fabric totaling the perimeter of the quilt plus 10". The strips are joined as shown in Figure 17 and pressed in half wrong sides together along the length using an iron on a cotton setting with no steam.

Figure 17
Join binding strips in a diagonal seam to eliminate bulk as shown.

Figure 18
Sew to within 1/4" of corner; leave needle in quilt, turn and stitch diagonally off the corner of the quilt.

lining up the raw edges, place the binding on the top of the quilt and begin sewing (again using the walking foot) approximately 6" from the beginning of the binding strip. Stop sewing 1/4" from the first corner, leave the needle in the quilt, turn and sew diagonally to the corner as shown in Figure 18.

Fold the binding at a 45-degree angle up and away from the quilt as shown in Figure 19 and back down flush with the raw edges. Starting at the top raw edge of the quilt, begin sewing the next side as shown in Figure 20. Repeat at the next three corners.

Figure 19
Fold binding at a
45-degree angle
up and away from
quilt as shown.

Figure 20
Fold the binding
strips back down,
flush with the raw
edge, and begin
sewing.

As you approach the beginning of the binding strip, stop stitching and overlap the binding 1/2" from the edge; trim. Join the two ends with a 1/4" seam allowance and press the seam open. Reposition the joined binding along the edge of the quilt and resume stitching to the beginning.

To finish, bring the folded edge of the binding over the raw edges and blind-stitch the binding in place over the machine-stitching line on the backside. Hand-miter the corners on the back as shown in Figure 21.

Figure 21
Miter and stitch the
corners as shown.

If you are making a quilt to be used on a bed, you will want to use double-fold, bias-grain bindings because the many threads that cross each other along the fold at the edge of the quilt make it a more durable binding.

Cut 2"-wide bias strips from a large square of fabric. Join the strips as illustrated in Figure 17 and press the seams open. Fold the beginning end of the bias strip 1/4" from the raw edge and press. Fold the joined strips in half along the long side, wrong sides together, and press with no steam (Figure 22).

Figure 22
Fold end in and press strip in half.

Follow the same procedures as previously described for preparing the quilt top and sewing the binding to the quilt top. Treat the corners just as you treated them with straight-grain binding.

Since you are using bias-grain binding, you do have the option to just eliminate the corners if this option doesn't interfere with the patchwork in the quilt. Round the corners off by placing one of your dinner plates at the corner and rotary-cutting the gentle curve (Figure 23).

Figure 23
Round corners to eliminate
square-corner finishes.

As you approach the beginning of the binding strip, stop stitching and lay the end across the beginning so it will slip inside the fold. Cut the end at a 45-degree angle so the raw edges are contained inside the beginning of the strip (Figure 24). Resume stitching to the beginning. Bring the fold to the back of the quilt and hand-stitch as previously described.

Figure 24
End the binding strips as shown.

Overlapped corners are not quite as easy as rounded ones, but a bit easier than mitering. To make overlapped corners, sew binding strips to opposite sides of the quilt top. Stitch edges down to finish. Trim ends even.

Sew a strip to each remaining side, leaving 1 1/2"–2" excess at each end. Turn quilt over and fold end in even with previous finished edge as shown in Figure 25.

Figure 25
Fold end of binding even with
previous edge.

Figure 26
An overlapped corner is not quite as
neat as a mitered corner.

Fold binding in toward quilt and stitch down as before, enclosing the previous bound edge in the seam as shown in Figure 26. It may be necessary to trim the folded-down section to reduce bulk.

Tips & Techniques

Use a thimble to prevent sore fingers when hand quilting. The finger that is under the quilt to feel the needle as it passes through the backing is the one that is most apt to get sore from the pin pricks. Some quilters purchase leather thimbles for this finger while others try home remedies. One simple aid is masking tape wrapped around the finger. With the tape you will still be able to feel the needle, but it will not prick your skin. Over time calluses build up and these fingers get toughened up, but with every vacation from quilting, they will become soft and the process begins again.

When you feel your shoulder muscles tensing up, take a rest.

Making Continuous Bias Binding

Instead of cutting individual bias strips and sewing them together, you may make continuous bias binding.

Cut a square 18" x 18" from chosen binding fabric. Cut the square once on the diagonal to make two triangles as shown in Figure 27. With right sides together, sew the two triangles together with a 1/4" seam allowance as shown in Figure 28; press seam open to reduce bulk.

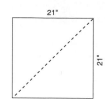

Figure 27
Cut 21" square on the diagonal.

Figure 28
Sew the triangles together.

Mark lines every 2 1/4" on the wrong side of the fabric as shown in Figure 29. Bring the short ends together, right sides together, offsetting one line as shown in Figure 30 to make a tube; stitch. This will seem awkward.

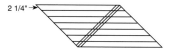

Figure 29
Mark lines every 2 1/4".

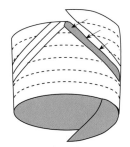

Figure 30
Sew short ends together,
offsetting lines to make a tube.

Begin cutting at point A as shown in Figure 31; continue cutting along marked line to make one continuous strip. Fold strip in half along length with wrong sides together; press. Sew to quilt edges as instructed previously for bias binding.

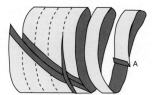

Figure 31
Cut along marked lines, starting at A.

Final Touches

If your quilt will be hung on the wall, a hanging sleeve is required. Other options include purchased plastic rings or fabric tabs. The best choice is a fabric sleeve, which will evenly distribute the weight of the quilt across the top edge, rather than at selected spots where tabs or rings are stitched, keep the quilt hanging straight and not damage the batting.

To make a sleeve, measure across the top of the finished quilt. Cut an 8"-wide piece of muslin equal to that length—you may need to seam several muslin strips together to make the required length.

Fold in 1/4" on each end of the muslin strip and press. Fold again and stitch to hold. Fold the muslin strip lengthwise with right sides together. Sew along the long side to make a tube. Turn the tube right side out; press with seam at bottom or centered on the back.

Hand-stitch the tube along the top of the quilt and the bottom of the tube to the quilt back making sure the quilt lies flat. Stitches should not go through to the front of the quilt and don't need to be too close together as shown in Figure 32.

Figure 32
Sew a sleeve to the top
back of the quilt.

Slip a wooden dowel or long curtain rod through the sleeve to hang.

When the quilt is finally complete, it should be signed and dated. Use a permanent pen on the back of the quilt. Other methods include cross-stitching your name and date on the front or back or making a permanent label that may be stitched to the back.

Metric Conversion Charts

Metric Conversions

U.S. Measurements		Multiplied by		Metric Measurement
yards	x	.9144	=	meters (m)
yards	x	91.44	=	centimeters (cm)
inches	x	2.54	=	centimeters (cm)
inches	x	25.4	=	millimeters (mm)
inches	x	.0254	=	meters (m)

Metric Measurements		Multiplied by		U.S. Measurements
centimeters	x	.3937	=	inches
meters	x	1.0936	=	yards

Standard Equivalents

U.S. Measurement		Metric Measurement		
1/8 inch	=	3.20 mm	=	0.32 cm
1/4 inch	=	6.35 mm	=	0.635 cm
3/8 inch	=	9.50 mm	=	0.95 cm
1/2 inch	=	12.70 mm	=	1.27 cm
5/8 inch	=	15.90 mm	=	1.59 cm
3/4 inch	=	19.10 mm	=	1.91 cm
7/8 inch	=	22.20 mm	=	2.22 cm
1 inch	=	25.40 mm	=	2.54 cm
1/8 yard	=	11.43 cm	=	0.11 m
1/4 yard	=	22.86 cm	=	0.23 m
3/8 yard	=	34.29 cm	=	0.34 m
1/2 yard	=	45.72 cm	=	0.46 m
5/8 yard	=	57.15 cm	=	0.57 m
3/4 yard	=	68.58 cm	=	0.69 m
7/8 yard	=	80.00 cm	=	0.80 m
1 yard	=	91.44 cm	=	0.91 m

Embroidery Stitch Guide

Buttonhole Stitch

French Knot

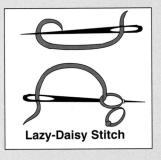

Lazy-Daisy Stitch

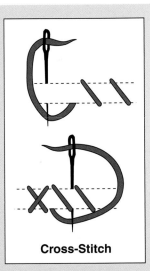

Cross-Stitch

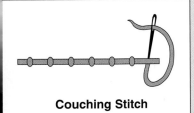

Couching Stitch

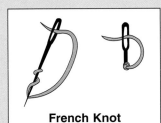

Chevron Stitch

Satin Stitch

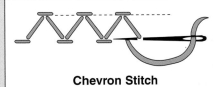

Herringbone Stitch

Stem Stitch

Fly Stitch

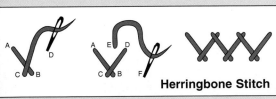

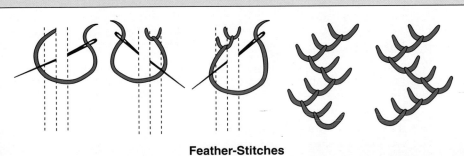

Feather-Stitches

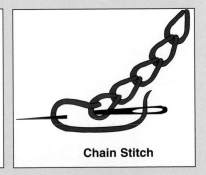

Chain Stitch

Special Thanks

We would like to thank the talented quilt designers whose work is featured in this collection.

Barbara Clayton
Baltimore Album Wall Quilt, 188
Tumbling Blocks Raggy Quilt, 32

Chris Malone
Chicken Wall Quilt, 152
Irish Chain Biscuit Quilt, 37

Christine Carlson
Popping Prairie Points, 46

Christine Schultz
Eight-Point Star Wall Quilt, 72
Magic Carpet Quilt, 56

Connie Kauffman
Autumn Door Banner, 166
Fall Flourish, 53
Granddaughter's Flower Garden, 85
Miniature Whole-Cloth Quilt, 118
Spring Door Banner, 50
Summer Door Banner, 7
Winter Door Banner, 110

Connie Rand
Underwater Wedding Ring, 101

Donna Friebertshauser
Cathedral Windows Sewing Projects, 27
Trapunto Desert at Night, 158

Holly Daniels
Barrel-Bottom Purse, 141
Gone Fishin', 171
Merry-Go-Round Medallion, 63

Jill Reber
Quilting Tote Along, 97

Judith Sandstrom
Baltimore Album Cross-Stitch Quilt, 144
Iris & Tulip Garden, 179
Kaleidoscope Stars, 175

Julie Weaver
My Garden Basket, 41
Redwork Hearts & Flowers, 127
Star-Spangled Yo-Yo's, 13

Marian Shenk
Apple-a-Day Pot Holders, 168
Baltimore Album Flower Basket, 205

Compass Garment Bag, 69
Crazy-Quilted Wall Quilt & Pillow, 113
Floral Reflections, 184
Golden Cord Pillow, 76
Grandmother's Floral Bouquet, 121
Spring Bouquet Pillow, 199

Pearl Louise Krush
Blossom Basket Medallion, 15
Penny Rug Posy Table Runner, 162
Redwork Tote & Sewing Kit, 130

Peg Johnson
Summer Sunset, 94

Sandra L. Hatch
All Points Lead Home, 90

Sue Harvey
Kitty Blues, 136

Susan Parr
Desert Rose Garden Path, 80
Garden View Wall Quilt, 23

Fabrics & Supplies

Page 90: *All Points Lead Home*—
Northcott Midnight Garden fabric collection and Fairfield Natural cotton batting.

Page 94: *Summer Sunset*—
Handpainted sky fabrics by Mickey Lawler from Skydyes.

Page 97: *Quilting Tote Along*—
Masterpiece ruler.

Page 136: *Kitty Blues*—Country Cats

fabrics from Balson-Erlanger, Fairfield Natural cotton batting and Mettler Silk-Finish thread from American & Efird.

Page 141: *Barrel-Bottom Purse*—
Warm and Natural cotton batting and Heat 'n Bond Lite fusible transfer web from The Warm Co.

Page 171: *Gone Fishin'*—Rainbow Sherbet fabric collection from Marcus Brothers Textiles.

Page 175: *Kaleidoscope Stars*—
Heirloom Circa 1840's Collection fabrics from Northcott/Monarch and Hobbs Heirloom Premium cotton batting.

Page 179: *Iris & Tulip Garden*—
Hobbs Heirloom Premium cotton batting and DMC hand-quilting thread.